Also by Richard Erdoes

Lame Deer, Seeker of Visions (*with John Fire Lame Deer*)

The Sun Dance People

The Rain Dance People

The Pueblo Indians

The Sound of Flutes

Picture History of Ancient Rome

Saloons of the Old West

The Woman Who Dared

American Indian Myths and Legends (*with Alfonso Ortiz*)

A.D. 1000: Living on the Brink of Apocalypse

Lakota Woman (*with Mary Crow Dog*)

Gift of Power (*with Archie Fire Lame Deer*)

Ohitika Woman (*with Mary Brave Bird*)

CROW DOG

FOUR GENERATIONS OF SIOUX MEDICINE MEN

LEONARD CROW DOG and RICHARD ERDOES

HarperPerennial

A Division of HarperCollinsPublishers

Photographs follow page 152.

A hardcover edition of this book was published in 1995 by HarperCollins Publishers.

HarperCollins books may be purchased for educational, business, or sales promotional use. For information please write: Special Markets Department, HarperCollins Publishers, Inc., 10 East 53rd Street, New York, NY 10022.

First HarperPerennial edition published 1996.

Designed by Nancy Singer
Photograph insert designed by Maura Fadden Rosenthal
Line drawings and photographs by Richard Erdoes

The Library of Congress has catalogued the hardcover edition as follows:

Crow Dog, Leonard, 1942–
    Crow Dog : Four generations of Sioux medicine men / Leonard Crow
Dog and Richard Erdoes. — 1st ed.
      p. cm.
    ISBN 0-06-016861-7
     1. Crow Dog. 2. Crow Dog, Leonard, 1942– . 3. Brulé Indians—
Biography. 4. Brulé Indians—History. I. Erdoes, Richard. II. Title.
E99.B8C753   1995
929'.2'089975—dc20   94-40695

ISBN 0-06-092682-1 (pbk.)

97 98 99 00 ❖/RRD 10 9 8 7 6 5 4

Crow Dog

one

I AM CROW DOG

Look at things not with the
eyes in your face but with the
eyes in your heart.

Leonard Crow Dog

I am Crow Dog. I am the fourth of that name. Crow Dogs
have played a big part in the history of our tribe and in
the history of all the Indian nations of the Great Plains
during the last two hundred years. We are still making history. I am talking this book because I don't read or write. I
never went to school—where they try to make Lakota
children into whites, where it takes them eight years to
teach you to spell *cat*. Talking and listening, not writing,
that's in our tradition. Telling stories sitting around a fire
or potbelly stove during the long winter nights, that's our
way. I speak English as it forms up in my mind. It's not the
kind of English they teach you in school; we don't use
five-dollar words. I always think up the story in my mind
in my own language. Then I try to put it into English. Our
Lakota language is sacred to me. Even now, as I am talking, our language is getting lost among some of us. You
can kill a language. The white missionaries and teachers
in their schools committed language genocide. We are trying to bring our old language back. Trying to purify it. So
now I'm telling my own story in my own way—starting at
the beginning.

It's a medicine story. White historians say that we came over from Asia, when ice covered the Bering Strait so that one could walk over it. We don't believe this, not only us Lakotas, but nearly all the Native Americans on this turtle continent. If there was any crossing of people on the Arctic ice it was the other way around, from Alaska to Asia. We were always here; we came from this earth. We were put here for a purpose, by Wakan Tanka, the Creator. We were put here in the center of the world, and at the center of these United States. Look at a map. Rosebud, our reservation, is smack in the middle. My story is a spiritual winter count of our people.

It was Ptesan Win, the sacred White Buffalo Woman, who made our people holy and taught them how to live. She was the spirit of waonshila, mercifulness. She was grace. She was beauty. When she appeared, the people were starving. There was no game and nothing to eat. The chiefs sent out two young hunters to look for game. But these scouts found nothing. They saw neither buffalo nor deer. Then the winyan wakan, the woman sacredness, appeared to them in the morning. Ptesan Win came out of a cloud. The cloud turned into a hill. Ptesan Win walked the hill in the shape of a white buffalo calf who turned itself into a beautiful maiden dressed in white buckskin. In her hands she carried sage and her great gift to our people, chanunpa, the sacred pipe. Four days before she appeared, the hunters had foreseen her coming in a dream.

The sacred woman spoke to these two young men: "Go back to your people. Tell them to get ready to receive me, to prepare the sacred tipi. Prepare the sacred sweat lodge. Do all these things. You already have the fire, peta owihankeshni, the fire without end. Light this fire for me. Igluha. Act well. Perform all I told you. In four days I will come to your camp."

The young men treated Ptesan Win with awe and respect. They honored her. They went back to their village without meat, but bringing with them spiritual food. Their nourishment was the wind, and it filled up the people's bellies as if they had eaten buffalo hump. And the hunters told their chiefs, who ordered everything prepared for Ptesan Win's coming. The people at that time were not what they became. The men knew a little about hunting. They had stone axes and wooden spears whose sharpened points were hardened in fire. They hunted the mammoth and other animals that have long since died out. They killed mammoths and buffalo by chasing them with burning branches over high cliffs to fall to their deaths. The women gathered wild fruits. The people's language was still rude. They did not know how to pray. They did not even know that there was a Tunkashila, a Grandfather Spirit, the Creator.

At daybreak, just as the sun rose, the sacred woman arrived at the camp, as she had promised the two young scouts. She wore her hair loose, on the right and tied with buffalo hair on the left. She was carrying the sacred pipe, carrying the stem in her left hand and the bowl in her right. As she approached she was singing her song:

Niya taninyan	With visible breath
mawinaye	I am walking.
oyate le	Toward this nation
imawani.	I am walking.

Her voice was sweet, and the men, women, and children who had assembled to greet and honor her saw that she was beautiful beyond words. Besides the chanunpa, she carried a sacred stone into which seven circles had been carved. These circles represented the seven sacred rituals of the Lakota nation. She brought with her chanshasha, red willow bark tobacco. The chief led her inside the sacred lodge, where sage had been spread to sit on at the place of honor. The chief's name was Tatanka Woslal Nazin, or Buffalo Standing Upward.

Ptesan Win told the people that she had been sent by the Buffalo Nation to instruct them in the ways of Wakan Tanka, the Creator, whom she also called Tunkashila, the Grandfather Spirit. She taught them how to use the sacred pipe and how to pray

with it. She taught them the sacred songs. She taught them how
to perform the seven great ceremonies. She instructed them how
to make offerings to Wakan Tanka. She told the men to protect
and nourish their women and children, to be kind to them and to
share their wives' sorrows. She told the women that without
them there would be no life. She taught them the manner in
which to bear children, how to do quillwork, and to stay away
from men and sacred things during their moon time. She taught
the people how to live like human beings, how to put things
together, and to understand Tunkashila's holy ways. She made
the Lakota into the people of the sacred pipe. After she had done
all this, the woman took leave of the people, promising to return
after four years. As she walked away, the people saw her turning
into a ptesan ska win, a white buffalo calf, and also into a tahca
win, a deer woman, and a hehaka win, an elk woman. They also
say that she turned herself into buffalo of four different colors—
black, dark brown, light yellow-brown, and, finally, white—as she
disappeared into the clouds. The Creator had given her the
power to carry the pipe to the Lakota people. She was a woman
sacredness, a spirit of the spirit. When the descendants of Chief
Tatanka Woslal Nazin had died out, the pipe was passed on to
Chief Hehaka Pa, Chief Elk Head. The Elk Heads were the pipe's
keepers for generations. After that the pipe passed to the
Looking Horse family at Eagle Butte, on the Cheyenne River
reservation in South Dakota. The present keeper is Arval Looking
Horse. The sacred pipe is made from a buffalo calf's leg bone.
Age has made it so brittle that it can no longer be smoked, but
when you touch it, power flows into you like an electric current.
The power is so strong that you burst into tears.

Now here is something that has never been told. The way
they tell the story of Ptesan Win today, when this sacred woman
appeared to the two young hunters one of them had impure
thoughts and stretched out his hands to touch her, to possess
her body. Lightning struck him and burned him up until only a little heap of bones and ashes was left. But this is not true. Both

young men were respectful of Ptesan Win. Nobody was burned up. This untrue story was made up a hundred years ago by missionaries who always tried to make our beliefs look savage and nasty. When they put the story into books, everybody started to repeat it this way. That's one kind of religious genocide.

I think there must be a reason why Ptesan Win came to the center, to our people, to the spirit of this continent. After her, the nation split up into seven tribes, the Oceti Shakowin, the Seven Council Fires: the Sichangu or Brulé, also known as the Burned Thighs, that's my own tribe; then the Oglala, the Scattered Ones; the Hunkpapa, Sitting Bull's people; the Mnikowoju, the Planters Beside the Water; the Itazipcho, the Without Bows; the Oohenunpa, the Two Kettles; and finally, the Sihaspa, the Blackfeet (who are not the same as the Blackfeet of Montana, who are not Sioux). So these are the seven western Lakota tribes, the Tetonwan. Sioux is a word that's part French and part Ojibway, a white man's word for us. We are Lakota. We full-bloods also call ourselves the ikche wichasha—the wild, natural human beings.

My father told me that after Ptesan Win came four chiefs—a medicine man, a man of knowledge, a warrior, and a hunter. They dwelled together in the Black Hills. The White Buffalo Woman had taught the people sacredness. The four chiefs taught the people how to survive, how to live in this world, when to sleep and when to get up, how to make bows and arrowheads, and the different ways to make a fire. They taught them their language.

They told the people, "You will see the waters flow, the thunder coming, and you'll have the winter, the spring, the summer, and the fall, the four seasons of the human mind, the four sacred directions. Go back into yourself and dream it. Go by the four winds. Snow falls from the north, rain from the west, the sun rises in the east, warmth comes from the south. Above the sky, between the earth and the moon, the Great Spirit roams. There's nothing between our world and the stars but the Great Spirit. Pray to the clear sky. Drink clear water from the spring and it will clear your mind." This the four chiefs taught the people.

We Lakota didn't come from another nation or country. We came from across the Missouri, from three daybreaks and three nights away, from the east. And we Lakota claimed this land; it belongs to us. Before that, so long ago that we can hardly remember it, we came from the land of the Great Lakes. We were then a lake and woodlands people. Then the French gave guns, matchlocks, to the Ojibway. We had only bows and arrows. So we were pushed toward the west. And they had horses and we had not gotten them yet. It was not the Ojibway's fault. It was the white man who started the fighting among the tribes, who pushed Ojibway onto Lakota land, and Crows onto Cheyenne land, Crees on Blackfoot land, always pushing the tribes westward to make room for himself, pushing them with guns and cannons, piling one tribe onto another, stopping only when they reached the western ocean. So for a while, the great prairie became our hunting grounds and we turned into a prairie people, a nation of the Great Plains. We need space to roam, to ride. We are a tipi people. But we are not drifters. We try to stay on our own ground. We are Tunkashila's people. He chose this sacred land for us. Our grandfathers chose it. When the grandfathers had the buffalo and owned this land—the Great Dakota Reservation, as the whites called it in 1868 in the Treaty of Fort Laramie—all our dreams and beliefs and sacred sites were centered here. The wasichu, the white man, always talks about those murderous Sioux, always on the warpath, killing settlers, burning and scalping. But that is not true. We were, and are, a peaceful people. Wolakota means "peace." We even welcomed the wasichu. Only when we saw them building roads through our land, wagon roads at first, and then the railroad, when we watched them building forts, killing off all the game, committing a buffalo genocide, and when we saw them ripping up our Black Hills for gold, our sacred Paha Sapa, the home of the wakinyan, the thunderbirds, only then did we realize that what they wanted was our land. Then we began to fight. For our earth. For our children. That started what the whites call the Great Indian Wars of the West. I call it the Great Indian Holocaust.

It began with some of our eastern Dakota cousins, the Sisseton, Santee, Wahpeton, and Yankton. They lived in Minnesota, where they had been put on a reservation. The government, which had taken their land, had promised to feed them. But corrupt white agents stole the food and other supplies. The Dakota were starving to death. The white superintendent told them to eat grass. That started what the whites called the Great Sioux Uprising, the revolt of a desperate, dying people. Out of the prisoners the army took, thirty-eight Dakota warriors were condemned to death and hanged. They sang their death songs. Then the last of our eastern tribes were chased across the Missouri and beyond.

It was a killing time. Many hundreds of our people and of the Cheyenne were exterminated, most of them old people, women, and children. They were easy to kill. As one colonel, who was also a clergyman, told his soldiers, "Kill 'em all, big and small, nits make lice."

After the Lakota and Cheyenne had wiped out Custer, the soldiers swarmed over our land. So many buffalo were killed that they became almost extinct. They had been our main food. Then we were driven onto the reservations and fenced in.

I can trace my ancestry back for nine generations. We Crow Dogs had always had the "earth ear," maka nongeya, having the whole earth for an ear. It means you know what's going to happen before it happens. And you can also listen backward, way back, know the generations gone by. And I have my spirit computer, Inyan Tunka, the ancient rock computer, a finding stone. So I have the rock spirit in me. And I have the wakiksuyapi, a special memory, a hot line to the spirits, the remembrance of long-dead relatives, the understanding of signs. Also I can speak the Lakota language as it was spoken hundreds of years ago. In my dreams I can speak to my ancestors. I carry our history inside me.

Before we were put on the reservation, and before the census takers got hold of us, sons had names different from their fathers. So Chief Iron Shell's son was called Hollow Horn Bear. You got a childhood name and, after your first vision quest, maybe a dream gave you your grown-up name. And later, maybe you performed some great deed and were honored with still another name. Men could have different names during their lifetimes. But sometime after 1870 the missionaries and census takers made us all take Christian first names, like Tom, Dick, and Harry, while our Indian names became our last names and were frozen in time. So in the five generations since, we have all been named Crow Dog. Before that, each ancestor had a different name, according to his or her vision. I have seen a trail. I walked it backward. I saw the footprints of our ancestors.

My earliest ancestor was Mato Mani, Walking Bear. He got his name because he was hunting all the time. He had two wives—a Lakota and an Arapaho woman. He had a son and a daughter. The son's name was Mato, Bear. Just Bear. He took after his father; he did a lot of hunting. He had a charm that brings the animals to you. And there was Mato Kangi, Bear Crow. This one had three wives, who gave him four sons. The first was a Lakota woman, the second a Cheyenne, and the third was from the Pawnee nation. There was always a lot of marrying between the tribes and, in the old days, a lot of capturing of wives from another tribe during a raid. Two of this Mato Kangi's sons were spiritual, what the white man calls medicine men. We had many of them in our clan, our tiyoshpaye. We are medicine people. Going farther back there was Mato Shunka Manitou, Bear Coyote. He was a great warrior. He was a Tokala, a member of the Kit Fox warrior society. The Tokala had a song:

Tokala kin hemacha   I am a fox,
Taka yakapi channa   I am supposed to die.
Iyatan michila.   Whatever is dangerous,
                           let me do it.

In battle, the Tokala didn't care whether they lived or died. That gave them an edge. Still farther back there was Shunka Numpa, Two Dogs. He had two wives, a Lakota and a Cree. And there were the Iron Shells and Two Strikes, famous chiefs and warriors.

My father, Henry, took up where I stopped. He said, "It started with that damned cow. It belonged to a Mormon passing through with a wagon train. That cow strayed. A young man, High Forehead, shot it. Then they butchered it. It wasn't much of a feast. That cow was nothing but skin and bones and hard chewing. The Mormon went to the soldiers' fort and made a big stink. He shouldn't have done it. That cow was sick and ran off to die someplace. There was this Lieutenant Grattan. He was the kind of wasichu who has an Indian for breakfast every day. He said, 'With thirty men I can ride over the whole Sioux nation!' That's what he said. So this fool, Grattan, went to the Indian camp. Conquering Bear, whom they also called Brave Bear, was the chief there. He was my grandfather's uncle. He belonged to our tiyoshpaye. That's why it all starts here. Grattan told the chief he must give up the man who shot the cow. Conquering Bear told him he couldn't give up the man because he was a Minneconjou, not a Brulé. Also, he didn't want to give up High Forehead to be put in a tiny cell inside prison. Why all that trouble about an old, broken-down cow?

"Grattan came up with his soldiers and two cannons. He shot up the Indians' camp. One of the cannon balls killed Conquering Bear. Then the warriors got mad and killed Grattan and all his men. The first one named Crow Dog was in that fight and counted coup. He earned eagle feathers. The way I see it, Grattan had it coming. This happened in 1854. So from there it starts—Crow Dog history."

The white man has a family—papa, mama, two kids, and a poodle—in an apartment inside a high-rise. He puts his parents into a nursing home. He doesn't know his cousins. He doesn't want to know them. He's thinking about whether he can afford a new car. He has six doormen watching his building so that no poor, or black, or chicano guy can go in there and rob him. That's a white man's family. We have the tiyoshpaye, all the people having a common grandfather or great-grandfather: aunts, uncles, granddads, grandmothers, grandkids, cousins, nieces, nephews. Whites call this the extended family. The Crow Dogs, Hollow Horn Bears, Two Strikes, and Iron Shells all come from common ancestors, so we all make up one large tiyoshpaye. And then all these men formed their own, smaller tiyoshpayes. Many of them had several wives, who, in turn, had several kids each. So now we have relatives in the Rosebud, Pine Ridge, Cheyenne River, Oak Creek, Standing Rock, and Lower Brulé reservations, at Fort Yates, Fort Belknap, and Fort Peck, in Oklahoma, and even in Canada. There are so many relatives spread far and wide even I am losing track.

two

THE BUFFALO HUNTER

The buffalo is our brother.
He gives his flesh so that
the people may live.
The buffalo is sacred.

> Lakota proverb

Old Man Crow Dog, the first of that name, was a buffalo hunter. He knew the ways of the buffalo and of the animals in the forest. He was born in 1836 and died in 1912. A government paper says he was born earlier, in 1832. Maybe so. Before he took on the name Crow Dog he had six other names. One of them was Mato Sicha, Bad Bear. When Crow Dog was a young man, just at the end of his boyhood, he hunted with bow and arrow. His arrowheads were made of chipped stone. My father, Henry, still had his arrow straightener, a round stone with a hole in it. My father kept it as a souvenir. He was a good bowman, but not as good as his close relatives Hollow Horn Bear and He Dog. The best was Numpa Kahpa, Two Strikes, who got his name from killing two soldiers, riding on a horse, with one arrow. Some say that he shot an arrow clear through a buffalo and it went on and killed a buffalo calf. I don't know which is true, but Two Strikes sure was a great arrow shooter.

My father still saw his grandfather, Crow Dog Number

One, carry a bow, even though by this time he owned a Winchester. He told my father, "Always take two bowstrings. If one breaks, you still got the other. Always be ready, because any-time you might run into something. Then go for your arrow bag! The wind can turn an arrow. Judge the wind if you want to hit something. Get the right wood for the bow, get the right wood for the arrows. You have to feather them good. By the feathers you can tell what tribe the arrow is from. Go to a good bow maker. Don't try to make them yourself. The bow maker has a certain power. Maybe it's an herb he uses, a bow medicine. Often he is a bad hunter. You supply him with good hump meat, he makes you a bow. A fine bow is worth two good horses."

My father remembered those things and he taught me. Later, my great-grandfather had iron-tipped arrows and, during the 1850s, got his first trade gun, a muzzle loader with a silver dragon mounted on its stock. Without the dragon you wouldn't accept such a gun, because without the dragon it wasn't good. They made those guns until 1860. Henry had it before I was born. He said it shot straight. He sold it to a trader for two dollars for food.

When my great-grandfather was young he kindled a flame with a fire stick of sharpened hardwood. You twirl it around in some soft wood with a little heap of tinder about so big. I can still make a fire that way for a ceremony where you're not allowed to use matches. Later, he carried a "strike-a-light" in a quilled bag around his neck—a U-shaped piece of steel, some flint, and tin-der in a little box to keep it dry. He also had a knife made from buffalo bone with a very sharp point, a real man-killer. He lived in a tipi made of buffalo skins.

From a white man's point of view, Old Man Crow Dog was still living in the Stone Age—savage and uncivilized. In the white man's view you are civilized when you have a flush toilet and a microwave. But that's not how we look at it. I think that the first Crow Dog was a lot more civilized than a white man of today, watching wrestling on TV. He lived in a time of change, lightning-swift change. My father, Henry, said, "Old Man Crow Dog jumped from inside the body of a Stone Age aborigine into the body of a modern man." Henry spoke English badly but liked to use a few five-dollar words that had come his way. *Aborigine* was one of them. Old Man Crow Dog lived long enough to ride in a train. He never rode in a car, but might have seen one of the earliest kinds. Henry was the first to own an automobile, an "Indian car"—that is, an old rattletrap. After he was put on the reservation, the first Crow Dog was told that he must have a Christian first name. "Pick any one you like," said the census taker. "You pick it" was the answer. "How about Jerome?" said the census taker. Jerome it was. Henry thought it might also be possible that a missionary baptized his grandfather without his knowing what was going on. So from then on he was Jerome Crow Dog. He moved from a tipi of buffalo skins into a canvas tipi, because by then all the buffalo were gone. An old photograph shows Jerome with his wife, Catches Her, standing in front of that tipi. Later he moved into a one-room log cabin with a dirt floor and a kerosene lamp for light. Just before he died, someone in Rapid City showed him how to make a phone call. By then they had electric light in that town. I would have liked to know what an old bow-and-arrow man would have thought about all this, the sudden jump from one age into another.

Jerome was a Brulé. We are all full-blood Brulés. The word is French, meaning "burned." In English we are the Burned Thighs, or Sichangu in the Lakota language. We got this name because of a fight during which enemies set the prairie around our camp on fire, so our people's leggings and moccasins burned.

Jerome was a good rider, a horse master. An old photograph shows him riding bareback. He didn't need a saddle. He loved his luzan (fast) horse. He could tame a wild pony. He could doctor a sick one, blow into its skin or use shunka wakan tapejuta, the horse-curing herb that shines like silver. He cured limping or a lump somewhere, any horse sickness at all.

He also was a great horse stealer. He raided far and wide, got horses from the Pawnee and Crow. "He had that way with horses," my father told me. "He had that power, a horse medicine. He went on a raid, and he crept up and put a halter on that pony and just walked off with it. The horse never made a sound, it just went along. None of those Crow or Pawnee, sleeping in their tipis, woke up. His medicine was that strong." My father still knew his grandfather's horse-raiding song:

Pahani wichasha kin	Pawnee man,
shunk awanglaka po	watch your horses;
shunka wamanon	a horse stealer
tuktektel	sometimes
miye yelo.	I am.

Getting horses when raiding an enemy tribe got a man war honors. It was like counting coup. It earned a man eagle feathers. In Crow Dog's vision, he saw a strange thing in the clouds. There was thunder and lightning, and all of a sudden he had this vision. It was as if he were blindfolded, like having buckskin covering his eyes. He peeked through it, lifted it up, and saw an Indian riding his horse. In him he recognized himself. And he recognized the sacred horse power given to Crow Dog. So he became a horse dreamer through the power of Wakan Tanka. He was given the gift of putting on a horse dance. He had four times four riders doing it, riding horses of the same color. The men wore black masks. There were no holes for their eyes in those hoods, so the horses did all the dancing. They never bumped one another. They knew this was sacred. The masks had horns on them and the riders used no saddles, or blankets, or bridles. Both men and horses were painted with lightning designs. They called the horse dance pejuta wacipi, medicine dance. It brings rain and cures sick minds.

Crow Dog also put on the shunka alowanpi, a horse parade for warriors who are going out to fight an enemy. And he put on warrior honoring dances. Crow Dog taught all these things to the people. He taught them the songs, so that when he was no longer around they would remember them and how to perform those ceremonies. Thanks to him we still know them today.

My father told me, "Old Crow Dog Number One was a fighting man. In battle he made the bear sound: 'Hrrrnh, watch out! Crow Dog is coming!' He had the right to carry a chief's staff, shaped like a white man's sheepherder's stick, crooked at the top. He counted many coups with it. He also had a bear claw necklace. He had to kill the bear himself before he was allowed to wear it. He always wore a blanket around his shoulders. So the missionaries called him an 'unregenerate hostile nonprogressive aborigine' or a 'blanket Injun.' He liked that. He was proud of it."

Jerome was a loner. He lived way out on the prairie, as far out as he could. He went by the sun, the moon, the stars, and the wind. He had his campfire. He knew how to strike a spark without matches. He harvested from the earth and the animals. He was a buffalo man, an herb man, a pejuta wichasha. He saw an herb and, in his mind, the herb told him how to use it.

My father remembered the old man telling him stories, rocking back and forth, sometimes stopping to hum a little song, "Always moving, I was, from place to place, always moving. Following the buffalo, going to the sacred Paha Sapa, the Black Hills, roaming as far up as the Big Horns, and east all the way to the Missouri but never as far as the Mississippi. Ah, hokshila, son, that was a life for a man to live. For a woman and a kid, too. On a horse, after buffalo, buffalo covering the earth as far as you could see, the thunder of their hooves ringing in your ears. The great rumbling sound of the herds. The smell of roasting meat, the laughter, the drums going, the dancing. And nothing to spoil it. Ho, hokshila, you can never know what you're missing." Then he would stop and look sad. He dreamed of his youth when the country was still wild and beautiful, without fences, telephone poles, or pig farms.

Jerome didn't meet a white man until he was nearly grown up. White beaver men and traders had been around since about 1810 or so, but they always came up the Missouri, bringing whiskey and the smallpox to the Mandan, almost wiping out that tribe, but they didn't come as far west as Crow Dog country. There was just one little fur trading post at what is now Chadron, Nebraska. But somehow Jerome never was there. He grew up as an ikche wichasha, a wild, natural human being.

Old Man Crow Dog had the power to see things coming. He saw it in his mind. He would say, "Tomorrow will come bad weather for some time." And that would happen. He told the people, "Soon there will be no more buffalo and people will starve. Make wasna! Make wasna!"—that is, pemmican. And it was as he said; the buffalo were being killed off by the whites. He foretold such things. He could say to a person that he was going to die unless he ate a certain medicine, and that person would go out looking for that herb. And soon enough he found that root and got the medicine to make him well. Jerome told them to go south or east, this way and that, for an hour, or a day, or a week, to stop at a certain tree or rock, and they'd find food or water. Or he told them how to find a spot where they could find and kill a weak animal, and butcher it, and be hungry no more. He saw these places in his mind. He told the women where to find timpsila (wild turnips) and chokecherries when there was no meat. He could always foretell the weather. His four wounds helped with this. It was the bullets inside his body that told him what kind of weather it would be.

My father was fourteen years old when Jerome died. So he knew him well. He told me, "When my grandfather was alive we had to get our drinking water from the creek. We got our water like the animals, like the deer and elk. My grandfather, when he was young, didn't even have a pail. He carried his water in a bladder bag. Every woman had a skin bag then. Getting water from the creek, first thing in the morning, was women's work. When they met at the creek, that was a time for them to chat, to gossip. It was not only that he had no pail, he had only a few of the white man's things. He once traded some skins for a miloglas, a mirror for his wife. In his old age, of course, he had to live pretty much like a wasichu.

"Before he had to go to the reservation, my grandfather had been a great hunter. He was open-handed and had a generous heart. He gave feasts for the hungry, even if he himself was starving. He always shared his meat with the old and the sick. He was a giver. He always told me, 'You must follow my trail. Don't be stingy. Tunkashila has made this earth for us to live on, so that our people should live forever. So the half-starved must share with those who are altogether starving.' He said this whenever our government rations ran out. He sometimes said things that were hard to understand, like 'The pain you have to learn like the animal learns it. The herb itself gets sick. The thunder gave thirst to the earth!' It took me a long time to figure him out. He liked us to think for ourselves, to guess at what was in his mind.

"When he was young, my grandfather was very good-looking. He had the love power, the elk power. Women who met him had that love light in their eyes. In his earliest photograph he looks very young, smooth skinned, with strong cheekbones. He was close to fifty when that picture was taken, sometime around 1880. He looked about twenty years younger. His eyes were keen like a hawk's always looking for things to be seen. When he was old, the way I knew him, his face had broadened and his mouth was like a gash. He looked like the chief he was. His hair grew white, but not totally, and began to curl a little. He tried to raise a mustache, but we Indians don't have much body hair. And he was a full-blood. All he could do was two tiny tufts at the sides of his upper lip. He was a good man, a loner, living way out on the prairie, far from other folk."

three

TWO BULLETS AND
TWO ARROWS

He got his name from a battle
in which he almost died
from his wounds.

Henry Crow Dog

Our shield design, our wotawe, looks like this:

TWO BULLETS–TWO ARROWS
CROW DOG FAMILY CREST
(WOTAWE)

It stands for the two arrow wounds and two bullet
wounds the first Crow Dog received in battle. All the
wounds were in front. From the first fight, where he was
hit by the arrows, he got his final name. Before that he
had a bear name. He then took the name Kangi Shunka
Manitou, or Crow Coyote, not Crow Dog. The interpreter
misunderstood it. His Lakota was poor. It should have
been Crow Coyote. The coyote was my grandfather's
sacred animal. It has to do with wounds he received in a

fight. Without the coyote he would have died and it would all have ended right there.

One time Crow Dog took a war party north to Cedar Valley. The party was made up of young men from the Kit Fox warrior society. They are the sash wearers who pin themselves to the ground and fight it out where they stand. But Crow Dog did not go out to fight. He went for a ceremony he wanted to hold at that place, he went there for a vision. The young men he took along because this was close to Crow country. The Sioux and that tribe were at war most of the time because the Crow worked for the white soldiers as scouts. At this time they even had a white man fighting among them. So that party was out and roaming. Crow Dog made out the figure of a man standing on a hill. Crow Dog's horse raised its ears forward, and the two eagle feathers my grandfather was wearing caught the wind and the feathers began to talk, telling Crow Dog, "There are enemies over there, behind those hills." So they all stopped. They saw this man hiding. Then Crow Dog sent two young men ahead to find out, one to the north and one to the south. Soon the scouts were back. They had not seen anything. The wind, the feathers, told Crow Dog that something was wrong. He told his men, "We'll not go on. We've got to find out what's beyond those hills. We'll camp right here." He also told them, "Put the tipis right up to the riverbank so that horse riders can't go around, so that on one side the river will be your shield." They did this. They put up the camp so that nobody could run a circle on them. But still my grandfather smelled the danger, and the eagle feathers did not stop whispering. Then a coyote was whooping four times. Crow Dog understood that the coyote was saying, "Something is going to happen to you."

Just as it was getting light, a large party of Crow was riding up, coming from behind. They had found a ford upriver. Suddenly, there they were. Hollow Horn Bear was with Crow Dog that day, and so were Hollow Horn Bear's son, and Kills in Water, and Kills on Sight. Kills on Sight was wounded early on. He was hit bad; they unhorsed him. Two Crow came at him from both sides. Crow Dog came up at a dead run and killed the two Crow. He put Kills on Sight on one of the enemy horses, and Kills on Sight took off, so badly hurt he could hardly stay on that pony. In the meantime, two more Crow were going after Crow Dog. He had his hands so full with the others and with helping Kills on Sight that he had not even noticed them. As he turned around, they were already very close. They had bows. Crow Dog took two arrows, one below the collar bone and one in his side. That one went into his water bag, his bladder, but it didn't really penetrate. The one under the collar bone was the bad one. It went very deep and he couldn't pull it out. He could not fight well with that arrow sticking out in front. So he broke it off at the point where it was going into his body. He had dismounted to help Kills on Sight get onto his pony and now he got on his own horse again. They came at him from front and back. Crow Dog had a sacred warrior stick, a coup stick. One end was crooked and the other end had an iron spear point. He used that on those Crow. More Crow went after him, and he got very weak from his wounds. A large part of the arrow with the point was still in his body. The point was barbed and pulling only made it worse. He fell off his horse. He couldn't do much then. I'm not going to make it, he thought. He was looking death in the face.

The Crow left him where he fell, thinking that they had killed him. Crow Dog crawled under some stinkwood bushes—that's coyote medicine. Then he blacked out. He couldn't move. He was lying like that for a long time, for days even. He was thirsty but had nothing to drink. He was too weak to make it to the nearby creek. He was cold inside and outside. He wasn't even sure that he was still alive. Then he heard the coyote whooping, "Huuuuuh, huuuuuh, Crow Dog, I'm coming! Human being, listen, I'm coming over."

Pretty soon that coyote came and cuddled up to Crow Dog and warmed him. He whooped like one coyote speaking to another, "Huuuuuh, Crow Dog, I've come to doctor you. I brought you a special kind of sage. Pick it up. Doctor yourself with it."

Crow Dog had the wolf and the coyote power. He could under-stand their language, understand it spiritually. Then a second coyote came, and then a third, and, finally, the fourth. This one told Crow Dog to eat that special sage and to roll up some of it in a ball. And the coyote carried that ball of sage in his mouth and went to the creek. He dipped it in the water and soaked it and brought it back that way to Crow Dog, who used it like a sponge, drinking the water, and when it went dry, the coyote carried it back to the creek and soaked it some more and brought it, again and again, to keep Crow Dog from dying of thirst.

One of the other coyotes brought Crow Dog taopi tawote, wound medicine. The coyote chewed it up into a mush and told Crow Dog to put it on the spot where the arrow had gone in. It made the flesh tender, so that Crow Dog could pull the point out. And he put the same medicine on the wound in his side and it began to heal fast. He told all this himself to my father, Henry.

On the fourth day after the coyotes had come to help, they made Crow Dog understand that he was well enough to walk. They talked among themselves and Crow Dog understood them. And they whooped, indicating that he should follow them. The coyotes scouted ahead for Crow Dog, warning him if enemies were close by. These coyotes were wakan. A message from such a sacred coyote could reach New York faster than a telegram.

And a crow appeared, caw-cawing, flying ahead, also showing the way. Crow Dog followed that bird and followed the coyotes' tracks on that spiritual trail, followed them all the way home to his people's camp. When Crow Dog came back the tribe honored him with okicize wacipi, a warrior dance, and a waktegeli wacipi, a men-coming-back-in-one-piece-after-killing-an-enemy dance. After returning from death to life, Crow Dog changed his name to Kangi Shunka Manitou, meaning Crow Coyote, in order to honor these wakan animals who had helped him to survive. But years later those damn census takers misunderstood it. Maybe their half-blood interpreter mistranslated it, and they put his name down as Crow Dog. And because by then everybody also had to have a

Christian first name they wrote him down as Jerome and he was stuck with that. He grumbled for a while, but now we are proud to be called Crow Dog.

Now about the two bullets Crow Dog took. He was a little over forty years old, maybe forty-five or -six, when he was in the Custer fight. Not much is known of what he did there. He might have been wounded early in the fight or there could have been some other reason. We just don't know. Spotted Tail was the head chief of the Brulé at that time and he forbade his men to leave the reservation to make war upon the white soldiers. He was Crow Dog's cousin and had been a great warrior once. He had often fought side by side with Crow Dog. But then the whites had taken him prisoner and brought him east, where he had seen big cities with their crowds of people, and he had been shown the factories turning out a thousand guns in one day, and when they let him go back home he was no longer a warrior. He told the people, "There are too many wasichu to fight. Don't leave the reservation." So those men who left and joined Crazy Horse and Sitting Bull did it secretly and did not talk much about it.

After the Custer fight, Sitting Bull took the Hunkpapa people to Unci Makoce, Grandmother's Land—that is, Canada. Crow Dog and a few others went to join Sitting Bull there. They told the people on the reservation that they were going hunting. But what they really wanted was to join Sitting Bull to honor him. On the way they came across a lone buffalo bull, but they did not kill him. Crow Dog told his friends, "We're going to Sitting Bull, so we're not going to kill and eat tatanka on this journey. We will eat deer instead." So they went hunting, and every day they brought back two deer. They stopped at a place called the holy Medicine Rocks, where Sitting Bull had held a sun dance just before the Custer fight. There Sitting Bull had received a vision that the white soldiers would be defeated. These medicine rocks are covered with designs scratched into them— figures of men, horses, and buffalo. These holy rocks are now part of a Montana ranch.

It was near Medicine Rocks that Crow Dog ran into a party of white soldiers. Crow Dog tried to talk to them in sign language, but they didn't understand it and opened up on him with their guns. He was on his horse, riding without a saddle. Crow Dog took two bullets, one in his belly near the groin; the other I am not sure where it hit. I was a young boy when my father told me and I forgot. It is such a long time. He had a fast horse and made it back to camp. There a medicine man named Sitting Hawk took care of him. Sitting Hawk told Crow Dog, "The two bullets are still there inside you. I'm not going to try to take them out because that would kill you. You will carry these bullets until the day you die. Someday you will go back to this earth, and long after your body has turned to dirt these two white man's bullets will remain there in your grave. They'll be the evidence that you fought for your people. So I'll leave those bullets alone, but I will put a medicine into you that will help you." And that is why Crow Dogs use the sign of two arrows and two bullets.

That happened between Standing Rock and the sacred Stone Hills, as we called them at that time when more and more white settlers came into our country and hardly a buffalo could be found anymore. The sad part was that Crow Dog had gone to this place to negotiate with the commander of the U.S. cavalry, which had a camp nearby. But he couldn't understand them and they couldn't understand him and just started shooting. The soldiers were building forts all over the country, and Crow Dog and his friends had gone to the sacred rocks to hold a ceremony that would help them to find a way to deal with the soldiers. That was also a time when missionaries, backed by the army, made Sitting Bull and Crow Dog accept the white man's religion and take Christian first names. But Crow Dog and Sitting Bull went on praying with the pipe and holding their ceremonies as before in places where the missionaries couldn't watch them.

There are different ways this story is told, depending on whether Henry told it or some of the other old men who had known the first Crow Dog. There was one old man who said it was not Crow but Pawnee arrows that had wounded Crow Dog. That's the only difference. It doesn't matter much. All of the old, long-dead storytellers agreed on the main points, and the legend of Crow Dog is now part of our Lakota history.

four

THE KILLING

If the Brulés had continued to lead
their old free life of hunting and
fighting, Crow Dog's cool courage and
mental alertness would have won him
high rank both in war and in the
tribal council, but on the reservation,
time and opportunity stopped dead.

George Hyde, *Spotted Tail's Folk*

I shall now tell how my great-grandfather killed the tribe's
head chief, Spotted Tail, and how he was the first Indian
to win a case in the Supreme Court of the United States.
Crow Dog was a leader of the Wablenicha, the Orphan
band, a part of our Brulé tribe. As the tiyoshpaye is a
clan, so the Wablenicha is like a few clans put together. In
a way the Orphans are all Crow Dogs, all related, all coming from a common ancestor. The most famous of the
Wablenicha chiefs was Pankeshka Maza, Iron Shell.

My father told me, "Jerome Crow Dog lived at this
creek north of here, where we are now. A place called
White Thunder, after a chief killed in battle one hundred
fifty years ago. The first chief of the Wablenicha, Kangi
Tanka Sapa, Black Raven, led his warriors on a raid
against the Pawnee and was killed together with some of
his men. So his people became orphans, in a way, and

were called by this name from then on. The famous chiefs were
Iron Shell, Two Strikes, and Iron Shell's son, Hollow Horn Bear,
and my grandfather, too. They were all related and did everything together.

"So they were all part of our bloodline. The Fool Bulls, too,
and the Eagle Elks, all related, all friends. Iron Shell was the head
chief. He was a great warrior who counted many coups. He killed
eleven Pawnee in one day. His thumbprint is on the Fort Laramie
treaty of 1868. My grandfather rode and fought alongside him.
Crow Dogs, Iron Shells, and Two Strikes always act together.
They fight on the same side, to preserve the old ways. At this
time the Crow Dogs had their camp at White Thunder Creek.

"Those early reservation days were hard. People lived on
wild turnips, fish, and roots. That was all. We were real orphans
then. The buffalo were gone. Hard times for Mister Indian. The
agents cheated on the meat issue: kept half and sold it and got
rich that way. The meat came walking, on the hoof, the stringiest,
sorriest animals they could find. My grandfather said that if he
had boiled his old, stiff moccasins that would have been better
eating.

"Iron Shell Number One, son of Chief Bull Tail, had seven
wives. He was a big chief and had to entertain, so there was too
much work for just one wife. He took an extra wife, and then
another, and then another and kept going like this. He had to,
because people came visiting, wanting meat, hides, trade cloth,
and all kinds of stuff from him. He was a great chief and had to be
a sharing man. So the wives had to tan and bead and cook and do
quillwork for enough gifts to go around. They all had children.
There was a whole community of Iron Shells. Iron Shell got his
name, Pankeshka Maza, from wearing shells in his braids. Iron
Shell was from the purity of color in those shells. Other people
couldn't find such a shell.

The great-grandfather on my mother's side was Nahca Cica,
Little Chief. He was small, but he brought in more buffalo meat
than anyone else. He got his own good medicine to heal. He had

some luzan horses who could run faster than any other. He was still fighting the whites when all others had given up. He was out hunting and met a white scout and a cavalry man, who knew he was a fierce fighting Sioux. They hunted for water, but it was all iced over. Little Chief had an ax and chopped up some ice. He melted it for a drink, drink for the horses, too. He fixed a fire so that the cavalry had a fire on the ice. He fed his enemies and watered them and they tried to pay him with bullets for having saved them. But he got away from them and escaped to Mni Chumpa, the Smoking Waters.

"Iron Shell's son was Hollow Horn Bear. I knew him well. He had a real full-blood face, the kind you don't find anymore. He had his portrait on a fifteen-cent stamp and on a five-dollar bill. He got a peace medal from the president once, to make him a peaceful, turn-the-other-cheek Christian, but it didn't work. He remained an unregenerate aborigine. Chief Two Strikes was the same, a great warrior who earned eagle feathers left and right, fighting the whites, the Pawnee, and the Omaha. The Arikara, too. He was a full-blood of the full-bloods. He became a ghost dance leader together with Crow Dog in the Badlands.

"Crow Dog, too, had two wives at one time, when he was young. You need a big bed for two wives. Jerome Crow Dog's wife's name was Jumping Elk. She was a Blackfoot woman with curly hair. He built a log cabin for her. It was very small, just one room with a dirt floor, but it was one of the first log houses among the Brulé. He had another wife before that, a Lakota winyan. I think her name was Catches Her. He had two brothers, one of whom was called Brave Bull, and one half brother, named Yellow Horse. This one was a huge one-and-a-half man. The other brother died in Pahaska, Oklahoma. We have relatives there in what used to be called Indian Territory. Some of our relations married Osage and Comanche and settled down in Oklahoma, close to the Kansas line. One daughter took up with a Kiowa. Low Dog, Red Dog, Fool Bull, Eagle Elk—these are all our relatives. Fools Crow, our oldest medicine man, was a grandson of our tiyoshpaye. He settled in Pine Ridge. He seemed to go on living forever, but he died two years ago. In 1974, Frank Fools Crow ran our sun dance at Crow Dog's Paradise, and we helped him several times running the sun dance at Pine Ridge. So we are everybody's cousins. We were also relatives and allies of the Wazhazha band, the Loafers. The Wazhazha and our Wablenicha often camped together.

"At this time, Spotted Tail, Sinte Gleshka, was the head chief of our tribe. He was proud, fearless, and very handsome. Even when he was surrounded by other chiefs, Spotted Tail stood out. He got his name from a raccoon tail that was part of his headdress. It was his wotawe, his medicine. He was a Brulé of the Red Lodge band, who were hunting buffalo near the Platte River. His father was Tangle Hair. His mother was called Walking with Pipe; she was a Siha Sapa, of the Blackfoot Teton band. Spotted Tail was about twenty years older than Crow Dog. He was a cousin of Chief Brave, who was killed in 1854, during the fight with Lieutenant Grattan's soldiers. Crow Dog was the chief's nephew. So he and Spotted Tail were relatives. The place Spotted Tail's people picked to do their buffalo hunting belonged to the Pawnee, old-time enemies of the Sioux. The Lakota people looked down on the palani, folks who planted corn like white farmers, living in permanent earth lodges, bad-smelling, we thought. We changed our campsite when it was no longer sweet. They didn't. We also hated the Pawnee for practicing human sacrifice. In 1838, the Skidi Pawnee had stripped a young Sioux woman naked, spread-eagled her on a wooden frame, and shot her full of arrows as a sacrifice to the morning star. The Lakota showed little mercy to any Pawnee falling into their hands and slowly pushed their enemies off their hunting grounds.

"In this long war Spotted Tail did great deeds. He was already counting coups while still in his teens. He was only fifteen years old during his first fight against the Ute, but most of the time he fought against the Pawnee. Blowing on his eagle bone whistle he charged into a Pawnee village and went right into their earth lodges to get at his enemies. Together with Two Strikes he was in the midst of the Grattan fight, riding down and killing the soldiers. Sometimes he fought alongside Red Cloud, and years later, side by side with Crow Dog. While still not yet thirty, Spotted Tail was made an Ogle Tanka Un, a Shirt Wearer. This was a great honor. It meant that he was looked up to as a war leader. From then on he wore a painted war shirt fringed with Pawnee scalp locks.

"During the Grattan fight the lieutenant himself and all his thirty-one soldiers had been killed. In 1855, General Harney came out with many soldiers to punish us for this, even though the battle had been started by the whites. Our people called Harney the hornet, because he stung us so badly. The soldiers had guns and cannons. Our people had only bows and arrows. So we were beaten. Many warriors were killed, their camp overrun, and the women and children taken prisoner, among them two wives of Spotted Tail and Iron Shell, who had led the fight. Iron Shell was lucky to escape. Spotted Tail was not so lucky; his horse was shot from under him. On foot, he put up a good fight and he killed two dragoons. But he came away with two bullets in him, besides two deep saber slashes. It was like Crow Dog's four wounds. This happened in 1855, at Mni to Wakpala, or Blue Water Creek. General Harney said he would let his dragoons loose on the Brulé unless the tribe gave up its best-known warriors. So Spotted Tail and two others surrendered themselves and were taken to Fort Leavenworth and there put in the 'iron house' as prisoners. Two of Spotted Tail's four wives stayed with him through all this. The whites wanted to try and hang Spotted Tail, but in the end he was pardoned and they let him go back to his tribe. He had been treated well and he'd made friends with some of the officers at the fort. After he came back he told the people, 'We shouldn't fight the wasichu anymore. They are too powerful. There are too many of them. They have bigger weapons.'

"He went on fighting the Pawnee but stayed clear of trouble with the whites, who called him a friendly and a progressive. In

1865, he fought the wasichu for the last time. The whites built the railroad straight through our hunting country, so his own people forced him to take up the gun again. He couldn't stand aside when it was a case of life or death for the tribe. He took part in the burning of Julesburg, which the whites themselves called a helltown, full of scalp hunters, gamblers, pay women, buffalo skinners, and whiskey sellers. Again they dragged him to prison in chains, and again he was let go after a year. In 1866, the government made him head chief of the whole Brulé tribe. From then on, he worked with them. The whites put him up in a white, two-story clapboard house. They put him in a starched shirt and a black suit, taking him to Washington to meet President Grant. He fooled them by going to the White House in his black suit, all right, but with a Hudson's Bay blanket over his shoulders. The 'Great White Father' treated him and Swift Bear to a train ride. They weren't impressed.

"The government gave him and his people a reservation, then called an agency, at Whetstone, near Fort Randall. It was on the Missouri River, in the eastern part of South Dakota. Later the agency was put where it is now, at Rosebud, in the western part of the state. During 1876, the year of the Custer fight, he kept most of his young men on the reservation. He was a big chief supported by the government. But he was not just a yes-man.

"He had given his sons to Captain Pratt, founder of the Carlisle School for Indians in Pennsylvania. For this the whites called him a 'wise, education-loving Indian, helping to make little heathen savages into civilized Christian boys.' But when he went east to visit the school and found that his sons had to wear stiff collars that chafed their necks raw, and were beaten with a cane for speaking their own language, and were trained to repair shoes instead of becoming chiefs, he got mad. He took his sons out of the school and back to Rosebud.

"Spotted Tail had to walk a very fine line. He tried to save his people from being wiped out. He tried to preserve their old beliefs and ceremonies. So he tried to beat the wasichus at their

own game, playing politics. He had been three times to
Washington. He had seen that the whites were as grains of sand
at the seashore. He had seen factories turning out a thousand
rifles a day. He knew that he had to fight the white man with his
mind and not with weapons. He played a cat-and-mouse game in
which the white man always turned out to be the cat. It could not
be helped. He did the best he could. He managed to save our
tribe from being shipped to Oklahoma's Indian Territory. Crow
Dog had never been taken prisoner. He had not seen the big
cities of the East with their factories. He had never been on a
train. He could not imagine the numbers and the power of the
whites. He thought that Spotted Tail was too soft on the
wasichus, too ready to give in. Crow Dog became the head of
those who wanted to live in the old Indian way, the ones the government called 'hostiles who stood in the way of civilization.'
Spotted Tail became the leader of those the whites called friend-
lies and progressives. Crow Dog and Spotted Tail had been
friends, but little by little they became rivals and, finally, enemies. It was not their fault, but the fault of the situation they
found themselves in, a situation forced upon them by the whites.

"After they put us on the reservation and fenced us in, Crow
Dog was made chief of the akicita, the tribal police. One day he
was out scouting all over the reservation. He had another policeman with him, a half-breed who could speak a little English. Crow
Dog saw smoke and went to look and see. It came from a campfire. Around it sat some white ranchers and cowhands drinking
coffee. They were running a large herd of cattle on tribal land.
Crow Dog couldn't speak English, or write, or read, but he knew a
thing or two. He told those ranchers, 'You are running your
steers on our land. You should pay us for this.' He had his policeman translate it. The white men said, 'We have already paid to
your chief, Spotted Tail. Look, here's the receipt for three hundred dollars. Here's your chief's X mark and his thumbprint.'

"Crow Dog accused the chief in front of the people. He said
that Spotted Tail had kept the money for himself instead of giving

it to the tribe. He told the great head chief to his face, 'You are just a white man's stooge.'

"Spotted Tail said, 'I am the chief. I have many mouths to feed. I have to entertain many visitors, both Indian and white. It is for this that I kept the money.' This was true, but Crow Dog didn't see it that way. He thought that he, or Iron Shell, or Two Strikes, had a better right to lead the tribe. Both men were proud and strong-willed. So there was bad blood between them.

"Spotted Tail was a great chief. He did not drink or use the white man's tobacco. But he had a weakness for women. He could not resist them, and they could not resist him. One of his nicknames was Speaking With Women. In our language that meant as much as 'making love with women.' When he was young, Spotted Tail fell in love with a pretty girl who was about to marry a wealthy chief named Mato Makuwa, or Running Bear. Running Bear had already paid many horses for her, but she liked Spotted Tail better. The two men got into a fight over her, going at each other with knives. When it was over, Spotted Tail was badly wounded and Running Bear was dead. After Spotted Tail was healed, he took the girl as his first wife. Altogether he had four wives, each with a fine tipi for herself and her children. He was a good husband, a good provider, and a loving father. But he had the elk power, which charms women. There was nothing wrong with this from the Indian point of view at that time. We do not think about such matters as white missionaries do. A man called Medicine Bear had a pretty wife, whom Spotted Tail wanted for his fifth wife. Medicine Bear was a cripple and no longer young. The woman went to live with Spotted Tail. Crow Dog was angry, because Medicine Bear was a relative and friend of his. When Crow Dog and Spotted Tail next met, they quarreled. They dared each other, 'Go ahead and shoot!' In the end they walked away from each other. This is one of many such stories about them, and it's hard to tell which of them are true. The anger between the two men had grown so hot that it became a matter of life and death.

"On August 5, 1881, Crow Dog and Spotted Tail met for the last time. On this day Crow Dog took the seats and wagon box from his buggy to load it up with firewood for the agency. That's how he made his living. He was then no longer chief of the tribal police. He and his wife delivered the wood and started driving home. Near the council house Crow Dog stopped and got down from the wagon and knelt to tie his moccasins, whose strings had come loose. At this moment Spotted Tail came out of the council house. There had been a meeting, and hot words had been exchanged. Spotted Tail was so angry he jumped on his horse and took off. Two Strikes, He Dog, and Ring Thunder followed a little behind the chief. Farther back, at the tail end, came Turning Bear.

"Spotted Tail came riding down the road and saw Crow Dog tying his moccasins. He said, 'This is the day when Crow Dog and I will meet as men!' Grandma called out to warn Crow Dog. Crow Dog got up and drew his gun, which was hanging at the side of the wagon. It was a Winchester. Spotted Tail went for his six-shooter, but Crow Dog was faster. He hit the chief in the chest above the heart. Spotted Tail fell from his horse. But he got up and walked a few steps toward Crow Dog. He was still holding onto his six-gun. But then he fell down once more—dead. My grandmother stood up on the wagon frame and Turning Bear shot at her. He missed. In Rosebud they heard the shots and some of Spotted Tail's men mounted up to go after Crow Dog. My grandma told Crow Dog to ride one of the team horses, so she had just one horse to pull the wagon. Crow Dog whipped the other horse and made it back to his place. His wife soon came back with the wagon. They hadn't laid a hand on her. Nobody bothered them for a while. Nobody wanted to go to Crow Dog's home, because they were afraid he might try to kill somebody.

"It was all very sad. Crow Dog and Spotted Tail were related. As young men they had fought side by side. Without the wasichu coming in, maybe they could have remained friends, instead of becoming enemies.

"The Spotted Tails are still around, just as we are. They have their own way of telling this story. That's their right. We don't fight anymore. When we meet we shake hands, talk about the weather or who will be the next tribal chairman. We speak the same language and have the same problems. We are friends now.

"While the killing of a Crow Indian or a white soldier was a brave deed, killing a man of one's own tribe was the worst thing a man could do. Black Crow, a member of Spotted Tail's band, was Crow Dog's close friend. When he heard about the killing he rode to Crow Dog's place, offering to help. He said to Crow Dog, 'Cousin, before the white man's law does anything to you, you must purify yourself.' So he made a new sweat lodge and the two of them went in. But before they did, Black Crow loaded up Crow Dog's gun and made Crow Dog shoot it four times into the sacred rocks as they were being heated up for the sweat. That way the spirit of Spotted Tail wouldn't bother Crow Dog. Then they had a real hot sweat and purified themselves.

"Spotted Tail's relations painted the dead chief's face red and put some buffalo fat into his mouth so that he would have plenty to eat on his journey along Tacanku Wanagi, the Spirit Trail. Then they put him on a scaffold after the traditional manner. The agent didn't like it and told them to take him down and bury him in the Christian way. So they took him from the scaffold and buried him on that hill overlooking the agency and put a marble monument over that spot. A lot of Crow Dogs and Spotted Tails are buried up there, all crumbling in the earth together. And Spotted Tail's big chief's house, the one the whites had built for him, also crumbled into dust. Only the rocks and the mountains are forever.

"Black Crow and some others went back and forth between the two families, trying to make peace. It was decided that Crow Dog would pay six hundred dollars in blood money to Spotted Tail's relations and also give them many horses and blankets. Somehow Crow Dog's people got the money together, and the thing was settled the old Indian way. But again the whites were not satisfied. The marshals came, arrested Crow Dog, and took him to Fort Niobrara. They took Black Crow, too, because he happened to be there. From Fort Niobrara they took Crow Dog to Deadwood to be tried. In court Crow Dog did not lie. He told them, 'I'm the one who killed Spotted Tail.' He spoke for himself with the help of a translator. His lawyer spoke for him too. They sentenced Crow Dog to be hanged and put him in jail pending appeal. He asked to see the judge. He said, 'Judge, I've got to go back to my place. Prepare myself to die. I've got to have a giveaway, give away whatever things I own, my horses, wagons, chickens, things like that.' The judge asked him, 'If I let you go, how do I know you'll come back?' Crow Dog answered, 'Because I'm telling you. I am Crow Dog.'

"The judge let him go. Crow Dog had a big giveaway at his place. His wife made him a special buckskin outfit to be hanged in. Then the judge got cold feet. Maybe Crow Dog won't come back. They sent a marshal to look for him. This man went to Crow Dog's place and told him, 'Chief, I'm going to take you in. You must come with me.' Crow Dog said, 'No. I promised to come back by myself.' It was evening. The marshal said, 'Tomorrow I'll take you in.' Before daybreak Crow Dog sneaked off. He had already given his team away but borrowed it back for going to be hanged. He took his wife along. He wore his special white, beaded, and fringed outfit. The two drove more than a hundred miles to Deadwood. When he got there his lawyer was all smiles. Word had come from the Supreme Court that when one Indian kills another on the reservation he won't hang because the government has no jurisdiction. So Crow Dog was the first Indian ever to win a case before the Supreme Court. The judge told him, 'Crow Dog, I congratulate you. You kept your word. You came here by yourself and now you and your wife can go back by yourselves. You're free.'" Somebody translated it for him. That is how my father told it.

This was a landmark case in Indian history. I still have a copy of that paper, "ex parte Crow Dog." It reads: "The first district of South Dakota is without jurisdiction to find or try an indictment for murder committed by one Indian upon another in the Indian country, and a conviction and sentence upon such indictment are void and imprisonment thereon is illegal."

We still bring up this ruling to prove that federal courts and the FBI have no business on the reservation, but it's no use. Federal law enforcement has been made legal—one-sidedly—on all Indian reservations for what they call the ten major crimes, leaving the tribal courts to handle only such things as drunk and disorderly, traffic tickets, or wife beating. The Crow Dog case is also racist. If Crow Dog had shot a white man he would have been hanged for sure. A saying among the wasichus was always "If a white man kills an Injun, that's justifiable self-defense. If an Injun kills a white man, that's murder. If an Injun kills an Injun, that's one damn Injun less."

When Crow Dog got home he prayed with the sacred pipe. He asked the Great Spirit to forgive him for what he had done. Black Crow came again, riding on his horse, and built a sweat lodge at the same spot as before. Then Crow Dog's relatives came to be in on the final purification, and Crow Dog and Black Crow went in and made themselves sacred and smoked the pipe. They made the sweat really hot. They wanted to suffer. When they got out, Crow Dog's relatives got hold of a big bunch of good sage, the kind they call deer's ears, and they wiped him with it from head to toe. Then he put on his buckskin outfit. Black Crow advised him: "Cousin, from this day on, whatever you do, you'll dwell by yourself. You'll have your own cup, your own dish, your own pipe, all the things you need. When the pipe comes around, if the people don't understand you, if they have not forgiven you, don't smoke from that pipe. Use your own pipe. If they invite you, you can smoke with them. When the dipper with the water comes around in the ceremonies, don't drink from it unless the people say it's all right. Use your own cup."

After that Crow Dog dwelled by himself. He had paid the blood money and the white men had let him go free, but the guilt was still upon him. He didn't go to visit other people. He didn't go from house to house, from tipi to tipi. And many people wouldn't come to his place. So he led a lonely life. All he did was cut poles and sell firewood. Then a white Catholic priest came to see him. He asked Crow Dog to come down to the church one Sunday. There they put up a great feast for him. They asked him if he wanted to go through the white man's religion. Crow Dog said, "Hou." So through the white minister he repented. The priest told him that God had forgiven him. This way Crow Dog became a Christian, but he still went to the sweat lodge and prayed to Tunkashila. The main thing was, the Spotted Tails had forgiven him, the Great Spirit had forgiven him, and now Jesus had forgiven him too. The forgiving was complete, but still he kept seeing Spotted Tail's face in his drinking cup. The blood guilt is still there. Spotted Tail's blood is still dripping on me. It lasts four generations. My son will be free from it.

In 1991, Chief Spotted Tail came to Crow Dog's sun dance. He wore his war bonnet. He pierced. He hung from the tree. I prayed together with him. I fanned him with my eagle wing. So now we are friends. The bad feeling is gone. It's over.

five

HOLDING HANDS
THEY DANCE IN A CIRCLE

There was no longer hope for us
on this earth, and the Great Spirit
seemed to have forgotten us.
                    Red Cloud

The 1880s were "years of thin grass and little rain" for the
Lakotas. In summer there were droughts. Prairie fires ate
up the grass and the trees. The winters were so cold that
trees cracked apart and men's bones ached. The snow-
storms never stopped. These were hard times for white
ranchers and farmers, too. During the great blizzards of
those years all their livestock froze or starved to death.
The whites could leave and try their luck somewhere
else. The Lakota, stuck on their reservations, could not.
We had been forced to sign away the bigger part of our
reservation. Our sacred Black Hills had been taken over
by gold diggers. The land left to us was the kind where
nothing grows. On the Cheyenne reservation people were
dying of hunger. At Rosebud only half of the children survived. They were too weak to fight the whooping cough
and diphtheria the white man had brought. The kids' legs
were thin as sticks, their eyes hollow, and their bellies
swollen. Some people died of hopelessness. The government picked this time to cut our rations, the beef issue at
Pine Ridge by one million pounds, at Rosebud by two mil-

lion, and even part of what little food did arrive was stolen by thieving agents. One commissioner reported that "the Sioux have fallen into a state of consternation, like men on an ice floe that is about to break up." We were so hard up that men ate up the seed corn and butchered the stud bulls upon which their survival depended in the coming years.

On January 1, 1889, there was a total eclipse of the sun. It caused great fear among the Indians, who thought "that the sun had died" and that the end of the world had come. They were just ready to give up. In Nevada, more than a thousand miles southwest of Rosebud, a Paiute holy man and dreamer named Wovoka had a vision. He told his people that when the sun died he had gone up to heaven and there met God and all the people who had been dead for a long time. And God told him to go back to life and tell the folks on his reservation to be good and love one another and not fight or steal or lie. And he brought with him from heaven a new dance and a new song, which would bring the buffalo back and make everything all right again.

This new dance and new religion was the ghost dance, and Wovoka became its messiah. His message spread like wildfire from tribe to tribe. A man came in the dark of night and told Crow Dog, "A new world is coming. It will roll on top of this one, which the white man has spoiled, like a carpet. Oyate ukiya, Oyate ukiya, a nation is coming!" The man also brought with him a new dance and new songs. The man's name was Kicking Bear and with him was a friend called Short Bull. They had been with Crazy Horse at the Custer fight.

My father told me, "Kicking Bear and Short Bull had gone far away to a kind of Indian Jesus by the name of Wovoka. He had let them look into his hat, and in it they had seen the whole world, many buffalo, and tipis with meat racks, and their dead relatives whom the wasichu had killed. He also made them die and took them to his new land and had them talking to all these dead people, these ghosts. Then he had them come back to life again and gave them his new dance, and vermilion face paint, and eagle feathers. 'Go and teach your people,' that Paiute man had told them.

"Crow Dog had already heard people talking about this holy man who could make the ghosts of dead people and buffalo return to this earth. So Crow Dog, Low Dog, Two Strikes, and some others had sent Kicking Bear and Short Bull to find out whether it was true. How they could make it all the way to this Indian Jesus, traveling through hundreds of miles of land settled by whites, crossing roads, barbed wire fences, and railroad tracks, and never be caught by soldiers or police, that cannot be explained. It was Indian messiah medicine. Well, they did it, and they came back in one piece and brought the message."

The message was one of hope. The white world could be buried or, as some said, rolled up. And underneath, or on top of it, would reappear the beautiful world of the grandfathers. This message was rain for thirsting souls. One of Crow Dog's relations was Howard Red Bear, who, about 1969, died at the age of one hundred and two. He had been a ghost dancer. I remember what he told me about the ghost dance as it was in the old days.

"A man called Woman's Dress had been performing the dance and when the sun reached the center of the universe he ran into the middle of the dance circle, where the director was standing, and knelt down. Then he laid his body flat on the ground, face-down. He was lying there for a long time, like sleeping, and then, with the people still dancing, he woke up. The dance leader burned some sweet grass and smoked Woman's Dress up. When Woman's Dress stood up he was asked what he had seen and heard. Woman's Dress said, 'I went to another world. It was beautiful and filled with good things. From there I brought back some wasna.' Then the ghost dance leader told all the sick dancers to come to the center of the hoop.

"Woman's Dress was standing in the same place before he fell into the spiritual world of his vision. He stood there like a tree that has taken root. He stood there holding hands with the people on either side of him. Then the circle of dancers opened up to allow the sick to come in and eat of this vision meat. There were many sick people to eat the medicine, and what was left was placed in a special wooden bowl called a canwaksila. The director took the sweet grass up again and began to smoke up all the sick people. As they chewed and swallowed this otherworld meat, they could feel it going down into their bodies and through their veins. After that they felt much better."

Near the White River, at the point where one road goes to Rosebud and the other to Parmelee, there my great-grandfather ran a ghost dance. The circle hoop is still there. On a nice summer day you can still make it out. At that spot an old man named Black Bear fell into a vision world of the ghost dance. As Black Bear lay on the ground, the rest of the people continued to dance. After a while Black Bear got up on his feet and faced north with his arms and hands outstretched, and in plain daylight the people saw a little flash of lightning in his hand, like a small looking glass. The ghost dance leader went over to Black Bear and smoked and fanned him off with sweet grass. He saw that Black Bear held a small shining rock, the kind of rock that couldn't be found on earth. A moon rock. And dancers came out of their trance with spiritual food in their hands—moon flesh and star flesh. There still hovers around that place a smell of burning sweet grass.

Old Jerome Crow Dog joined the ghost dance. He liked that new way of praying, of relating to the spirits. He became a leader, and many of our people followed him. He told them to make special shirts for all the dancers. So the people who followed Crow Dog made ghost dance shirts painted with pictures of the sun, the half moon, the stars, and also with pictures of birds, such as the eagle and the magpie. These shirts were supposed to make the wearer bulletproof.

Uncle Dick Fool Bull, who watched the ghost dance when he was a young boy, told me, "There was a man named Porcupine who put on such a shirt and invited people to shoot at him. Later he showed them some bullets that had just dropped off upon hitting, without going in."

Crow Dog told his people, "The Paiute did not teach us this thing. These shirts cannot stop bullets no matter what is painted on them." But they did not want to believe him.

When the soldiers ran all over the reservation, trying to put down the ghost dance, Crow Dog took his people way out into the Badlands where the whites could not follow them. Two Strikes and Short Bull joined him there. Short Bull had firsthand experience of Wovoka's power and was the fiercest believer in the new religion. Crow Dog started his ghost dance by having a woman shoot four sacred arrows into the sky. They had points made of bone dipped in buffalo blood. In the end as many as three thousand people danced with Crow Dog, Short Bull, and Two Strikes. Besides the ghost shirts they wore striped blankets and upside-down American flags.

It was hard for them to stay in the Badlands. Winter was coming on. It was cold, with a lot of snow on the ground, and they had only skimpy canvas tipis for shelter. They had no food except for whatever white ranchers' cattle they could find and butcher. But the Badlands was the only place people could still ghost dance. Up at Standing Rock the agent sent his tribal police to kill our great holy man, Sitting Bull, for protecting the ghost dancers. Everywhere people were running away from the soldiers, who they were afraid might kill them. The government sent soldiers and interpreters to Crow Dog's and Two Strikes' camp, telling them to return to the reservation or they would be wiped out.

Two Strikes said, "They will do it. They have already killed many of us. They have cannons. We have women and children here. I will not see them die. I will take them back to the reservation."

But Short Bull and his men pointed their Winchesters at the whites, and even at Two Strikes, shouting, "Kill the wasichus. Kill all who want to go back."

So here were Lakota men facing each other with loaded guns, ready to shoot. And the soldiers were ready too. It was only a matter of seconds before the blood of many men, women, and children would be painting the snow red. It was then that Crow Dog did a great thing, maybe the greatest in all his life. He sat right in the middle between the two rows of men screaming at each other and pulled a blanket over himself. There he was, a little heap in the snow, singing softly to himself. They all, whites and Indians, kept staring at this blanket with the man under it. They did not know what to make of it, but they all calmed down. They lowered their guns. They kept staring at that little heap, wondering what Crow Dog was going to do. At last Crow Dog threw his blanket off. He said, "I will not see Lakota kill Lakota. I will not see my people butchered by the soldiers. You can kill me if you want to. The soldiers or Short Bull, it is all the same to me. I am not afraid to die. But while I live I will try to save these women and babies. I will take them back to the agency."

Then Crow Dog and Two Strikes marched their people peacefully back toward Pine Ridge. Short Bull's band went with them. In the end only Short Bull was left standing there, clutching his Winchester. Then he went too. Thus Crow Dog saved the lives of a thousand people. In the same month, of December 1890, the soldiers massacred hundreds of Sioux men, women, and children of Big Foot's band at Wounded Knee, leaving women with babies nursing at their breasts dead in the ditch. They had no Crow Dog to save them.

Old Henry told me, "My grandfather was a ghost dance leader. He didn't dance often himself. Mostly he sat back and watched and listened. He supervised the dance. He was teaching them the songs and the sacred language to get the power. They were dancing in three circles. The earth is still trampled down there. Nothing has grown at that spot for years. But the songs and words are still growing in my heart, because he taught me everything about this Wanagi Wacipi, and I taught you, my son, so this ghost dance will never die."

After the ghost dance, my great-grandfather lived quietly by himself with his wife. He went back to the tipi rather than live in the tiny log cabin he had built years ago. One day, in September 1912, when Crow Dog was going toward Rosebud, he got sick all of a sudden and died. From that day his wife lived alone, but she and Crow Dog had already prepared. She had asked him where he wanted to be buried. And he had answered wherever they would accept him. After he died, the Catholic priest came and accepted Crow Dog. He had a good funeral. His wife had told him, before he passed away, "Old man, when you die and get buried, I'll tell them to leave a space next to you, so when I die we'll lie there together as we did in life. After all the hardships that you went through, I will follow you. I'll do that much for you." And when the old woman died, they put her right next to him.

When Frank Good Lance started in as a medicine man he told us, "Your grandfather was buried in the Catholic religion. Now, in the white man's religion, if a man killed someone, they don't bury him in the regular cemetery when he dies. They have outside graveyards for those men. But in the Saint Francis cemetery your great-grandfather is buried right in the center, in hallowed ground. Old Crow Dog had been forgiven. By white law he was supposed to be hanged, but the high court freed him. He went into death and came out of death. So here you have something to talk about, something to be proud of. You never have to be afraid to speak up. So let's not be afraid to be among the people." And he prayed for us with the sacred pipe and the eagle wing. Then he smoked us up with sage and sweet grass and purified us. We still have our sweat lodge at the same spot where he put one up for us, and we pray there. These are the sacred things that we're doing now.

Henry summed it up: "Jerome Crow Dog was a great man. He was always using what the white people call symbols. And we have taken after him in this. He wore an old coat a missionary had given him, but over his shoulders he always had an Indian blanket. This meant he had to walk the white man's road while remaining a Sioux in his mind. And he also wore a white man's hat with a visor, a woolen hat, something like a beanie, but he stuck an eagle feather on its top. He told me, 'This cap means that we live under the wasichu now, but the eagle feather means that we won't be whitemanized, that we'll be Indians forever.'"

six

HE WENT WITH BUFFALO
BILL'S WILD WEST SHOW

The Sioux are the wildest,
most wondrous riders
on naked steeds.

Buffalo Bill

The second Crow Dog's name was John, Henry's father.
He, too, was something of a loner. As Henry told me,
"Johnny Crow Dog doesn't worry about anything, just
himself and his family. He doesn't worry about who's big
chief, or who eats plenty peyote, or who smokes too
many pipes. He keeps out of tribal politics. He's a First
World War vet. He's that kind of man. Dad's life was really
hard after Old Crow Dog killed Spotted Tail. They made
him suffer for what his old man did. He didn't talk much.
He was a quiet man. John tried peyote once, in Macy,
Nebraska. That was in 1920. But he didn't join the Native
American church. He told them, 'You eat peyote. That's
good. But I am a rough man. I do things my own way. I am
not a man who goes to meetings and mingles.'"

John Crow Dog lived by himself. He had no education.
During Prohibition, he was a moonshiner—another reason why he lived way out by himself. One time he went
east with the big circus, together with two brothers. He
was a spin roper. They had to playact the Custer fight and
attack the Deadwood stage coach. They had to play cow-

boys and Indians. Among the other Indians in the show were Thunder Hawk, Standing Soldier, and Iron Eagle. John said that Buffalo Bill had been a fair man who paid them well and was friendly to the Indians. He drank a lot of whiskey out of an extra-big glass. He told John that Sitting Bull had once been in his circus and, in New York City, right on Broadway, had given nickels and dimes to poor white children who had been begging. Grandpa John brought back a poster with a picture of all the Indians riding around on their horses. Somebody read the headline to me. It said the Indians were the "wildest, most wondrous riders on naked steeds." I remember that much but nothing else.

When John went east he met a white woman there. She came out to Rosebud with him. He took her to the mountains and stayed there with her for a while. She hung around for close to a year, but life on the reservation was too hard for her. So John left her and she left him, but before she went away he gave her five hundred dollars from his lease money.

John lived like a badger, alone, but he had his pipe to pray with. He wasn't cut out to be a model family man. He always said that when he died, not to put him in a cemetery but to bury him someplace on his own land. He lived at the old Orphan band camp, at Upper Cut Meat. He trapped beaver and got prairie chickens for food. He dug the charming medicine. Use it and the deer come right up to you. A hunter is quiet, lets other people do the talking. If you talk too much, you spook the game.

Two holy men told John never to eat dog, that it was bad medicine for him. John listened, but one day he went with a half-breed friend, Sam David, a World War I vet like John, to Crookston, Nebraska. They both liked the moonshine and they were drinking. There was some food there that had been lying around for some days and they ate it. It was dog. John got sick right away. Later some guys came and made a big party. Nobody knows what happened. John Crow Dog was in the best health that night, and in the morning he was dead. He looked as if he had passed out, but when they tried to wake him they found out that he had been dead all the time. They brought him to my father's place, but Dad was out in the woods cutting timber. So they took him to Winyan Tanka, John's sister. She was living a mile from where we are now, on Crow Dog's land. For the longest time Jerome, the first Crow Dog, would not accept his allotment because he didn't think land, Grandmother Earth, should be cut up into little pieces and owned by single men or families. He didn't accept land until 1910, twenty years after everybody else did. So my older sisters found Dad cutting wood. They held a wake for Grandpa John. He had never been baptized. He belonged to no church. He wasn't Christian, just an old-time Indian. Uncle Dick Fool Bull said that since he wasn't baptized, he had no place to go. He was right. The missionaries wouldn't have him in their cemeteries. He also couldn't be buried in a Native American churchyard. So my father was sad. One Santee from Grass Mountain, Roy Vessor, said, "Well, we have land right here. Let's dig a hole for him." So they did that. Henry himself buried him. They took him up to the place across the hills where I always fast, and they dug his grave. That's exactly what John had wanted. He got his wish. At the time I was eight years old. I didn't think too much about my grandfather being buried on his own land. But when I was under the power of peyote I felt that my grandfather needed help, needed the prayers. So I told my father that I would make it good for him, and I think that my son will make it that much better for me, like what Jerome Crow Dog did for the Brulé Sioux. Henry went often to John's grave and always placed a rock there. Each Veterans Day we put up a flagpole for him and, wherever John is, he knows that we remember him as a son and a grandson. I want all this put down. I want my children to have a legend. It is important that they know the history of the Crow Dog generations.

My grandmother's name was Ta Mahpiya Washte Win, Mary Good Cloud Woman. Grandma could hardly speak English, but she understood some. She could do some reading and writing. She read the government letters and explained them. That was a strange thing for an Indian woman to do then. Some relations made fun of her for this, but she really helped. My grandmother was a hardworking woman, lending a hand with anything. She'd chop wood, haul water, do the gardening, dig wild turnips and dry 'em up, plant corn, do the washing, bead moccasins, fix up clothes for the whole family. She was a woman who did everything every day. I look at the girls coming up now; they don't do it anymore, they haven't got the strength. Grandmother Good Cloud Woman was strong-hearted.

seven

LET ME TELL IT IN MY OWN WORDS

I am the last true aborigine.
I am the last real Sioux left.

Henry Crow Dog

My father, Henry, loved to recount his life's story. I have it on tape. He said, "Let me tell it in my own words. Don't put it in fancy language! My mother's name"—John's wife's—"was Jumping Elk. John's father-in-law put this poshta, this hood, on Jumping Elk. They made the marriage by praying with the pipe in the four directions. They put the pipe in the hands of John and his woman. They tied their hands together with a strip of red cloth. They put a blanket over them. They took a turtle shell and put charcoal from the pipe in it and let the two of them touch it. The medicine man told them, 'Someday you'll turn into dirt and ashes, but the pipe will hold you together.' Then the medicine man gave them the staff. After they were married a while my mother told John that there was going to be a baby.

"I wasn't born in a hospital. I was born in the old way. John called on four older women, fifty to sixty years old, who no longer had their moon time. They gave my mother nine small red sticks, like from a matchbox, and she put them in a little parfleche. An older lady makes this. Every month you put one of those little sticks in there. They already know whether it's going to be a boy or a girl. If the moon opens up like a sickle, toward the left, it's a girl. If it's curling up a little downward, it's a boy. If it's a half moon, that means twins.

"Now it's birthing time. Two elder women watch Jumping Elk. They have a tanned deer hide and two crutches, about a foot long, and two small stakes. The medicine woman wraps a rawhide belt around the birth giver, wraps it around her waist. There are holes in the rawhide to tighten it like a belt. Jumping Elk pushed herself. She's not lying down like a wasichu winyan, she's kind of squatting. The medicine woman has an herb. She puts it around Jumping Elk's shin. That helps. Then the older women press with the belt. Before the pains come, one woman has four sticks. Every pain she cuts a short stick. My mother grabs onto a large birthing stick and holds on. She pushes three times. The fourth time the baby comes out. They catch me on a tanned white hide. There's a bowl, and water, and sage. They wash me and scrape the gook off me with a bone knife. The old lady sticks a finger into my mouth and pulls it out. Then I begin to cry. If I had not cried the woman would have slapped me on the back until I did. That's how I was born. That's how we all were born. Now they go to the hospital. The old way made you feel good.

"The world I was born in, it was the wasichus' world. I wished I had been born a hundred years earlier. There were no buffalo anymore, no game, nothing to be happy about. We were starving. The people lived on timpsila—wild turnips, berries, roots, and drank water. That was all. As for meat, we ate anything we could catch—gophers, muskrats, squirrels, anything. The family that ate medicine roots had power. If a man dreamed of an eagle, he had to follow that faith. Eat gray grass. If you eat that, chew that, you feel better. You could find that gray grass and drink water after. That filled you up. You could make your way with it.

"They gave us all the meat parts to eat that the white folks would not touch. Once I got a chicken's onze [anus] with a little meat around it. And that way we lived. The old Indian food was mostly gone. The government issue lasted two and a half, maybe three weeks. The last part of the month was always hard. So to get food we sold our old decorated tipi to a white man for five dollars. We had nothing.

"The tipis were all gone. Some people lived in dirt huts, and some fixed up shelters almost like sweat lodges, bent sticks covered with hides. We were lucky to have my grandfather's little log cabin. We had matches already. If we ran out of matches, in wintertime, we had to watch the fire so that it didn't go out. People were starving. We were having a hard time. At that time, when I was a boy, there were twelve thousand Sioux left, and then, suddenly, there were only six thousand Brulé. At one time Rosebud was down to maybe five hundred full-bloods and two thousand, five hundred mixed bloods—all kinds of races, mixed together, but they called themselves Indians. People talking Indian became few. Yankton, Sisseton, to the east, they start speaking English and forgetting their own language. I speak only broken English. They call me a good-for-nothing because I talk so much but, nowadays, if I talk for long I get tired. I talk myself to sleep.

"We used to go to the creek and hunt two kinds of rabbits. The little one, the cottontail, and out on the prairie the big one, the jackrabbit. We'd kill it, cook it, and have a big feast. I hunted, go someplace to find something to eat, anything to fill the pouch. We have forgotten how buffalo meat tasted. I once saw some buffalo that got away from the Black Hills herd, from Custer State Park. They advertised in the papers that anybody who saw a buffalo someplace should report to the agency. There was a reward out. Somebody got a hundred-dollar reward. Not me. I wouldn't snitch on the buffalo. They are relations.

"My father and grandfather had learned the old way. They could still use the bow. They could make a fire with flint and tinder. They still had all the survival skills. If the dogs start to bark, or even if they are too silent, what does it mean? You had to be trained. You had to exercise, to be able to run a long distance. Go a long time without food or water. But not too long, for then you get weak. If you don't learn those things, you gamble with your life. If you don't learn the signs on the ground, or the sounds in the air, or some tiny movement someplace, you could have an arrow or a bullet in your gut. And you had to learn the herbs, the hunting medicine, so you wouldn't be easy to target at.

. "Well that's the kind of education my father and grandfather got, but not me. When I was a kid most everybody had horses. We learned to ride almost before we could walk. Now there aren't enough horses left to go around. I'm over eighty, but I still ride, I still drag wood behind my horse. You've got to breathe into a horse's nostril, let him smell under your armpit to make him know you. You got to know how to gentle a horse, how to break him nicely without spooking him, without force. In the old days you depended on your pony.

"Everybody was afraid of school. In my grandparents' days they took the kids all the way to Carlisle, Pennsylvania. They took them by horse and buggy to the railroad station, some fifty miles away, and there put them on the train. Their parents and relatives went along by wagon, or on horseback, to the station. Then they watched the train disappear with their children. The little boys and girls in the carriages wept, and their families, left behind along the tracks, wept too. You can imagine the shock it must have been for those kids, who had come from tipis and tiny log cabins out on the prairie, to find themselves on that rattling, smoking, whistling train, being carried away at a terrifying speed. And the shock at the many stops along the way, in the ant-heap cities, with a thousand faces of curious wasichus looking at them, gaping at those 'cute little savages.' My uncle Jake Left Hand Bull had to stay at Carlisle for seven years without being allowed to go home or see his folks, not even on Christmas. They cut his hair real short, just like stubble. He had to wear a dark, heavy uniform with a stiff collar, like being a soldier in the army, and heavy shoes going up over his ankles. They hurt so that he could hardly walk. The kids were beaten for every little thing. They weren't told to become doctors, or lawyers, or teachers, but to be carpenters, or shoe repair men.

"I had trouble in school. I didn't speak a word of English, and the teacher didn't speak a word of Sioux, so how could we learn? We were not allowed to speak Indian, or pray Indian, or sing Indian. They treat us bad, hit us if we speak our language. I didn't care for their kind of food, either. Also they went only to the fourth grade, so I was in fourth grade for a few years. There were white kids and mixbloods and they harass me all the time. So I fight back. Then they say, 'That Indian boy's always fighting.' It was never the white boy's fault. Then the school superintendent said, 'Crow Dog's always fighting. So we better send him away as far as we can.' So they sent me to Pierre, a hundred miles from home.

"My father taught me everything I need to know. He didn't talk much. He just did it and made a motion—you saw me doing this, now you try it. He taught me how to use white man's tools, saws, drills, crowbars. I worked for a while for the railroad, laying track. From 1934 to 1950 I worked in Nebraska harvesting grain, digging spuds, and picking beets. I made two or three dollars a day. They call it migrant labor now. I was camping near Saint Francis doing WPA work, but the priests heard me having an Indian ceremony, heard the drumming and singing, and chased me away. On our allotment there was nothing. First we lived in a tent. I built my own house with my own hands. Without money. Nobody helped. I built it from wooden crates, logs, packing paper, old car windows, pieces of corrugated sheet iron. I found a big iron stove that a white man had thrown away, found an old door from a wrecked place, but it was a cozy home. I took care of my own.

"I have white friends. They are good people. Man to man I can relate, but white Americans as a whole, that's different. The white man made me a surplus Indian. I couldn't digest the white man's ways. They made me sick. I am a truant from school, a truant from life. I am a truant from the white man's life into the spiritual life. They cut me in half—a white man's half and an Indian half. Now, when I'm old, I try to put the halves together, because, though I'm a full-blood, I have to live in the white man's world. Under that system I need a doctor, a lawyer, a policeman, a judge, a psychiatrist, a pill, and lots of money. We didn't need such things when I was a kid. To tell the truth, now I need only my pipe. To hell with all the other stuff!

"The buffalo's gone. He was something! Now we have the holsteins, the Angus. Us buffalo people can't get used to the holstein. That's a surplus buffalo. Babies used to go to sleep on milk from the two natural milk bottles of their mother. Now it's pasteurized stuff from the holstein. But even the holstein milk is gone. Now it's powder, and formula. Old-time fellows used to go to sleep on cougar milk, on white lightning, the hard stuff. Slept like babies. Now we have insomnia. It used to be hump meat, raw buffalo liver, kidney. Now it's milk, cheese, powdered eggs, bread like cotton wool. It made me lose all my teeth. Maybe that was the plan: Make Mister Indian lose his teeth so that he can savor that soft white man's chesli [shit].

"Why did the white man come here? Why did Custer steal the sacred Black Hills from us? White men are crazy about gold. They have gold-rimmed glasses, gold watches, gold teeth. They were always rooting around, tearing everything apart, digging, digging, digging. They tore up the whole Black Hills to find gold, silver, and precious stones. They still work the huge gold mine, the Homestake mine, up there. Now they're after gas, coal, oil, and uranium. You can see the big trucks with the nuclear stuff coming through here from the Black Hills. We got to civilize the white man because he has gone crazy.

"They call us bloody savages, but when they have a war, suddenly we're good Indians. 'Here, take a gun, fight for your country!' So, okay, our young boys went over there to Vietnam, went to war, and some of them died there. But for whose country? We were fighting the last war against aborigines. That was like Crow and Rhee scouting for Custer. The white man has eyes, but he does not see. He has ears, but he does not hear. The clock of the universe, the spirit clock, has already struck twelve. It is time to set this clock right, time to stop and think. Let my voice be heard. Stop making weapons! Make relatives! Make a worldwide alowanpi, the relation-making ceremony. If you don't watch out, a time will come when the bullets won't work, the bomb won't work, the spaceships will fall into the ocean. The generals, the senators, the president himself won't know what to do. They'll end up eating snakes, nothing but snakes.

"The Great Spirit of the wasichu gave the white folks the Bible and the dictionary, because they always forget. The Ten Commandments—don't kill, don't steal, don't covet—they always forget. They have to look up that don't kill, don't rob, don't lie all the time. We don't have to be reminded, so we don't need a book to tell us.

"I have no education, but the spirits talk to me. I listen, and I learn about relationship, I learn about spirits. Over the hills there, one time, there were two antelopes, a buck and a female. Someone says, 'Go over there and shoot them and bring the meat.' But nobody could find them or shoot them. They were spirit antelopes. So they call that place Antelope Creek. You hear the noise sometimes, something like a hoofbeat. It couldn't be a bear, it couldn't be a coyote. You hear them, but you can never see them. Hooves, hooves, something strange. People hear it and think there must be some antelopes there. No, nothing. Just something spiritual with a hoof. I myself encountered it. One morning I looked for some horses. I went up that hill about half a mile. I went down to the creek. The horses were there. They were snorting and stamping with their ears pointing ahead, looking at something, smelling something, but there was nothing. Just air. Then suddenly I saw them, something like a ghost, you could kind of see through them. That was the first time that antelope buck and his female came back. They just sort of dissolved into air. I saw it, many years ago. The wasichu can't handle a thing like that.

"When I was young, Indian ceremonies, even a sweat lodge, were forbidden. They called it an Indian offenses act. So you talked and listened to the yuwipi spirits at night, in the darkness. By day you put up a good front, toting your Bible around, crossing yourself—that was a shield behind which a medicine man could hide. And we also kept our medicine bundles hidden where the missionaries couldn't see them.

"White people depict us in their books and movies as stony-faced folks with the corners of our mouths turned down, always looking grim. But we are not like that. Among ourselves we joke and laugh. With all that suffering and poverty our people can survive only by laughing at misfortune. That's why we have the sacred clown, heyoka, the hot-cold, forward-backward, upside-down contrary. He makes us laugh through our tears. And we have Iktomi, the spider man. He's a trickster, a no-good, but also an inventor, a creator.

"The man and woman thing, it's sacred. It's good. The missionaries always say, 'Don't do that with a woman or the devil will get you.' I tell them, 'You guys invented the devil, you keep him. It has nothing to do with us.' A man and a woman have to experience everything. The man is a human compass, the needle leads him to the woman. Those pious wasichus, that's like a short in a radio. A man has to connect to understand women. You have to go to bed early to make a baby. At Crow Dog's Paradise they ought to breed, to make more full-bloods. There aren't enough. Well, Leonard and I, we have done our part. The Crow Dogs always had the elk medicine, the love herb."

Winyan kin akoka,	You women from other tribes,
econpi yo!	keep away from me.
Cicinpi sni yelo	I don't want you!
Sicangu winyan	I want a Rosebud woman!
ecena wacin ye!	
Sicangu winyan,	Rosebud woman,
washte cilake!	I love you!

People would listen to my father for hours. He led a hard life, but he did not let it conquer his spirit. Under all the poverty and suffering, he was proud of who he was. He spoke of the "royalness of our bloodline." He told me, "We are the born government of this turtle continent, physically and spiritually. They call us aborigines because we are the originals on this earth. The Crow Dogs are royal blood—that is, full-bloods. We are the people of the center."

My father held on to our land, our allotment, which he named Crow Dog's Paradise. He never sold the land, even when he was starving. He never dressed up. He always wore the same floppy pants and out-of-shape hat. But it was different when it came to his dance outfits. They were beautiful and he made them himself. He was the greatest eagle dancer our tribe ever had. Watching him you forgot that it was a man dancing, not a bird. He spoke about this: "I was great doing the eagle dance. I could make myself into Wanbli, the sacred bird. I could think and move like a bird, move slowly, cock my head, turn it this way and that way— just like an eagle. I had big eagle wings with feathers from my shoulders down to my fingertips and an eagle's head and beak hiding my face. They all came to see Crow Dog dancing. A soaring song. The eagle has to soar, to fly high. I could crawl into the mind of an eagle. An eagle spirit took over my body." My father's dance was a prayer, a sacredness.

Old Henry didn't have much of the white man's learning, but whatever he learned he made good use of. He always said that he got his education from the spirit. He knew the old ways better than any man alive now. He could put it all together. He thought deeply about things. He wrestled with his thoughts. He was a teacher. He taught my sisters how to bead. His hands were always busy—making a feather bustle, a headdress, or painting a picture with a spiritual message in it. He was one of the first members of the Native American church in our tribe, the peyote church. He made a fire place for it at Crow Dog's Paradise. He made our place into a spiritual center where our old ceremonies were being performed. He and I never talked much to each other. We didn't have to. We understood each other without words, in our minds.

Henry Crow Dog was born on September 2, 1899. He died in the winter of 1985. He was still in very good shape for his age. It was night. The snow was deep. It was very cold. He went to visit my sister Diane who lives only about half a mile from us. We didn't notice him going out. We had a crowd of relatives staying over that night. He didn't know that Diane had gone out and that her door was locked. They found him lying at her doorstep. He might have had a heart attack, or simply frozen to death, or both. It was as he always had said: "I am the last real Sioux left."

We don't have men like him anymore.

eight

A STRONG-HEARTED WOMAN

My mother was a good woman.
She took good care of us.
Her life was hard,
but she never complained.
She stood up under whatever came down.

Leonard Crow Dog

My mother, Mary Gertrude, was like her husband, full-blood and traditional. Her life was sad—of her twelve children only myself and my sisters Diane and Christine are still alive. She lost so many of her children, but she was strong enough to carry on, to take on the burden. She was born in 1900. She married my father in June 1921. Sixty years later you could still see them walking hand in hand. My mother took good care of us, in the old Indian way. She was a member of the Native American Church and one of the first to sing during meetings. Up to then only the men did the singing. She sang well.

On my mother's side they don't use peyote, only the pipe. They are the Left Hand Bulls. They are related to many medicine men, to Chips and Moves Camps. They come from White River, on the Rosebud reservation, some thirty miles north of Crow Dog's Paradise. When my mother married Dad people told her, "You are going to carry a heavy load. You're going to lead a hard life, because the Crow Dogs live by themselves in the old way out on the prairie. When you marry Henry, you'll carry a heavy burden." She didn't mind. She had a broad back. She stood up for us and protected us always.

My mother had a broad, full-blood face, with black sparkling eyes and a determined mouth. She was always busy cooking, beading, or making moccasins. She spent hours bending over her old Singer sewing machine, the kind you work with your foot, because, until 1965, we had no electric light, just kerosene lamps with big reflectors. We had no running water and no indoor plumbing. So life for my mother was not easy. People liked her arts and crafts, and she earned money with it. She taught beading to her daughters and grandchildren. Doing so much work with tiny beads and thread so fine it was almost invisible made her shortsighted. Even though she wore glasses, she was bending so low over her work that her nose almost touched her hand holding the needle.

My father said, "Waktapo, my wife's grandmother, was a fine tanner. She still did brain tanning. It stinks but it's the best. She also used porcupine quills well. She made beautiful things. She was a Left Hand Bull, part Cheyenne. My wife took after her. She learned from her to make beautiful beadwork. But she didn't do the quilling much. You wear down your teeth flattening the quills. My wife has the Indian understanding. She keeps track of a whole trunkload of papers, with seals and stamps on them. Piles and piles of documents, allotments, treaties, promises, guarantees, all broken. A mountain of paper flying in the wind. When our house burned down, most of this was lost. We took to each other, never quarreled, never complained. She's a fine woman and a fine mother. She knows the Lakota ways."

When we taped my mother in 1983, she said, "Both our families, mine and Henry's, are traditionals. My father, my uncle, and my father's sister had ceremonies all the time at their places, and I was always there. So I know all those songs. And when I went to mission school, at Saint Francis, I was a choir singer, so I catch everything. All the songs, any songs. From then on, whenever there was a ceremony, they took me along. I sang the starting songs. The spirit comes for the songs.

"My father was a Left Hand Bull. And my mother's name was Camilla; her Indian name was Shorty, or Neck. I was the oldest girl in the family. My father told me to get married and not come back over there. 'Make your own life,' he said. 'Stay with your man. Don't ask for trouble.' He taught me that, and I did that. I was never parted from Henry. My mother told me, 'If you are unhappy, come over for a while, for comfort.' But I never had to go to her for that kind of comfort.

"My father was a traditional full-blood. He used to be a tribal policeman at Rosebud. He was a good man. He could speak good English. And my mother heard it and she learned by listening to him. I hardly went to school, but I could talk English. People asked me how come I can talk all that wasichu language? 'I listen and I learn,' I told them. 'And what I learn I use.'

"I met Henry when I was twenty-one years old. I met him at Saint Francis, at some doings there. But before that I already knew him. Well, that was June 26, 1921. First we stayed over at my mother's place and then we went to live at Ironwood. Then we went back to my mother's place again, and my father told me, 'Now you are married. So you have to have a house and make a living, the two of you.' So Henry brought me here, on the other side of the Little White River. We lived in the log house Henry built himself, right at this place here on Crow Dog's allotment land, right under those hills. Henry made the house large, because we were having kids. He used anything he could find to build this house. He was good with his hands and could make anything, build a house or make himself a dance costume or a war bonnet. He used tree trunks to support the ceiling. He painted the whole works sky blue with a yellow trim. He also built two outhouses a little away from the big house, and also a cook shack for hot summer days. So we lived in there with plenty of room, not only for us, but to have plenty of space for ceremonies—peyote meeting, yuwipi, dog feast, giveaway, any kind of ceremony. The house was always full of guests. When people came for meetings they slept on the floor. Whenever there was a ceremony the whole floor was covered with bodies.

"And cooking went on all the time, twenty-four hours almost. Indians are not like whites, who eat and sleep always at the same time according to the clock. We sleep and feed whenever we feel like it. So it was cook, cook, cook all the time. But it was nice, so nice. We stayed there for a long time, until the house burned down, and with all the troubles we had, it was still a good time of much friendship and laughter. The house burned down in 1976. We think somebody did it on purpose. The goons, maybe, who hated us because of AIM and Wounded Knee and who saw their chance when Leonard was away in jail. Well, we had no gas, no well, no electricity. We had nothing, but we managed. We got the water from the river. We had a stove to keep warm in winter, we had a cookstove. We lived there for over forty years. First, while Henry was building the house, little by little, we lived in a big tent. So we lived, sometimes hot and sometimes cold.

"Henry was a good worker. He was always cutting and hauling wood. He sold it. My mother gave us two horses and a wagon. We got a little lease check every December. We leased land to ranchers to run their cattle on, but we always had to wait until December or January until we got our money. The government fixed the amount the ranchers would have to pay us, but they fixed it way too low. Mister Indian always gets the wrong end of the stick.

"Left Hand Bull, my father, and the other Left Hand Bulls, they kept the pipe. They all smoked it together and prayed that way. My mother told me, 'That's holy in the Lakota way. Never forget, you're a Lakota. So if you sit there and pray quietly the Indian way, that's good.' My mother taught me how to pray with the pipe. Leonard's first wife, Francine, was a Left Hand Bull too. She gave him children, but they parted ways. They had a reason, I guess. Henry's father, I knew him. He and his wife were parted, but he was a nice, good man. We stayed with him for a while, but he never stayed for long in one place. He moved around, stayed by himself.

"There are women around here, old ones, who are bashful. They're afraid to talk, afraid to open their mouths. Some younger ones are that way too. I tell them, 'Speak up! You can talk. English or Indian, don't hold back!' I never was bashful. Maybe that's why Henry liked me. He isn't bashful either. I went to school as far as the sixth grade. I learned what I needed to know and made a living.

"Leonard had an older brother. During the war he worked in a cement factory and he breathed in all that cement. They didn't give them masks and all that. And when he came back, he was coughing all the time. He got worse, so they took him to the hospital for a while. When he came back again he told me, 'Mom, I can hardly breathe. I am drowning for air.' They took him to Rapid City and kept him there for a while. And he came back again and seemed better. But soon he was coughing once more, and the coughing never stopped. Then he died, from all that cement. At that time the war was still going on, though coming to an end. And nobody was back around here. We had no men to help us. So I had just my sister and my mother to help me. We buried him at Saint Francis. His name was Cleveland, Cleveland Crow Dog. He took peyote. He belonged to the Native American Church. He was a good singer. He had a soft, sweet voice, not like Leonard's. He knew every song. Everyplace we went, people wanted him to sing. He was that good. He was a nice boy, and even after all those years I still miss him real bad. He was a good boy. He was so young. And he died.

"Just like my daughter Delphine. She was nice too, but she had no luck. A drunken policeman beat her to death. He broke her arm and left her lying there in the road. It was snowing and so cold. They found her dead, her tears frozen on her cheeks. When he sobered up, that policeman asked my forgiveness. What can you do? I had twelve children, but they're all gone except three. They died so young. All gone, gone, gone.

"Leonard had an older brother whom he never got to know. We named him Earl Edward. In 1934 he was about two years old. We were living in Saint Francis at the time, near the church. Henry was working for the WPA, putting out square chunks of compressed hay for cattle and picking beets. What the whites called Indian work. John Black Tomahawk came over to visit us. He was singing powwow songs and Henry did the drumming. We were having a good time. Somebody heard it and thought we were having a peyote meeting. So he went and told the priests in Saint Francis. The priests ran things there. They said, 'Crow Dog is a heathen. He contaminates the flock, leading them to damnation.' They sent the tribal police to arrest Crow Dog. They told Henry, 'The missionaries don't want your kind here. You have two hours to get out of town, two hours or else.'

"Henry ran over to Uncle Dick Fool Bull. He asked, 'What shall I do? My little boy is sick with a cough.'

"Fool Bull told him, 'What can you do? They have the police. They have the power. You have your own allotment near the river. They can't chase you from there. Go there and pray.'

"So Henry packed up. He took down the tent that was our home and fixed up the wagon, hitched up his team. He loaded up everything we owned and put us all in the wagon. There was a blizzard. You couldn't see your hand before your eyes. And it was so cold! So Henry drove the team all the way to our allotment, with the snow and icy wind in his face. It was dark and you couldn't see. The horses were all iced over. There was hardly any road. It was slow going. And somewhere between Saint Francis and our land, our little boy died. Of the cold. Of the wind. His name was Earl Edward. Weeping, we made camp across the river from where the house is now. There was no house then. There was nothing. Henry and his friend Ed Red Feather went to the BIA office and got a coffin and all the things needed for the funeral. It was such a little coffin. Henry did not know where to bury our son. At Saint Francis they wouldn't have him, because their cemetery was for 'good Christians only.'

"Ed Red Feather told my father, 'You have been to the Native American church and you are welcome to return. You have a seat there. You can bring your son to be buried in our cemetery.' Sky Bull told the members of the church, and they made our dead son a member of the Native American Church and buried him that way.

"I was so sad. I went to a meeting and took peyote for the first time. And in my vision I saw the spirit with my dead children, and was encouraged, even though I couldn't stop crying. Grandfather Peyote comforted me and Henry through his spiritual power. One year later, on the memorial day of our little son's death, Henry and I were baptized in the Native American Church. We were baptized by Ed Red Feather. Whoever was Catholic in our family then left the Church. They said it was the priests who killed our little child.

"Henry went to a Native American Church meeting one time and didn't come home that night. My mother told me not to say anything about that, not to let those missionaries hear about it. It could cause trouble. My mother was a good woman. She never talked down any church or religion, white or Indian. She was raised a Catholic, but, at the same time, she prayed with the pipe and prayed in the Lakota way. From that time on, Henry always went to the peyote meetings.

"I was sick at the time, very sick. I had lost a lot of weight, but the white doctor had not helped me. Dick Fool Bull said to me, 'Sister-in-law, you ought to eat peyote, eat the holy medicine. You'll be all right, because you've got some kids and you are still young. That medicine can help you.' I went down-river to Dick Fool Bull's place and he gave me a cup of peyote tea. At that time I knew little about the peyote church and the sacred medicine, so I went to the meeting. I ate peyote all night and began getting well the next day. The herb made me feel so strange, so very different. I didn't think I could get well, so I prayed as hard as I could. The woman next to me said, 'Watch me praying. Do like me.'

"I said, 'There is something strange going on inside me, in my mind. Something wrong, maybe.'

"'No, that will help you. That's the medicine working on you.'

"And they prayed over me, and feathered me, and they were singing. I got to feel well, like soaring. My body, and my thoughts, and my mind, they felt good. It was a new kind of good feeling. Like looking down into myself from the outside. I felt good, and warm, and contented, and comforted. Toward morning, I felt well, better than I ever had in my whole life. I was light-headed, clear-headed, and my sickness was gone. All those germs had got out of me. So, from that time, I was never sick."

My mother died in 1987 of cancer. As long as her husband was alive she remained strong, but when my father died she lost heart. She lost the will to live. I wept for a long time. We miss her.

nine

THE SPIRIT PICKED ME
AND MADE ME WHAT I AM

My son Leonard had the
power from birth. Even before.
When my wife was pregnant,
when we'd drum and sing,
he'd dance in there. In her womb.
From this I knew what he was going to be.
So I knew he shouldn't go to school.
He could go to the white man's school,
be a surgeon or anthropologist,
but that was not what the
spirit had in mind for him.

                    Henry Crow Dog

How far can people remember their childhood? How far
back can you remember it? Can you remember being
born, being in your mother's womb? Can you recall a
dream that you were in another world? Can you understand it? I remember it. I could not see, but in the eye of
the mind, the eye of the heart, I can see it. During a ceremony, or when taking sacred medicine, I reexperience it. I
can recall it. When I was born I experienced earth joy, universe joy, happiness of the world. I could feel air filling
my lungs, on August 18, 1942. I was born spiritually. With
the gourd. The medicine man Horn Chips was shaking it.
For a day and a night I could not see, but I heard people

talking, heard a drum and a gourd, heard a song. And when I was so little I remember the joy that I could crawl. I remember the places that I wanted to reach and couldn't reach. And the first thing I held in my hand was a ball, tapa they call it, and a round stone. During a yuwipi ceremony, in the darkness, when the spirits come, I remember this.

As I grew up they saw that I was different. Tunkashila picked me from among the other boys to become a pejuta wichasha, a spiritual man. When I was about five years old I was walking with some other boys and I saw that my shadow was not like theirs; it was the shadow of a grown man. That was one of the first visions I had. I was a dreamer. And when it was time for me to go to school, my father would not let me, because going to a white man's school and learning the white man's way would spoil me for becoming a medicine man. And when the truant officers came to get me, my father chased them off with his shotgun. When I was seven years old my father purified me in the sweat lodge. Four medicine men helped to initiate me. My father made an altar. The spiritual power was in it. It entered all of us. My father taught me the right prayers and songs. We all went into the sweat lodge, inikagapi wokeya, we went in together. Within the circle, inside the sweat lodge, that's where they gave me the power— the inyan, the Tunka. Tunka, that's the sacred stone we use, the yuwipi wa sicun, the oldest god.

Then I was given this power. I saw the spirit go by, but I did not hear any voices yet. My father told me, "Before a ceremony, before doing anything important, always purify yourself in the sweat lodge. In the old days a man always purified himself in the sweat lodge after making a kill, after killing an enemy or a royal eagle."

One of the people who taught me from the earliest days was Good Lance. He was one of the few who still at that time wore their hair in long braids. He was a famous spiritual man among my people. He taught me the sacred ways, the prayers. I remember clearly, when I was about five years old, my Grandpa John, my father, and Good Lance showed to me, and explained, the four wopiyes, the four medicine bags that are kept by the Crow Dog family. One had belonged to Black Crow, Jerome Crow Dog's friend. And this wopiye he gave to Good Lance, saying, "You are the only one I trust. This sacred bundle is looking to be kept in the Crow Dog tiyoshpaye." Good Lance was a Crow Dog, but a vision had given him a spiritual name. One of these bundles got seven hoops. In another were eighty sticks with porcupine quill designs on them. My elders introduced me to these four wopiyes. They opened them up and taught me the meaning of all the things inside them. "Remember this," they told me, "it is sacred. In the future your grandsons will inherit this."

My older sister Christine told me that I was not like other babies. It seemed to her that I knew more than a baby should know, that I grew up right away. I was thirteen years old when I became what the whites call a medicine man, a wichasha wakan. It is not often that boys start out that young, but it happens. There are others besides me who were kept out of school, as I was, and who became spiritual people when still very young, especially those who perform the yuwipi, the tying-up ceremony, which I do.

At thirteen I went to the sweat lodge, the initipi, and had my first grown-up sweat. For four times a day for four days I did it. I came out very light-headed and I told my mother, "Mom, somebody spoke to me. They talked to me. They told me to prepare a place to communicate with them." So my mother said, "Son, that's sacred. You're going where, a long time ago, your grandfather was. You are going into manhood now. You've got to do what your voices tell you."

At about that time I also went on my first hanbleceya, my first vision quest. I stayed on our vision hill for four days and nights. I neither ate nor drank. A big shadow again stood behind me. On the third day he spoke to me: "I am the life of the generation, and I am the tree. I am the medicine, I am the things you experience. I will always speak to you. I will give you an altar. When you put up this altar, you must remember me. You must use the pipe and the four winds of the earth. So this is the message I am carrying to you. From now on you will be an interpreter for your people. Open your heart to them. Your grandfather is speaking to you now. I will be in you, and my spiritual words will grow inside you. That is the message."

From the age of twelve to eighteen that spirit power continued. A voice kept on saying, "My name is Sitting Rock. This is your Indian altar I am giving you. You will speak to each other through the eagle and you will speak to the eagle. Now you have come far enough to handle the two center feathers. I am Flying Eagle. I will interpret for you."

At the age of twenty-four I went on another vision quest and again a spirit man spoke to me: "I am Stand on the Earth Man. I have been chosen to teach you medicine. To give you herb power. That's why I am here."

At the age of twenty-nine, I went crying for a dream once more and again the spirit talked to me: "I am Lightning Man. I am speaking to you within the lightning power of the spirit. So that's the power I am giving to you, a new understanding." When I heard this my hair stood up and I heard a sound like knocking two flintstones together.

When I was thirty-two I again went up the hill. That time the voice said, "I am the spirit man. I am going to teach you understanding of human beings." From time to time I still hear the voice.

On the nonspiritual side, in everyday life, when I was five years old, I remember my father going through the valley, through the woods. Before he left, we always had breakfast, but before we ate, he always went out and prayed to Tunkashila, the Grandfather Spirit. And he always put out a morsel of food and spilled some coffee for the spirits of dead friends and relatives, to give them something to eat too. After that my father said, "Son, come along, hiyupo!" So I always went with him. We had horses and a wagon. Hardly anybody had a car in those days. I liked to ride in the wagon, beside my father. Later I learned to drive it. From early on I helped him get wood. We got a wagon load every day. Dad sold firewood. That was a part of how he made a living. He taught me how to gather up dry wood. "Oak is the good one, and you can burn it for ash. But you can't burn red elm or white elm. And look for good, dry pine."

He told me, "In this valley here, your great-grandfather, your relatives used to live. In different places. But when Grandfather Jerome killed Spotted Tail, they thought they should change their camp. So they sold everything and scattered. Everybody moved. But remember this valley. It's part of us. It speaks to us."

Then we'd bring the wood back, unload it, and have lunch. Dad cut logs for people, and tipi poles. Old Walking Crow had a sawmill. Dad helped him cutting boards. He and I also cut fence posts. He cut about a hundred fifty a day and I cut seventy-five. We'd sell the poles and with the money buy food and on Saturday we'd go to a ceremony and help put it on. We lived like that.

Dad wanted to show his appreciation for my helping him with the wood. So he made me a ball out of an old inner tube and a kind of catcher's mitt from a scrap of deer hide. He taught me how to play throw and catch. He also showed me how to play marbles with oak nuts. In wintertime he carved toys for me out of yellow wood.

Then Dad also taught me how to fix up a bow and arrow. For a bowstring he used rawhide from a female deer. It's so stretchy you can't break it. He used ash for the arrows. "These things," he said, "they used them way back years ago. They don't use bows and arrows anymore, but you could teach yourself how to play with them." But he told me, "You should never handle a gun, because your hands are still red with blood." By this he meant that Spotted Tail's blood was still dripping on us in the fourth generation. My sons will be free from that guilt.

I had few friends, because I didn't go to school, and we lived pretty far from the nearest settlement. The only friends I remember playing with as a child were two boys, named Abel Good Lance and William Centers. They lived with us for about a year and a half. I was about six years old then. They were orphans and my father brought them over from Pine Ridge. I learned from them to carve little ponies and buffalo from old cow bones. We also took yellow wood, which is easy to carve, and all winter long made our own toys. I still have some of my Indian toys from those days. It was not until I was ten years old that I got my first store-bought toy—a little car. Later on Dad bought me some real marbles. That was a big event for me. Later I made shooters, something like a slingshot, out of old Model A tire tubes. I never shot at birds or living things, just at targets. As I got older I made my own bows and arrows. Then we were joined by another boy, Vine Goodshield. We also played Sioux fighting Crow or Pawnee. I always wanted to be a Sioux. With time we got less isolated, maybe because some families got old beat-up cars, what we now call Indian cars, not secondhand, but maybe fourth- or fifth-hand. So then we played baseball. At age ten I had my own horse. Its name was Nick and I rode him all summer. The thing I liked best of all was swimming, and I was really good at it.

The only pet I had was a wild skunk. I had been playing in the woods and heard some noise from out of the bushes. I went to investigate and found a little baby skunk, so small he didn't have teeth yet. When he was about three months old, my father descented him. He was a good little pet, but somehow his scent bag came back and my father said it was time to let him go. But he kept coming back to eat, and then would leave again. Finally he came with his family for a handout. That went on for quite a while but finally they stopped coming.

My dad always hunted, because we were so often out of food. He never used a gun, in order not to offend Spotted Tail's spirit. He taught us how to smoke out rabbits up on the hills. We'd take some kindling and go looking for rabbit holes. Then we'd smoke them out and stand by with a stick, and when they came out of their holes we hit them over the head. Then we'd have rabbit stew for dinner.

Dad also taught us how to fish. Sometimes we ate mud turtles and sand turtles. The sand turtles we found along the road and the highway, where there is sand under berry bushes. The mud turtles we found down by the river, near our place. Mud turtles are real big, much bigger than sand turtles. They taste good, like chicken. After Dad cleaned out the shells he gave them to us as toys.

When I got into my teens my father taught me how to ride all kinds of horses—yellow, white, and spotted ones. I never used a saddle; that's not the Indian way. Mostly I rode a gelded stallion. He became my favorite. Then Dad showed me how to use an ax and a sledgehammer, a wedge and a saw. He showed me how to take care of chickens, hogs, cattle, and horses. It was better than going to school, where we learned nothing.

Sometime between age seven and fourteen I learned to dance from a medicine man—the hoop dance, the gourd dance, the eagle dance, and the rope dance, what we call spin roping. These are not good-time dances to have fun. They are sacred cere-monies, like prayers. The hoop dance represents the sacred hoop, the hoop of the universe, the circle without end, the circle of all living things—people, animals, and plants. Before he started teaching me, the medicine man took me into the sweat lodge to prepare me for becoming a dancer.

By the time I was nine years old I could dance with five hoops. I kept them whirling around my arms and legs, as well as around my waist, dancing very fast to the beat of my father's drum. I formed the hoops into shapes, into a butterfly or a bird. I could jump through the hoops easily, because I was still small and thin. Soon I had the confidence to dance with seven hoops. My father took me to powwows and I won many prizes. But I never forgot that dancing was a prayer and that the hoop was an altar, that it "had a face," as my father said.

When I was eleven years old, every time I danced I heard the spirit talk to me. It was a sound like clicking two stones together, and a whistling like from a bird. I was learning all the time. I could make more and more difficult movements—the eagle hoop, the chair hoop, throwing up hoops into the air while jumping through them. This last figure was called the lightning hoop. I could keep two hoops in my mouth and three whirling around my arms, and one going clockwise around my neck. At the same time I was stepping into a spare hoop, drawing it quickly over my body in a nonstop motion.

As I got older, I added more and more hoops, around my ankles, between ankles and knees, and around my chest. By the time I was twelve years old I danced with sixteen hoops at the same time. When I was fourteen I went to a big powwow with my dad and mom. As I was fixing up my costume I saw a big cloud come up over me and out of it I had a vision and heard a voice like a bird's, but I could understand it. It told me, "Hokshila, boy, this is the moment, the year, the place where you will get a new understanding and a new power." I told my father about it and he said, "The hoops were your preparation, a way to get ready. From now on you will learn to be a healer and learn how to help your people."

That day I danced as I had never danced before, with twenty-one hoops. People told me that it was the best dance they had ever seen. It was my last dance. After it I hung up my hoops. They were for a boy, but now it was time for me to become a man.

During the days I did the hoop dance I also performed the gourd dance, and right in the gourd, in the rattle, there was a spirit talking to me. As I was shaking the gourd, the spirits talked to me in little ghostlike voices, encouraging me.

I also performed the eagle dance. I could never do it as well as my father. Nobody could; he was the best ever. When he danced he turned into an eagle before your eyes. When you do the eagle dance you blow on your eagle bone whistle, and through it you communicate with the eagle. This sacred bird is a messenger making a bridge between you and the Creator. When you dance the eagle dance a power gets hold of you.

I did the rope dance, spin rope dancing, which stands for the tying-up ceremony called yuwipi. The rope should really be a rawhide, not just a lasso. My father said, "The rawhide makes a straight road; follow it."

I also did the stomp dance. Once I practiced it in a little grove of trees. There were some big oak stumps and, dreamlike, they turned into people with long hair and old-time buckskin outfits. I knew that they had long gone to another world and, as I watched, they turned back into oak stumps. Dancing often gave me visions like that.

I was growing up. I had six brothers born before me, but they all died. So I was the only son left, the only root. That put a heavy load upon me.

When I was fourteen years old, a whole string of bad things happened to me. Some boys came up to me and said, "Let's go for a ride!" I didn't know they had stolen the car in Colorado and changed the license plate. They didn't do a good job on it. They tried to put a new color on the car and messed that up too. But I didn't know anything was wrong. One of the boys suggested that I drive. They did this so that, if they were stopped, it would look as if I had stolen it. Naturally we ran into some police and they spotted that something was wrong with the license plate and that somebody had tried to repaint the car. They had us cold. They wanted to see my ID and driver's license and, of course, I didn't have any. The other boys said I had stolen the car. They lied and lied. At that time I spoke hardly any English. The police believed them, because I could not make myself understood. I did time in a reformatory in Littleton, Colorado. I learned to be a car mechanic at Littleton, and I am still good at fixing old clunkers. But being in the reformatory was hard for me. I was used to roaming, to riding, to swimming. I suffered from being cooped up. I was in there for one year and one month.

At age sixteen I worked for two months on a farm in Nebraska, for a Japanese man. Then I went back to South Dakota to work on a ranch, for five dollars a day. That was the only kind of work for an Indian then. After that I got into trouble again. Some kids had gotten drunk and rowdy and the police put them in a panel truck. I happened to be there, so the cops got on my case too. It made me mad. The panel truck was still standing there and I managed to creep up and open the door and let everybody out. They ran off in all directions. So they booked me for trying to escape and resisting arrest. But this time I was in for a very short time. It seemed that in those days every kid was in jail sometime. If you were a teenager and an Indian and were found someplace away from home, you had to be guilty of something. That was the attitude of the white police. And you had to go outside to find work. In court you couldn't understand anything that was going on. You couldn't understand the language they used. You got a white court-appointed lawyer you couldn't understand either. He did nothing for you because, win or lose, he got paid. So he spent as little time on you as he could get away with.

After that I did farm and ranch work again for about three years. I did a lot of planting and harvesting beets. When there was no more farm work I got a job at a body shop. I learned from one of my friends by watching him work. He used a torch, a heat torcher. You heat it to a certain temperature and you press it. If you do it right you can't even see where the dent was. But if you do it wrong, you crush the fender, you wrinkle that tin all up. So I did this to make a living. But it was tiresome and wore me out. I had to work on every car they brought in. Then I learned to cut glass for car windows. When you start cutting that glass, you've got to have strong hands and be careful. You can't mark it too well. You've got to use a heat glass cutter. You heat it and you mark the glass with a steel wheel. I was sixteen years old when I began doing that kind of work.

My dad said to me, "You are about ready to get married and

have children." I thought so too. Among the Lakota we get to be fathers and mothers early in life. I took on a new name—Defends His Medicine—which represented our sacred plant, peyote. Sage and peyote are our two great sacred medicines. The Native American Church, the peyote church, has always been under attack by the white man. It needs defending. That's why I took that name. So I stopped doing farm and ranch work, which kept me from being what had been shown to me in my vision. I became a spiritual man.

ten

THE PIT OF DREAMS

In 1956, when I was fasting,
a spirit told me,
"You will be a tool for the
ikche wichasha, for the simple man."
I give of myself for the people.
                    Leonard Crow Dog

A spirit had picked me to be a medicine man. Grandfather Peyote had chosen me to be a road chief of the Native American church. Before I could even begin along that path I had to go down into the pit and be buried in it and come to life again through the power of Tunkashila. And I had to have a vision to point the way. I had to go up the hill, "crying for a dream," as they call it. But even before that, I had to be purified.

To be purified you have to go into the sweat lodge. My father called on Good Lance, who had the power and the knowledge, to help purify me. He also asked another relative who was a spiritual man, Frank Arrow Sight, to help. They instructed me, "Before you do anything of great importance in your life, you purify yourself in the initi. Going on your first vision quest could be the greatest moment in your life, so preparing you for it must be done right. This sweat bath must be something special. It is sacred."

We have our sweat lodge at the edge of Crow Dog's Paradise, close by the stream. Whape washtemna, Indian perfume, grows there. Waterbirds fly over that spot. The way we do a sweat, we stick sixteen willow saplings in the ground in a circle—the number sixteen is sacred to all Indian people, not only the Lakota. So four times four willow wands make the frame, the skeleton of the sweat lodge. You bend them at the top and tie them together so that they form a dome, like a beehive. You cover them up with canvas, a tarp, or blankets. In the old days it used to be buffalo robes, but these are hard to come by now. At every step of making the sweat lodge you pray.

In that little sweat lodge, the whole universe is contained. It is the Creator's home. In the center we make a hole, a perfect circle. We place the sacred rocks in this hole. Inside we make a carpet of sage to sit on. Sage is a holy herb and makes the spirits come in. The earth one takes out of the center pit you make into a little mound outside the lodge. It represents Unci, Grandmother Earth. And beyond that you make peta owihankeshni, the fire without end. For wood my father used dry branches from the trees. They had to be laid in a certain way—first four sticks running west and east, and seven sticks running north and south. As my father laid the sticks down, he said a prayer.

The door of the sweat lodge always faces west. Only at the home of a heyoka, a thunder dreamer, or "contrary," does it face east, because a heyoka has to do everything differently from anybody else. Never does the lodge entrance face north. From the door to the Grandmother mound, it runs in a straight line. This is inyan chanku, the path of the sacred rocks. Along it the red hot stones are passed into the lodge.

Good Lance told me, "Let yourself see the generations as you set the wood on fire. Think of passing the sacred flame from generation to generation." When the fire had gone down my father placed the first twelve rocks on the glowing embers. They represent the twelve sacred eagle feathers handed down from grandfather to grandson. I had to go down on all fours to crawl into the lodge. "That is to teach you to be humble," said my father, "to show that you are no better than your four-legged relatives." We were naked as we were born, because the sweat lodge is Grandmother's womb, the earth womb, and I was to be reborn in it. We entered the sweat lodge clockwise. My father sat at one side of the entrance, Good Lance at the other. My cousin brought in the heated rocks, one by one, on a forked stick. My father grabbed them with a pair of deer antlers and put them into the center pit. He placed the first seven rocks, which represent the four sacred directions, the center of the universe, the sky above, and the earth below. They also represent the wakichagapi—if you have loved ones who died, you remember them by this. My father sprinkled sage and cedar over the rocks. As it burned it made a whispering sound, like a spirit voice. Then more rocks were placed in the pit. Finally, my cousin passed a pail of water into the lodge and lowered the entrance flap over the door.

Inside we were huddling in total darkness. All I could see was a red glow from the heated stones. I could feel their warmth. Now I knew that I was truly in Grandmother's womb, in the darkness of the womb, the darkness of the soul. In the warmth and moisture, I felt that this was myself before being born.

My father said, "The inipi uses all the powers of the universe. The fire, the water, the earth, the air are here, within the sweat lodge. Feel the power of inyan wakan, the sacred rock. All living things are in here." The scent of burning sweet grass and sage was around us like a blanket. I tried to catch this smoke with my hands and rub it all over me. My father prayed. He sang the songs. Then he poured cold water over the red, hot rocks.

All at once the initi was filled with white steam. It curled around us and enfolded us. It was very hot, so hot that I thought the steam would burn me up. My lungs seemed to be on fire. But I knew that this was a blessing, that it was the breath of the Creator purifying me. And out of the hot whiteness I heard my father's voice: "Immersed in this cloud, you will be cleansed. You will be prepared."

I prayed to Tunkashila as I had never prayed before, and I felt the spirits coming in, talking to me in spirit talk, touching me. Then the flap was opened. Good Lance sang, "Grandfather, you are the light of the world. Take care of us. Teach us, Grandfather, each morning, each evening. We ask you to have pity on us. Prepare our minds for this purification."

More rocks were brought in. Then the flap was lowered over the entrance. More water was poured over the rocks, and again Grandfather's breath enfolded us. And again I heard my father's voice: "Cultivate your mind, for all medicine goes there. Center the mind on the spirit. Ask the sweet grass to show you the way. Your vision will tell the rest."

This was a four door sweat, meaning that the flap was opened and closed four times, and each time everything was repeated. I had the privilege to talk every time the flap was lifted, but what we talked then I'll keep to myself. After the fourth door we were given cold spring water to drink. And my father said, "The moment we drink the sacred water of life, we receive its blessings. The moon brought all the waters together, from a tiny drop, to a lake, to a river. Let your mind flow like the water."

We finished by smoking the pipe. It united us as if we had been one body. The pipe bowl of red stone coming from the sacred quarry, the only place in the world where you can find it, that is the flesh and blood of the Indian. The smoke coming from the pipe is the Creator's breath. Then it was over. I had been made ready for the vision quest. I had been reborn.

While I had been in the sweat lodge, my older sister Delphine made a flesh offering for me. My aunt was cutting forty tiny squares of skin from her left arm. As I passed her, I saw a tiny trickle of blood making a red line from her shoulder to her elbow. She was making a sacrifice to help me get through being alone on the hilltop for four days and nights without eating or drinking. The tiny squares of her flesh were carefully wrapped in red cloth, which was tied to my sacred pipe. I would take this with me on my hanbleceya to comfort and encourage me, to make me know that someone had suffered to help me get my vision.

We still have our allotment land. Part of it is down near the road, by the river. It is where we have our sun dance every summer. The other part is up on the hill. That is Crow Dog's sacred place. Before giving me the pipe with flesh offerings, Arrow Sight asked me if I was prepared to fast for four days and nights. I nodded. Then he put me up there. There is a stream running through our land with a tree trunk across it. So we crossed on that and walked up to the hilltop. There is a flat place up where, in 1974, we brought the ghost dance back. There's cedar and pine at this place. Eagles circle over it. You hear the coyotes yapping, singing to the moon. It is beautiful and lonely up there. All you hear are the sounds of nature, animal talk, the wind blowing through the trees. In the center of all this is our family's vision pit. It is formed like an "L" pointing the wrong way. First you go down and then crawl across until you come to the dead end. That is the spot where we sit and cry for a dream.

Arrow Sight told me to take my moccasins off and walk to the sacred ground barefoot. On the way, he let me stop four times. Each time he sang "Tunkashila, I am coming to see your power. Anpetu, today, see me, see me. With the sacred pipe I am coming to you to sacrifice myself, to learn, to see my sacred roots. I give myself to the sacred pipe." Tunkashila is the grandfather word for Great Spirit. Frank Arrow Sight made me walk four times around the vision pit. He made me put up four sacred direction flags: red material first, then the yellow, then the white, and then the black. So we put up these colors at four points around the vision pit. And then we put up a center pole with an eagle tail feather tied to the top and a deer tail farther down. Then I connected the four direction flag sticks with four hundred chanli, tobacco tie offerings. Finally we made an altar out of gopher dust—an Iktomi, or spider man, altar.

After that Arrow Sight took wachanga, sweet grass, and smoked up all the flags and sacred things and made everything holy. "Go around, clockwise inside the hanbleceya grounds four times," he told me. "Think only good thoughts. From your vision quest bring something good back, something good for yourself, something good for your people. Stay inside the tobacco ties, stay inside the four colors. I go back down now, back to the sweat lodge and your father. But through spiritual power, we will be with you, we will feel physically and spiritually whatever you feel—your fears, your hopes. We will be praying for you." Then he left me alone up there with my thoughts.

I was afraid. I did not know what was going to happen. I might be rejected. I might not be given a vision. I would be up there alone for four days and nights, without food, without water. It would not be easy.

The first night, sometimes I sat close to the pit entrance, my head above ground. All I could see at first was a red circle. That's all. Then I crawled back into the hole, all the way, and I heard somebody walking on the left side—a rustling, like a scattering of kindling. I heard birds, heard an owl whooping four times. That is what I heard and saw the first night. All the time I was sitting there, praying, holding onto the pipe with my sister's flesh offerings tied to it, I was thinking that somewhere near were some of my ancestors' graves. I felt their presence. Then, at dawn, before the sun came up, at the west I saw a spark, a little red hoop, and I saw something like a lightning bug coming in the entrance. It made a clicking noise, like knocking small stones together. And I heard a voice: "Some things are still sacred. The spirit will direct you."

During the day I stayed in the pit. I lost all sense of time, of feeling. I was like dead. I wanted water but tried not to think of it. I was in a different world, in a different dimension. As the second night started, I looked out. Wiyatki, the Big Dipper, was halfway up. The evening star went down. It clouded over. It was pitch dark. Darker than dark. I prayed hard. And a white, shiny, fast ball came from the north. As it was coming toward me I gripped my pipe. A voice was coming out of it: "Power is going into your body. It is coming. It does not speak, but you will know. The iktomi power is given to you." Then it hit me like a blow, like being struck by lightning. I crawled back into the pit as far as I could. I heard people talking but could not see them. Then I saw tipis, horses, deer, buffalo. I was in another time. I heard children playing and laughing. I heard somebody saying, "Wauntinkte, we're going to eat."

All during the next day I was half awake and half asleep. I didn't know anymore what was real and what was not. I was really hungry. I wanted water. But then I saw a woodpecker on top of one of the pine trees. Did I really see it or was I dreaming? I heard him hammering against the tree. Then I heard someone say, "You are standing on wakan makoce, on sacred ground. Be happy. You are suffering now, but you are being given a power that will help you later in life." So, toward evening, on my third night, I crawled out just a little. The morning star was shining on me. I wasn't myself. I was facing toward the east. I felt spiritually as I had never felt before. And a man appeared to me, a soldier. It was Ruben Red Feather, who had been killed in action during World War II. He had been dead so long, but here he was. I think he wanted to help me in some way. I saw lightning, and the morning star reflected the lightning to where I stood. It turned into a rainbow, which was like a funnel, funneling the rainbow right into my eyes. And in there I saw a man's face, with five points sticking out all around like horns. It was a star who spoke to me: "He has seen you. Wowakan, power from the star, he has given you."

The next morning and afternoon, I stayed in the pit. I no longer felt hunger or thirst. In the middle of the day I saw a gopher's face. It came out of the altar. When it looked at me I felt that a strange power entered me. The gopher was swinging its tail and sprinkled me with sacred gopher dust. It rained down on me.

On the fourth day, just as the sun was coming up, just when it peeked a little over the horizon, I saw a blinding whiteness reaching all the way up to the sky. And I saw the universe filled up with green and blue, just the colors. Then I saw a man walking a mile off with a standing-up feather in his hair. He was carrying six sticks, six roots. And he was singing: "From Four Directions, Grandfather will see you. I bring the roots you will use in the Iktomi altar."

I turned toward the south and prayed. The sun was halfway out when I was given another vision. Right behind me I heard a voice from a spirit, from a hairy spider. An eagle was flying over me. A real eagle, not a dream eagle. I had my eagle bone whistle. I blew it four times in the four directions. Then a black cloud formed over me and water sprinkled down on my head. And the voice said, "The spirit will take care of you. Tunkashila blesses you with the water." That was all I heard on the fourth day, standing there with the pipe.

It seemed like forever until Arrow Sight came to bring me down. The sweat lodge was ready. I was hungry and thirsty. Arrow Sight said, "Before you talk, before you sweat, there is a young boy to feed you." They gave me water and corn, and that young boy, George Four Horns, gave me four spoonfuls of everything they had prepared for me. Inside the sweat lodge I told them what I had seen and heard. I left nothing out. I added nothing. Arrow Sight, Good Lance, my father, they all interpreted it for me. "It is all good. It made you a medicine man. But that's only one vision quest. You must go on three more before you can be the four different kinds of spiritual man combined in one person. But you have enough power now to take it from here. You are a medicine man. From now on you have to travel Grandfather's road. There is no looking back."

eleven

THE HOLY HERB

I'll jump into the sacred medicine,
dive into it. I want to know,
experience the knowledge the
sacred herb can give me.
It elevates me into another world.

Leonard Crow Dog

I am a member of the Native American Church, the peyote church. Some people criticize me for that. They say
that the sun dance is a Lakota belief, but peyote comes
from another tribe. I shouldn't mix the two up. But I was
born into the peyote way. I like it because it unites our
people. Whatever religion, whatever ceremonies a tribe
has, peyote makes them as one. I see nothing wrong with
holding onto my old Lakota beliefs while, at the same
time, I also practice the peyote way together with my
brothers and sisters from all tribes. When we sit in a
meeting with people from other Indian nations, we might
not speak their language, but spiritually we understand
one another. In our songs our languages become one.
Anything is good that brings our people together in a
spiritual way, from the Yukon to the Rio Grande, from the
Atlantic to the Pacific.

Peyote power is the knowledge of God through peyote. It is our Indian medicine, our holy herb, our sacra-

ment. It is not a chemical drug but a natural plant. It elevates my mind into another world, into a higher dimension. With the peyote I went to a lot of good places and met a lot of good people. Grandfather Peyote has no mouth, but he talks to me; he has no eyes, but he looks at me; he has no ears, but he listens. He is a song brought by the wind. The peyote way is thousands of years old. It is as old as the earth.

The word *peyote,* my elders told me, comes from the Uto-Aztecan *peyotl,* meaning caterpillar, because the peyote cactus is fuzzy, like a caterpillar's back. In Lakota we call it *unchela,* or simply medicine. When the Spaniards came to Mexico, peyote was already there. The priests called it the "devil's root, which keeps the Indians from salvation." They burned alive all Indians they found using this sacred medicine. In the United States, the missionaries called peyote "a barrier to civilization" and put in jail those who prayed with it.

There is a tale of how peyote came to the people. My father told it to me. Somebody had taught it to him. Long ago, long before the white man came, there was a tribe living far to the south of us. Those people were suffering from a sickness, and many died of it. An old woman had a dream that she would find a medicine to cure her people. So she went out to search for this plant. She took her young granddaughter along. They got lost in a desert. They were getting weak from hunger and thirst. They lay down to sleep under some bushes. They thought they would die.

Suddenly, toward morning, an eagle flew above them, from the east toward the west. The old woman prayed to this sacred bird for help. Then she heard a voice, saying, "I have a medicine that will help you." The voice came out from a peyote plant. It was a big Grandfather Peyote, with sixteen segments. The old woman cut the top part off, the green part, and they ate this. The peyote juice inside refreshed them and made them strong. The old woman and her granddaughter got peyote power.

When the second night came, the old woman prayed to the spirit, "I am lost. Have pity on me." And a voice answered, "You are lost now, but after two more nights you will find your way home." When they awoke at dawn, the old woman and the girl partook again of the sacred medicine. It made them feel strong, as if they had eaten a big meal. The old woman told the girl, "Granddaughter, pray with this new herb. It has great power in it."

During the third night, the woman had a vision that showed her how to use the peyote spiritually. In the morning she told the girl, "Granddaughter, we must find more of these holy plants to save our people." Then she heard many voices calling: "Over here, over here, I'm the one to pick." The peyote plants were leading them to their hiding places under shrubs and bushes. The old woman and the girl filled a whole hide bag with them.

During the fourth night, the old woman heard the voice again: "Toward the sunrise, you'll see three mountains. Behind the one in the middle you'll find your camp." So in the morning they walked that way and found their village. And the people were happy to have them back. Though they had not eaten in four days, the medicine had kept them strong. The people were still dying of sickness, but the old woman had been shown in her vision how to use peyote ceremonially to cure the people. So she did this, and the people got well. Through the peyote they received new understanding. It gave them a new mind. And they brought this medicine to their neighbors and instructed them in its use until the peyote way was accepted by many tribes.

Peyote doesn't grow in this country, except for a small area in southern Texas. We have to go into Mexico to harvest it. The Huichol, Yaqui, and Tarahumara have always had it, but not the tribes north of the Rio Grande. About one hundred fifty years ago the Comanche had a chief called Quanah Parker. In his youth he had been a great warrior. He traveled down into Mexico and there a bull gored him. He was about to die, but an Indian woman cured him with peyote. He took the medicine back to his tribe. He also had the ritual as the woman had taught him. It was different from the Huichol and the Yaqui way, though they all used the same sacrament. Quanah Parker founded the Native American Church. It was part Indian religion and part Christianity. His ritual became known as the crossfire ceremony, because a Bible was used in it and prayers to Jesus were in its songs. And they smoked cornhusk cigarettes in their meetings. Later non-Christian Indians founded the moon fire ceremony. They don't use the Bible and have the pipe instead of the cornhusk cigarettes, but we all get along with one another. We all pray with the same medicine. From the Comanche peyote spread to other tribes, farther north.

Peyote came to us in Rosebud around 1903. I was told that some people from the Winnebago tribe, John Bearskin and Mountain Wolf Woman, taught this religion to some of our Lakota men.

In 1922 we got the first charter for the Native American Church in South Dakota. Eagle Hawk, a college student, and Joe Good Breath were the ministers. Francis Little Stallion was a leader, Fanny Little Stallion a delegate. Orange Star was a helper, and Ed Red Feather and Jim Blue Bird were directors. Jim Sky Bull became the overseer.

My grandfather on my mother's side ran into trouble on the Rosebud reservation. That was in 1918. He went to Kansas and met up with some Potawatomi and Oto. They invited him to join in their peyote ceremony.

He first went into a sweat bath for purification. At that time they did not chop up the peyote as we do now. They cleaned the middle part out. They got a whole basketful of fresh green buttons, maybe about three or four hundred. Then after they had partaken, they offered some to their Sioux guest. So he took the medicine and, in the middle of the night, all of a sudden, he felt like he was behind bars. It was as if the tipi poles had turned into bars. And he could not find the entrance to the tipi. But then suddenly he experienced the greatness of the holy herb: "A new power got hold of me, so many things peyote is showing me. It makes me understand myself. The peyote spirit is releasing me from what is binding me." He was sitting among his new Potawatomi and Oto friends, joining them in their prayers. As he prayed, the morning star came up and the tipi poles moved aside and opened a path for him. Then he heard a mockingbird talking to him: "You have been released from what was tying you up." He stayed with these people for six weeks, going to meetings all the time, sometimes inside a house, sometimes in a tipi. When it was time to leave he told these friends that he wanted to take these ways back to his people in South Dakota. So they instructed him in the rituals and taught him the songs. And in this way he took the new knowledge with him.

My grandfather John Crow Dog first took peyote in Macy, Nebraska, at a powwow in 1921. He followed the sound of the water drum. It led him to where some Winnebago had a meeting. He joined them and took the sacrament and came to know the medicine. But he didn't join the church. He told them, "You eat peyote. That's good, I respect it. But I'm a loner. I do things my own way. When I die, just plant me someplace. I don't need a cemetery. I stay by myself, far from other folk. I ain't a membership man."

My father came to the medicine in this way. In 1929 he visited his cousin John Good Shield, who lived close to Jim Sky Bull. John Good Shield complained to my dad that his uncle Noah Little was an alcoholic. He thought maybe Sky Bull could help. So they went up to Sky Bull and took in a meeting. My dad took the medicine and was under the power for four days. He had a good vision. He felt something sacred. They gave my father water and corn, chokecherries, and jerk meat. My father got up and thanked all these people for what they had done for him. He told them, "Anytime you need help, I'll help you. I'm a poor man, but whatever I have I'll share with you. I'll be coming back. I'll cut wood for you, bring food, whatever. Grandfather Peyote has spoken to me." So from that time on my father went to the meetings and became a member of the peyote church.

A Native American Church ritual is beautiful. It is as tightly run as a Catholic Mass. All the things we use in a meeting—the drum, the staff, the gourd, the fan—must be handled in the right way. Whether it takes place in a house or tipi, the setup is always the same. There are differences between a moon fire and a cross-fire meeting, and between a Lakota and a Navajo one, but in the main parts they are all alike. If you looked down on a peyote meeting it would appear like this:

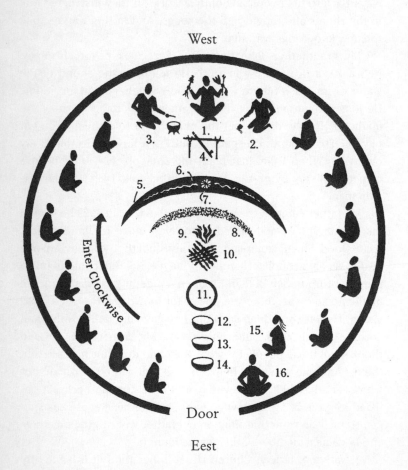

West

Enter Clockwise

Door

Eest

At the west, in the back, opposite the door of the tipi, sits the road man, or road chief. We call him that because he leads us on the road of life. He has a shawl around his shoulders that is half red and half blue. To his right sits the drummer, and to his left the cedar man, who uses cedar as incense during the meeting. At the east, by the door, sits the fire man, who tends and shapes the fire and also acts as doorkeeper. Close to him is the water carrier, always a woman. Among the Lakota she is either the wife or daughter of the road chief. The road chief has with him the holy things—the staff, the gourd, the feather fan, the eagle bone whistle, and a bundle of sage. In front of him is an altar cloth. Some members bring their own staffs, gourds, and fans in a decorated wooden box. If it is a crossfire meeting, there will be a Bible. If I run a meeting there will be a rack in front of me, made of two upright forked sticks with a crosspiece. This is for the sacred pipe to rest on. In some places they smoke cornhusk cigarettes instead of the pipe. In front of the pipe rest is the half-moon altar. It is made of sand and is shaped like a crescent, a half-moon. From one tip to the other we make a groove that represents the road of life. The top of the altar is flat. On its center we place the chief peyote, the Grandfather Peyote. Farther down from the road

1. Road Chief (also Road Man)
2. Cedar Man
3. Drummer
4. Pipe Rack
5. Halfmoon Altar
6. Path
7. Grandfather Peyote (also Father Peyote and Chief Peyote)
8. Ashes
9. Fire Glowing
10. Place Embers
11. Water
12. Corn
13. Chokecherries (Wojapi)
14. Meat (Wasna)
15. Water Bearer
16. Fireman (also Door Keeper)

man are the ashes, also shaped into a half-moon. Then there is the fire place itself, with its glowing coals and the fire power. And then down the line in a row is the sacred food—the pail of water, the corn, the meat (which could be wasna, or pemmican), and then the chokecherries or other fruit.

The water represents the water of life. There can be no life without it. The spirit dwells in the water. The corn is the food of the Indian who created this corn, who bred it from a small kind of grass thousands of years ago. The meat, or wasna, represents our brother, the buffalo, who gives of his flesh so that the people may live. The chokecherries stand for the generations. We put a branch of chokecherries on the sacred tree during the sun dance.

Outside the tipi, on the right side of the door, is a stack of wood to keep the fire going.

I call the sacred things we use in our meetings the elements. They are there for a reason. First, the drum represents the Indian's heartbeat. Sometimes, during a meeting, your heart beats along with the drum. That scares some people who have come for the first time, because the drumbeat is so fast. The drum is at the center; it is the spirit of peyote. Long ago, the drum was made of wood. Now it is an iron or metal kettle with three legs or no legs at all. In a crossfire, if the kettle has three legs, that represents the Father, the Son, and the Holy Ghost. The drum is a water drum. It is filled with the water of life. The spirit is there and you put a prayer in it. The water gives the drum its special sound, the peyote sound. It is the Great Spirit's tune. The hide is the spirit's skin or, in a crossfire, Jesus' skin as he is beaten by the soldiers or, maybe, the Indian's skin as he is beaten by the police. Early on we used buffalo hide, but now it is deerskin. At dawn every morning, the deer comes to the water. So hide and water go together. Some use moose hide. The hide stands for all the four-legged animals who give us food.

It takes skill to tie a drum. You take seven round pebbles, wrap the hide around them, and tie them with rope to the kettle. In a crossfire meeting the pebbles stand for the seven sacraments; in a moon fire they represent the Oceti Shakowin, the seven camp circles of our Lakota Nation. The rope used in the tying should be made of twisted rawhide. After the drum is tied, the rope should form the design of the morning star at the bottom, or, as some say, an "earth crown." A male deer horn is used to tighten the drum. If a pregnant woman is present at a meeting, the baby inside her will dance to the beat of the drum. It, too, will "be in the power."

The drumstick represents the stick the government uses to beat the Indian or, in a crossfire, the stick they whipped Jesus with. If the hide is heavy, like hide taken from the neck, we use black wood—that is, ebony. If the hide is thin, we use a drumstick carved from rosewood or black walnut. The drumstick represents the green, growing things, the trees who are our friends. It is said that inside the drumstick are the memories of loved ones who have passed away.

The staff is the staff of authority and unity. In a crossfire they call it Christ's walking stick. They also say that the staff is to remind us of the spear Christ was pierced with. Our thoughts and prayers travel up that staff, and the vision from above travels down to us, the Grandfather Peyote vision. With the staff you can communicate with the wind and the thunder. The staff is the tree, and the staff is a man who dresses himself nice, in a blanket of beads. Sometimes eagle feathers are tied to the staff. The staff is a bridge, a hot line to the Creator.

The gourd is a rattle. You keep time with it while you sing your songs, keep time with the drum. The gourd itself is the Indian's head. Our minds are inside this gourd. It is a shelter, a tipi for our thoughts. The red horsehair tuft on the top represents the rays of the sun, because we are all part of this universe. Some say that it is a Lakota war bonnet. Inside the gourd are little stones of different sizes. Some are crystals taken from ant heaps. The stones are the voices of the spirit. Sometimes all these voices unite into one—that's Tunkashila talking. The gourd is a communicator. It speaks the Lakota language. Good thoughts travel up and down its handle. The fringe on the handle, made up of twelve strings, in a crossfire meeting represents the twelve apostles. The beadwork around the handle is a rainbow. The finest peyote beadwork is done by the Kiowa. They use the tiniest beads, with the most beautiful colors.

Another of the elements we use in our meetings is the feather fan. It has twelve feathers tied to a handle that is beaded and fringed like the gourd handle. The greatest symbol of the Native American Church is the waterbird. You can see him embroidered on the shawls of women who are members and on the silver jewelry they wear. The eagle and the waterbird have power. They carry our prayers to the spirit above us. The woman who brings in the water for the meeting always uses a waterbird feather to bless the water. We also use an eagle feather or the two center feathers. They represent peace. Only the road man can handle the eagle feather. He fans people off when he is doctoring. The eagle feather symbolizes the sacredness of all birds.

When we move the fan, the feathers waft our thoughts and prayers to Tunkashila. They also catch good songs out of the air. Sometimes the feathers are trimmed in a sawtooth design. For the fan we can use many kinds of feathers—scissortail, magpie, pheasant, red flicker, blue jay, hawk, or macaw feathers. We can use either one kind on a fan or mix them up.

Scissortail feathers we use to honor the mothers of all Indian nations. In Oklahoma and Texas they stand for the sun and the four directions.

Magpie feathers are for doctoring any sickness. Besides the center feathers there are white and black feathers at the edge of the wing. They represent an Indian maiden, with black hair and white buckskin dress. If there's a dead animal lying in the road, the magpie will pick at it, clean it up. In the same way, he'll clean up a sick body. My dad heard a magpie sing and he found a song in that: "Look to the spirit, look to the spirit!" So we use this song now. I got a song from the roadrunner. If I sing it to you, you can hear a roadrunner's cry in between the words.

Then the hawk. This is a powerful bird, a hunter. He is close to the earth. You can tame him. He represents understanding.

We honor the blue jay. The blue jay represents the sky and the day, beauty, everything that looks nice. We also use the woodpecker. One of the road men of the Native American Church had a vision that woodpecker feathers could be used in curing, that they could dissolve gallstones, break up the rock inside the human body. So some use the woodpecker for this. The yellowhammer makes a real fine weed nest; he stands for the family.

If someone takes peyote for the first time, if he does not yet know the medicine, they fan him with nightingale feathers so that he can learn the Native American Church ways, the ritual, and the use of our sacred things.

We don't use crow feathers in our fans. The crow is for mourners. To remember somebody who died, we pray with these feathers for four days. Then we keep these feathers sacred.

Every road chief would like to have a fan made of macaw feathers, because they are the most beautiful. But now they are very hard to come by. I think they came to us first in 1936. An Indian brought them who could not speak English, but somehow we could understand him. Macaw feathers have been used for dances and ceremonies for more than a thousand years. When archaeologists dug up Pueblo Bonito, in New Mexico, they found thirty macaw mummies, going back eight hundred years. Many ancient pueblos used macaw feathers long before Columbus, which proves that there was communication between our North American tribes and Indian nations two thousand miles south of us. A macaw can learn to talk in any language. That is why a macaw fan is a translator. And because of the colors—red, blue, green—it stands for the rainbow. Holding a macaw feather fan during a meeting, I had a vision. In it the sun was coming up under a rainbow. I saw a man wearing red and blue macaw feathers like a blanket. And on his head he wore a macaw feather war bonnet. I caught songs out of that vision.

Another sacred thing we use is the eagle bone whistle. It connects us to the sacred four directions of the universe. We use it so that the Creator hears us. The whistle represents the sun. At midnight there is a pause for prayer and some good words. Water is passed around and drunk. Right after the midnight water the road man goes outside the tipi and blows his whistle to the east, south, west, and north. When we hear the whistle we think of our friends and relatives who have passed away. When the road man blows the eagle bone whistle, he may feel the presence of a dream eagle.

To the left of the road man sits the cedar man. He has the rawhide bag of dry cedar. At certain times he sprinkles cedar over the glowing embers. This is our incense. It is pleasing to the spirits. It connects us to all the plants in the universe. We inhale the incense, smoke ourselves up, and rub that smoke on our bodies. The cedar is the blood vein of the generations. During a peyote meeting, one among us has to go to another world and come back. The cedar stands for everlasting life. All other trees change their colors and lose their leaves in fall, but the cedar stays green. We smoke up not only the people but also all the instruments we use in our ritual. We "cedar" them. Besides cedar we use sage for incense and, sometimes, sweet grass.

When a family walks in the peyote way we say "they have a fire place." Fire—the great power of the sun, the fire without end, the spark passed on from generation to generation—is central to the peyote ritual. Fire is everlasting life. Fire is Tunka, the rock, our oldest god. It is inyan, the stone. It is the spark coming from flint hitting on flint, which lit the fire of generations past. When we light up the sacred pipe and smoke it, we make "fire talk."

The fire in the center of the tipi is a bed of glowing coals. It is easy to have it in a tipi because there is an earth floor. In a house it is not so easy. You can build it on a tray filled with earth or on a not-too-heavy U-shaped slab of concrete. There are different ways to do this. The sacred number four plays a big role in a peyote ceremony. The night is divided into four parts. At the beginning of a meeting the fire man uses the poker to shape the coals into a half-moon design. It represents the generations, and also the woman power, because the chief peyote on top of the half-moon altar stands for the first peyote picked by the woman in the legend. It also stands for night, because all meetings last from sundown to sunrise.

At midnight, the fire chief shapes the coals into a heart, because you should believe in this sacred medicine with all your heart, soul, and mind. That heart is alive. It pulsates. Then, at about four A.M., you form the coals into a morning star, because the Anpetu Wichapi is a sacred spirit in ancient Lakota belief. In a crossfire meeting they have this design because in the Bible Christ says, "I am the bright morning star." If a person wants to convert to the peyote religion, this is the right moment, the moment of light, of enlightenment. Then, at daybreak, we put the coals into the shape of a cross. That represents the sacred four directions of the Indian religion. In a crossfire ritual it is, of course, Christ's cross of the Crucifixion.

I still have my grandfather's fire flints. With those and powdered cottonwood for tinder I can make a fire for a special ceremony. I can still do that. Then I use seven kindling sticks. When I get a spark and a little flame, I let the wind and the flint power start the fire. Hardly anybody can do that anymore. And we don't take just any wood for our fire but what has been chosen for our meetings. Red elm, ash, cottonwood are the ones we use.

The water represents the water of life, the sea that was there before anything else, out of which Maka, the earth, our turtle continent, arose. The moon pulls the water, making it ebb and flow. That is woman power, and for that reason the water carrier is always a woman.

The tipi also has many symbols. In some tribes people pray and walk around the tipi before entering it. Sitting inside, forming a medicine wheel, they represent the sacred hoop, the circle without end. In this way the tipi represents unity. The tipi floor connects us with Unchi, Grandmother Earth. The walls stand for the sky, the poles all reaching up to the Creator. To the top of the center pole we sometimes tie an eagle feather. Because the tipi is like a mother giving shelter to her children, it also honors women, who in the old days made the tipi and put it up and took it down. The tipi also represents the buffalo, because before the coming of the white man tipis were made of buffalo hides.

The entrance of the tipi is shaped like a horseshoe. The concrete slab that serves as the fire place when a meeting is held inside a house also is often shaped like a horseshoe. Horses are gone now, but their spiritual hoofprint is still there. My dad told me, "If you lift up the hoof and look, there is a design there. You see a star, and a cross, and at the back a little half-moon." I didn't believe him and wanted to see for myself. I got hold of a horse and looked, and sure enough the designs were there. After the tipi has been put up, if you look from underneath, you see that the tipi poles have formed a twelve-pointed star. So, this is what I can tell you about the elements we use in the Native American Church and their meaning.

Peyote is our spiritual power. Peyote makes us relate to Grandfather, the Creator. When you partake of the medicine, you know that you are in the power, you do not see things that are wrong, you see things that are right. It's like a mirror. You can't evade it. It scares you because you have to face yourself. When I take part in a meeting I feel that I matter, that the universe couldn't go on without me.

Peyote and I got to know each other from early on. When I was a kid the missionaries used to tell me that I'd be nothing but a no-good savage if I prayed the Indian way. And the same thing happened to my four sisters. The priests at the mission school at Saint Francis told them that peyote comes from the devil. We all had a hard time holding onto our beliefs.

I was six or seven years old when I first took peyote. The medicine affected me. I was thinking real old thoughts and singing a very old song. Every weekend I'd go with my father with the team and wagon to a meeting. When I was seven I really started to sing. A man called Chasing Hawk was hitting the drum and I was catching on to those songs. I never forgot them. After learning to sing I learned to "feed the spirit," feed the fire outside. Then I learned to poke the fire inside a house or tipi, forming it up into a half-moon or cross. In time I became a road man, running meetings.

Peyote is not a "substance" or chemical gimmick. It does not create addicts. It is a natural plant, a kind of cactus. You don't take it for recreation. You wouldn't want to, because it doesn't taste good. As white Christians go to church on a Sunday, so members of the Native American Church go to meetings once a week, usually on Saturday night. They do not partake of the medicine except at that time, performing the ceremony in the traditional way.

At nightfall, the road man opens the meeting with a prayer. You must know how to behave. You never go in front of someone who is taking the medicine or someone who is singing. You should be able to stay in your place for the whole length of the ceremony. The road man places the chief peyote in the center of the altar. It is a big button of sixteen segments that sometimes has been in the road man's family for generations. The person who puts up the ceremony fills the pipe and gives it to the road man so that he can start the ceremony by smoking the pipe. After midnight the road man fills the pipe again and gives it back to the sponsor. The road man starts out with the opening song. He sings four songs of four verses. Then he passes on the staff, the fan, and the gourd to the person on his left. That person then starts to sing, holding the staff and fan in his left hand and the gourd in his right. The drummer then comes and hits the drum for him. If a person cannot or does not want to sing, he passes the elements clockwise to his neighbor. At first women did not sing, but now they do. My sisters are both good singers. Sometimes several persons sing along in harmony. We sing four starting songs, four midnight songs, four morning songs, and four quitting songs. Some of the songs have words in them and some do not.

Some of the sounds are like words, an echo from the peyote spirit—ha na ha na ha na; ha na yo yi; na he he he na yo witsi na yo. These are like words coming out of the medicine itself. It means something like "The peyote recognizes you. It is going to give you a voice to use during the night." When peyote is working on you, it gives you the words and tune you need. I have myself made up many songs. Some songs seem to come out of the peyote, not out of me. You have to be in the right mind to sing, in tune with the medicine. If the peyote spirit is at odds with you, you'll have difficulties singing. Your words, your songs are going to go out of track.

Of the four songs I sing, the first two are rather slow, but the third and the last I always sing fast. The drummer sees me shaking my gourd. He notices that I am speeding it up, and he keeps pace with me. He flips the drum over to change the sound, making it higher. As the medicine goes around from person to person together with the staff and gourd, so the drummer also goes around, coming to all who want to sing.

At first they did not want women in the meetings at all. But, as I see it, peyote is for all humankind—how can woman be left out? She is the birth giver, she stands for the generations. So for many years now women have participated, praying and singing, bringing in the morning water, blessing the sacred food. There's only one difference: Women can pass the staff along to the next person, but they should not hold onto it while singing. Because the staff is a man. As the elders say, "Women should not wear a war bonnet."

At the time of the midnight water there is a pause. The road man gives a spiritual talk. Everybody else also has the privilege to speak, to say something good, to ask help for his or her troubles. That is also a good time to get baptized, to be married in the Native American Church way, or to be doctored. The peyote way is a from-birth-to-death religion. In order to join the Church you must be baptized into it and then you are a member. A newborn baby can also be baptized with the medicine. When I wanted to get married I went to Uncle Leslie Fool Bull, and he told me that I and my future wife, Francine, should study the sacred medicine and come face to face with it and then we could marry during a meeting. I already knew the peyote and it knew me, but my bride came from a family in which they knew only the pipe. Uncle Leslie did not teach us. He told us, "Grandfather Peyote will be your teacher." So for a month we attended Native American Church services together. Then we purified ourselves, and Uncle Leslie married us.

When my children were young, just four, five, or six years old, I let them come into the meetings, sitting on Grandpa's or Grandma's lap. They felt happy. They already got an understanding when they were under the spiritual power. Little Richard was standing up, holding the staff, and dancing. Ina and Bernadette only smiled. I asked them if they saw anything. They told me that they saw all kinds of little birds, little dolls, and snowflakes. When the snowflakes hit the dolls they turned into raindrops. Some people say not to bring little kids in who don't know the medicine yet. But I think that it is right to bring the children up in the peyote way and let them sit in on a meeting. They learn something good there, so that later in life they won't start drinking and kill themselves in car wrecks on the weekend. Weekends are for ceremonies, for praying inside the tipi and feeding the fire. I like to have the children with me, trying to sing along.

Peyote is also there when a girl is on her first moon. In the old days, when a young girl became a woman they performed ceremonies in her honor, such as the ishna ta awi cha lowan, the for-her-alone-we-sing ceremony, a buffalo ritual, and connected with this the tapa wanka yap, the sacred throwing of the ball. We hardly do these ceremonies anymore, but in the Native American Church, in a half-moon fire, we still honor a girl after she has her first period, because in that state she is sacred. The girl might not even know why she is honored, why she is the first to be given the water to drink, why she is the first to be served the sacred food, but the remembrance of our old ceremonies is there in the sacred medicine.

And, finally, Grandfather Peyote is there at the time of your death. He will take away the fear of dying and fill your mind with wowahwala, with inner peace. Then he will gently take you by the hand to another world.

A meeting ends at daybreak, when the morning star is fading from sight. The roadman says a prayer: "Great Spirit, bless my people, take care of them. Take care of the coming generations. Bless the universe. Remember those who have passed on. Bless the water, bless the ikche wichasha, the natural, human beings," meaning the Lakota and all other native beings. Then we drink the morning water and partake of the sacred food—the corn, the wasna, the chokecherries. We untie the drum, put the staff away, and clean up the fire. Then, down the line from the first man who drank the water, we shake hands and say "hihane washte," good morning. We leave the tipi, one by one. Outside we stretch and watch the sunrise with a great feeling of friendship.

Peyote can be your doctor or your psychiatrist. He can analyze you. Sometimes he can cure a sickness through the power of the medicine. There was an old man whom no white doctor could help. So together we took peyote buttons. It transported me into another world, giving me the power to help this man. The medicine made this old man into a young boy, and at water call, I blew my eagle bone whistle and we prayed for him. At daybreak this man got up and danced around the fire place and everybody got scared, because he seemed to be a different kind of human being from what he had been before. I told my helper to sprinkle some cedar over the fire so that we could pray for the man. We smoked him up and I fanned him off with my eagle wing. And that old man got well and is still living. Of course it does not always work like this. In order to be cured a person has to allow the peyote to help. He or she must have confidence in the medicine. Sometimes the peyote uses me as a tool to cure someone; sometimes it does not. I do not know how this power works. I just accept it. Whatever the medicine wants to do, it does. Some white men call it witchcraft. We had missionaries forcing their way into our meetings, kicking and scattering our sacred things, telling us that peyote is "from the devil."

Now we have a charter, and the Native American Church is incorporated under the laws of South Dakota and other states. I have a certificate showing that I am a road man. I have a permit from the state of Texas identifying me as a custodian of the church, allowing me to harvest the peyote legally anywhere I can find it.

As I said before, peyote does not grow in North America. South of Laredo, Texas, it grows on a narrow strip on both sides of the Rio Grande and at one point it goes up to the city of Miranda, some thirty miles inside Texas. But that is the northernmost place you can find it. I call the whole area our peyote gardens, because the Creator chose the spot where we could harvest our sacred medicine. In the old days they let you go wherever you wanted to and pick it for free on both sides of the border. Sometimes you gave the owner of the land a small donation. It was still like that when my father took me down there for the first time. But already the second time I went to the gardens things were changed. There was a law that they can sell the peyote as a sacrament only to authorized members of the Native American church. And the law treats the medicine like a drug or a doctor's prescription. It must meet "certain standards." It has to be "pure" in the Food and Drug Administration's way. So now they have a machine to "sanitize" the peyote. It runs hot and cold water over the plants and shakes the peyote clean so that there is no sand in it, to make it fit for Mister Indian to use. They grade it like eggs—big or small. We must harvest according to the rules. The medicine is pure as the spirit made it, as you find it. But the government says it must be made sanitary, like aspirin or Alka-Seltzer. There are two kinds of peyote, from the same type of plant. One has twelve white spots on top. This peyote can be made into a tea or a mush. The other has ten spots and must be sun dried. After you dry it the button is the size of a silver dollar. When you dry it the right way, the juice, the power, stays in there. But the machine shakes the juice out and some of the power goes with it. Then the medicine is weakened.

White doctors and chemists are forever fooling around with our holy herb. Even the army and the CIA have experimented with it. They analyzed it chemically, put tiny bits under the microscope, distilled it into powder, made it into squares like sugar cubes, trying to "find its secret." And they photographed different kinds of peyote plants. I told them, "It's no use. You can photograph the plant, but you can't photograph its spirit."

Going to harvest peyote is like a sacred pilgrimage. Before you start the harvesting, at sunrise, you must say a good, strong prayer to the four directions of the universe, to the sky above, and to Mother Earth below. Whenever you find a Grandfather Peyote, you say a prayer. You never cut the whole plant. You don't cut clear to the root. You cut off only the top, the button, and the plant grows again. After six months, when you go there again, you will find a pink flower. And after another six months, there will be a fresh green peyote there. It seems that women are better at finding the medicine than men. Peyote likes women on account of the grandmother and her little granddaughter who found the first peyote in the legend. It is a long, hard drive from Rosebud to get to the peyote garden and back, maybe two thousand miles altogether. But we don't mind it. Getting the medicine is part of our lives.

We do not go to meetings to get high. You partake of the medicine to understand the Creator and yourself. You do not expect to get a vision, and most of the time you don't. You have no craving for peyote as such. You use it as a means to come close to the spirit and to one another, because it is a medicine that unifies. But visions and dreams are at the center of what we believe in. We are dream people. You can have a vision during a vision quest, or in a sweat bath, or in a yuwipi ceremony, or just walking in nature. And you can experience a vision through the power of peyote.

I still remember the first great vision the medicine gave me. I saw a worm that time, a caterpillar, because peyote means caterpillar in the Aztec language. It was all made out of a puzzle, and it was the drum hide, and its head was inside the drum kettle. It had a whistle, and each time I hit the drum it whistled, just like the voice of a roadrunner. At morning I saw a man's head in the drum kettle. He had seven eyes and they were the seven knots around the drum, and the circle of eyes was the rawhide and it was a rainbow. The hide became a cloud. All the time it was a good tune, a good sound coming up, and with the water spray coming up from the drum as I was beating it, I felt it was Life. I heard voices in the water—a man, a woman, a child, and a deer. Toward morning I heard it. And the staff was the leader, taking care of the herd, of the people. And the gourd—somebody a long way off could hear its voice, calling, like bringing sheep to water. So I stood up with the staff and all the sheep were coming, and their faces were men's skulls, all black with no features.

The fan was the sweeper, bringing blessings. The fire, right in the fire, whatever we do or say, there's a man with a green buckskin outfit. I could see his blood veins—that was the cedar, grains of red in the wood—and I heard the voice: "Wana cekiya, it's now time to pray." That man said it four times. But then it was a woman's voice. The cedar smoke went straight up. "Wana, here, now, here is the greatest power! He is listening to you."

And the altar was the map of this continent. I saw a man and a woman lying down, saw everything there—good health, death, sickness, everything between life and death. That man, on one side, one half of him was flesh, the other side bones. From his knees down he was all foggy, like smoke. I sat there praying. He was kicking one leg fast, with the drum. I heard a sharp little voice: "It should be done the right way!" I still think about what it means.

I see something every time I go to a meeting. During a cross-fire ceremony, I saw a light shining on the sacred medicine. And I saw a man in the cloud, when I was under the power, a man with long hair and a red and blue peyote blanket, holding up his hands, and he was singing a song. I was looking up and down. I saw the words. I can't read or write, but all of a sudden this voice went into me and let me catch that song. It was a big butterfly. He was wearing a costume with peyote buttons and that butterfly's eyes were shining, and the butterfly turned into a blue jay and went straight up and I heard a voice: "Hecetu welo—you learn." I took some buttons and learned that song. And the man next to me was singing that same song through the power of the medicine. With this power I can be in two places at the same time. Through the songs coming out of the medicine, I could hear my dead sister's voice.

There was a time when I was ashamed of being an Indian because the white man forced me to live after his ways and made me feel small, but peyote blew that away from my mind as with an eagle wing. With peyote I can see things I can't see with my eyes, I can see the real reality underneath what the white man calls reality. Peyote will make you relive your own birth. It is like a tape recorder; you reverse it back. Something you could not understand as a child, twenty-five years later you can bring it back and understand what happened. Peyote speaks with the language of your mother's womb. Peyote is a keyhole through which you can look into another world. My body and my mind can be the key to unlock a door to go into another dimension. Peyote is an old man with white hair. He is listening to you. Peyote is asking me questions. Sometimes I am ashamed to answer. Peyote can make you into an artist. Some of our greatest Native American painters got their gift from the holy herb. You can see it in their work.

Under spiritual power you will see how far you are from the Great Spirit and the roots of Indian medicine and how far you've been taken away from nature, but then peyote will make you feel that the spirit is close to you and it will bring you back to nature, to the black-tailed deer and the buffalo. Peyote is something on which you can stand. It is a great power. There are other powers in our beliefs, not bigger and not smaller than peyote—the power of Grandfather's breath in the sweat lodge, the power of the sacred pipe, the power of the rock in a yuwipi ceremony, the power of the dream during a vision quest, the power coming from the sun dance tree. Peyote is one of these powers that cannot be explained. I was picked inside my mother's womb. I was born with the shell, the caul, the birth veil. I know how I came to be. I am a road man of the Native American Church. I am my father's son.

twelve

ROCK DREAMERS

He wanni yank	To see you
auwe	they come,
tunkan kin sitomnia	all the sacred stones
wanni yank	to see you
auwe.	they come.

Mato Kuwapi—Chased by Bears

Tunka unshi ulapi yeyo	Stone spirits have pity on us,
tunka unshi ulapo yeyo	stone spirits have pity on us,
he mitakuye ob	with my relatives
lena kicu welo.	I make you these offerings.

Yuwipi offering song

Yuwipi is a ceremony using the power of the sacred rocks. Peyote is a new, all-over Indian religion that came to us early in this century. I am a road man of the Native American church. I am also a yuwipi man. Yuwipi is a Lakota ceremony as old as the rocks and the mountains. Nobody knows how old. Yuwipi is power from Tunka, the rock, our oldest god. Tunka, or inyan (another word for rock), I work with this. It is taku wakan, something sacred. The yuwipi is part of me. It is inside me. It was already inside my grandfathers and great-grandfathers. Tunka, inyan, the rock. So in a yuwipi ceremony there is the power grounded in Tunka, or inyan, and also the power of lightning, of the buffalo, the eagle, and the black-tailed deer. Yuwipi is the oldest way. Tunka was here before everything else. He is the foundation. Everything will perish someday, but Tunka, the rock, will never die. He will be there forever. We address the Great Spirit as Tunkashila, Grandfather. The word *tunka* is in there, part of the Creator's name. Through dreams coming from the rocks we can heal, or find a missing person. There are large sacred rocks people visit to pray over.

There is a circle stone, a buffalo stone, pte hiko. We use him in a ceremony to find buffalo. The stone is round, like the sun and the moon. He is related to the wakinyan, the thunderbirds. We got this stone from Ptesan Ska Win, the White Buffalo Calf Woman. The buffalo stone—I still have it. Right in this stone is the print of a buffalo hoof and there are also sacred designs on it. And in this stone is the power of the wind. In the old days, a powerful medicine man could send such a rock to look for buffalo, and by the wind and by takuskanskan, the power that makes things move, the rock returned and told the people where to find game. The stone makes a sound when the buffalo is near. It shows us where to find survival food. The buffalo are gone now, but we still use this stone in our ceremonies. It helps us to find things.

I have a rock that has a human face. It has eyes, ears, a nose, and a mouth. This, too, is sacred. I found it when I was looking for the white medicine, pejuta ska hu; the whites call it locoweed. If you don't know how to handle this medicine, it can make you crazy. The wagmuha rocks, the little stones in our gourds, are ant power rocks. They soak into the pejuta ska for days and months through rainwater, and then the yuwipi men use these stones and a turtle shell and soak the medicine for many days, and that's how we use it in the yuwipi ceremony. The stones, the rocks, Tunka, inyan, are sacred because the spirits dwell in them. Giant rocks, like the Medicine Rocks in Montana, where Sitting Bull held a sun dance one week before the battle in which Custer was wiped out, are wakan, sacred. These rocks are covered with ancient designs cut into them by our forefathers.

The round pte hiko stones for finding buffalo, some the size of a baseball or a golf ball, are wakan.

And the tiny crystal and agate stones we pick up from the ant heaps to put into our gourd rattles are all wakan. Big or small, there is a power in them. There is a reason we use the tiny ant rocks, some not bigger than a pinhead, in our gourds. The ant is sacred too. That little bug works in mysterious ways. He makes his ant heaps. He forms a family, like a tiyoshpaye. Inside the ant lives a spirit. It makes the ant look for shiny little crystals and agates to put on top of his house, as if that tiny living thing had a sense of beauty. If you turn a red ant on its back, you find a wigh-munge on the belly, a medicine web. Wablushka, the ant, doesn't have a heart. He doesn't need it. He lives by the universe. At some time the tiny agates were wood, pine trees. Over millions of years they turned to stone. The Great Spirit changed them from wood into rock, into rock power, wa inyan sicun. It is the rebirth of the thunder and the lightning. Tunkashila has given the tree the power to be reborn as a rock. The medicine man has to use the little stones in a spiritual way. He puts four hundred five of them in a gourd rattle. With the sound of the gourd he can talk to Wakan Tanka. Talking stones, I call them, not only the tiny ones from the anthills but also the larger ones that people keep among their own sacred things. Crazy Horse carried a sacred pebble tied in his hair behind the ear, which made him bulletproof.

Yuwipi is for healing, it is a finding-out ceremony—to find a missing person, find something lost, find the reason for some grief, find the cause of a sickness, find the identity of your future. A yuwipi man is a stone dreamer who has been going on many vision quests to renew his powers. The spirit picked me to be a yuwipi man when I was still a boy. The yuwipi ceremony itself is a child, a child of life born in the generation of dreams.

A yuwipi ceremony takes place when somebody with a problem asks for it. You must ask in the right way, with the pipe. The medicine man, the yuwipi wichasha, does not accept pay for his help, but the one who wants to be helped, the sponsor, has to

provide the food for all who want to participate. Like other ceremonies, this one begins with a sweat. While those who will partake in the yuwipi purify themselves in the sweat lodge, the
women prepare the sacred food. Inside the medicine man's
house a room has been made ready for the ceremony. All furni-
ture has been taken out. All the windows have been covered with
blankets so that not even the tiniest bit of light can enter from
the outside, because the ceremony has to be performed in total
darkness. Everything that could reflect light is taken down from
the walls or covered up—mirrors, pictures, photos, anything
made of glass or having a shiny surface. People coming into the
room even take off their wristwatches. Now the room is empty,
waiting to be made sacred, waiting for the spirits. Blankets are
folded up and put along the walls for the people to sit on. The
floor is covered with sage.

Many elements are used in the yuwipi ceremony—tobacco
ties, eagle feathers, eagle wings, an eagle bone whistle, deer tails,
drums, gourd rattles, and, most of all, the chanunpa, the sacred
pipe.

First, a square is laid out inside the room, made of chanli
wapahta, tobacco ties. The chanli are made this way: You cut a
little square of colored cloth, maybe an inch and a half across.
On this you put a little pinch of tobacco. Then you fold it into a
tiny bundle that you tie into a long string. Four hundred five
chanli are tied on that string. They stand for all the different
kinds of animals, for all the kinds of plants in the universe. They
also represent the spirits that might come in to help. So you form
this string into a square. The medicine man is on the inside. The
sponsor, the drummer, the singer, and all others who want to be
cured or have their problems solved sit on the outside of the
space made by the string of tobacco ties. In the old days the
chanli, the little bundles, were tanned deer hide filled with chanshasha, red willow bark tobacco, but now somehow it is changed
and we use colored material and Bull Durham.

In my ceremony, we place large cans at the four corners of

the sacred square. They are filled with earth, and into each we put a peeled willow stick, to the top of which are tied strips of colored cloth offerings, the waunyanpi. These colored flags represent the sacred four directions—black for the west, red for the north, yellow for the east, and white for the south. They also stand for the generations. It means that the sacred square now stands for the whole universe. Between the black west flag and the red north flag, at the top of the sacred space opposite the door, we place the center staff. Its upper half is painted red, the lower half is black. In between is a narrow yellow stripe. The red represents the day, the black stands for the night. The thin yellow stripe is the dawn or the sunset. To the top of the staff we tie a single center eagle feather. It represents wanblee, our sacred bird, the Great Spirit's messenger, the go-between from Tunkashila to the human being. This feather is also for the spirits to come in. Then I put another eagle wing feather under the other one. That represents all the flying relatives, the winged ones. This feather creates a good spirit, good understanding.

Halfway down the staff we fasten the tail of a black-tailed deer. The deer is fast and has a powerful spirit. If there is any person present who is sick and wants to be doctored, the deer will come in, go around, and walk through. If it turns back to where someone sits and turns its back on him, you can't cure that person. Early in the morning the deer comes to the creek to drink. He can smell and hear a human being from half a mile away. If somebody is far behind him he knows. He can see in the darkness of the night. On his eyes you see a yellow part and a white part. And in the morning the sun comes up, yellow and white shining upon all living beings. The white is your bone, and the yellow is for when you get into the spiritual power and you see little golden sparks in front of you. On the horns you see the four colors, because the deer horn has four colors. In the beginning, when the deer horn is growing, it is pink, or redlike, then it turns a little bit whitelike, then yellow, and then black. So there are the four direction colors. There is a powerful medicine we get from behind the deer's ear. It's some kind of fat. You use this medicine to find healing herbs and roots and to pray with it. For this reason we have the blacktailed-deer medicine to help cure people during the yuwipi. Together with the center staff I have four smaller willow sticks with cloth offerings tied to them.

Sometimes I also use a buffalo skull altar. Tatanka, the buffalo, is sacred. He stands for the four winds of the universe. He is our brother. During a yuwipi ceremony I took part in, a buffalo spirit came out of the earth into the meeting. He rumbled and bellowed, and his hooves made the ground shake beneath us.

In front of the center staff we make an earth altar. This is most sacred when made from gopher dust, from earth taken from a gopher hole. Gophers have power. It is a medicine. Before going into battle, Crazy Horse always sprinkled gopher dust over his horse's back. The altar is round. It is made smooth with an eagle feather or a sprig of sage. The medicine man traces a design on it—maybe an Iktomi design, a spider, a thunderbird, wakinyan, design, or a wicite, a human face. It is up to the yuwipi man to pick his own design. This altar represents Unci, Grandmother Earth. Around it I always place a circle of chanli.

On each side of the altar I place a wagmuha, a gourd rattle. The gourds are made of tanned deer or buffalo hide, just like a ball filled with the little ant rocks. Sometimes feathers are attached to them. Often during a yuwipi ceremony these gourds fly through the air all by themselves. When the spirit enters, he picks up the gourd and makes a noise with it, makes it talk. He may hit your body with it to make a cure. Sometimes there is a spark, a tiny flash of lightning at the point where the gourd makes a hit. Bad spirits do not like the sound of the wagmuha. They run away from it. If you put a sprig of sage behind your ear, if you are lucky you can understand what the gourd is saying. The gourd travels around the room or tent so fast that you can never catch it. The sound of the rattle is not music; it is the sound of spirit voices. Tunkashila put the spirits into the yuwipi ceremony. They are visiting spirits, soul spirits. When the wagmuha, or the eagle feather, touches a person, that's a gift of power from the spirits. The spirit is a nest touch. Someday everybody should be a nest, a nest builder for the future. Good things happen when you have a son or daughter. Tunkashila sees it. So he touches you like that. The spirit talks in his own language, hanbloglaka, dream speaking. Only the yuwipi man can understand it. He is the interpreter.

Before getting to the heart of the ceremony we smoke up the room with wachanga, smoldering sweet grass. Its good scent drives away evil spirits and adds to the sacredness of what is going to take place. Someone could make a flesh offering at that time. Then the medicine man takes off his shoes and shirt and stands ready to be tied up. We use rawhide for the tying. We take a big hide and cut it all in a circle. We cut it about an inch wide, for bowstrings as well as the yuwipi. We use the skin from the back of the animal, opening it up on top where the bone is covered by a white gut. It makes a string as strong as nylon. You roll and twist it together to make a long rope. The rawhide represents itazipe ikan, the bowstring. The spirit strikes with a bow.

There are two helpers standing with the medicine man, the yuwipi wichasha. They first tie his hands and fingers together behind his back. The finger ties represent the wakinyan, the thunderbirds. Next the helpers cover the yuwipi man with a star blanket. They cover his head and his face, all of him. In the old days they used a buffalo robe, but now it's a quilt. They make him into a bundle, wrap him up like a mummy. They tie him with the long rawhide thong, tight around his neck and then down and all around his body, using seven knots to do the job. They follow an ancient vision. They have to do everything right. A mistake could endanger the yuwipi wichasha's life. They make the string tight to unite the man with Tunkashila, the Everywhere Spirit. The one who is bundled up senses what the people feel. The tying is for concentration. People have one or two minds, but in this ceremony everybody is going into one mind. It pulls together the medicine man, the spirits, and all who have come to the ceremony. The helpers lift the medicine man up and lay him face-down upon the sage-covered floor. All this is called wichapahtepi, meaning "they tie him up." Hokshila unpapi, the cradle bundling, the little baby ceremony, that's one of the meanings of the yuwipi. They cradle bundle each other. We have performed this since the beginning of time. It symbolizes the baby wrapped in its cradleboard. While all this is taking place the yuwipi man prays to the four winds of the earth.

After they have laid the yuwipi man on his bed of sage, the helpers step outside the square of tobacco ties, leaving him alone in the center. He lies there so that the spirits can come in and use him. While all this has been going on, the yuwipi wichasha has prayed to the four winds of the earth. Now the moment comes when all lights are put out, plunging the room into darkest darkness, into womb darkness, blacker than a moon-less night. It is like floating in a river of black ink. It is the dark-ness of the grave. Then the drums begin to pound in step with your heartbeat. You feel it pulsating in your veins. Then the singing starts. There could be one singer and one drum or there could be several.

Uncle Bill Eagle Feathers used to say, "That man all bundled up like a mummy, he is like dead. It is up to all who participate to bring him back to life." When I am lying there I am a foundation, a receptacle for the spirit. So you are empty for that, lifeless. You make yourself completely empty to let the spirit energy come into you, to fill that space. At the fourth song the spirits come in. They speak to me in little voices. They use dream language. Wrapped up in my star blanket, I understand what they are say-ing. They are telling me the answers to what the sponsor and the other people present want to know. They can hear the voices, too, but they can't understand them. If they put a sprig of sage behind their ear, or in their hair, the spirits will talk to them. When I am tied up and they sing the songs, I feel the powers of the singers coming into me and my power going into them. And I travel while I am tied up, to all kinds of spirit places. I could travel to the place where Sitting Bull is buried, and still my body is lying there all wrapped and tied up. I could travel all over and, at the same time, spirits could come in from far away—Crazy Horse's spirit, maybe. The spirits of people who used to live, who have passed on, speak directly to the one who is tied up.

One sign that the spirits have come in are sparks of light flickering in the darkness, flying all over the ceiling, dashing all over the place, sometimes making a sound like two pebbles clicking together. These are the spirits of wakinyan, the thunderbirds. The wakinyan works with the sun, with the light that is everywhere. The sun is life; it lives within us, even in the dark. Wakinyan and inyan, the stone, are related. Two flint rocks knocked together make a little spark, a tiny bit of lightning. The rock and the wakinyan go together. Nobody can explain the yuwipi lights flitting through the darkness. The white man's science can't. It is the work of Tunka wasichun, rock power. Sometimes an eagle comes into the ceremony. You can't see him, but you hear his cry far above you and you feel the touch of his wings.

Sometimes I do a kind of yuwipi ceremony called iktomi lowanpi, spider ceremony. For this I use only seventy-five tobacco ties. It is for somebody who is in trouble and needs help in a hurry. So this is a shortened ceremony. I trace a spiderweb design on the earth altar. Iktomi, the spider man, Tunka, and wakinyan are closely related. It is all part of the yuwipi. A spider ceremony is a scouting. If anything is going to happen in the future, you scout for it. We have the power to do this. The Iktomi lowanpi is a one-track identity spiritual power given to our tiyoshpaye. It will always be in our family. The spider man is speaking to me when I am tied up, like a voice out of the womb. He is talking in a high, sharp voice, a voice you hear only in the yuwipi. A voice of the fathers and grandfathers.

In the end they sing the sixteenth song, the wanagi kiglapi olowan, the spirits-going-home song. When the lights are turned on again, the yuwipi man sits in the center, untied and unwrapped. Then he interprets what the spirits have told him, where to find a person or a thing lost, how to cure someone's disease. The yuwipi man could do some doctoring at that time, lead a sick person to the altar, smoke him up with cedar or sweet grass and fan him off with the eagle wing. Maybe he gives him or her a special medicine, a kind of root, for which the white man has no name. Then the sacred pipe goes around, clockwise, and everybody smokes it. Those present have the privilege to speak, to say something good, to ask questions. After the last person has smoked, we say "mitakuye oyasin," all my relatives, and the ceremony is finished.

After that we eat the sacred food. There will be a kettle of dog soup, because the yuwipi is also a dog feast. The dog is a sacrifice. The dog is sacred. If you leave your home, the dog will stay around until the last bit of food is gone. A dog will stay by the side of his dead master and starve rather than leave. Every once in a while the dog will bark toward the east and the west. When somebody dies he'll be calling to the family, barking. The dog sees the spirits, the dead souls. The dog knows when someone is about to die, but you don't know it. They choke the dog toward the west. We let a man pull the rope on the dog only for the yuwipi, heyoka, and memorial ceremony. The dog does not suffer. The rope kills him instantly. My father always painted a red stripe from the dog's nose and down the spine before choking him, because the dog is sacred. They also scent the dog, cedar him, or fan him off with sweet grass. The women singe it, cut the neck, and let the blood come out. They pray while doing this. Besides the dog we eat other sacred food: wojapi, which is a chokecherry pudding, and corn wasna, which is corn and kidney fat pounded together; we drink a kind of herb tea. We also drink the pejuta sapa, or "black medicine"—namely, coffee. That is not sacred, but good, hot, and strong. And then it is over. Maybe it is already close to sunup. Time to say good-bye, go home, and go to sleep.

thirteen

THE GHOSTS RETURN

Maka sitomniya ukiye,	The whole world is coming,
oyate ukiye,	a nation is coming,
oyate ukiye,	a nation is coming,
wanbli oyate wan	the eagle brought
hoshihiye lo,	the message,
ate heye lo,	says the father,
ate heye lo,	says the father,
maka owanchaya ukiye,	the whole world is coming,
	the buffalo are coming,
	the buffalo are coming,
kangi oyate wan	the crow has
hoshihiye lo,	brought the message,
ate heye lo,	says the father,
ate heye lo.	says the father.
Kangi oyate wan	The crow nation is coming,
uyike lo,	
ate heye lo,	says the father,
ate heye lo.	says the father.

Ghost dance

On January 14, 1890, my great-grandfather Jerome Crow Dog came out of the Badlands with his people to surrender. He and his band were the last of the ghost dancers, the last to dance the wanagi wachipi. In March of 1973, I, Leonard Crow Dog, brought the ghost dance back. At the right place, at the right time. I started from where the first

Crow Dog had stopped. I brought it back at Wounded Knee, during the seventy-one-day siege, when I was the spiritual leader of AIM, the American Indian Movement. My great-grandfather's spirit gave me a vision to do this. The vision told me to revive this ceremony at the place where Chief Big Foot's ghost dancers, three hundred men, women, and children, had been massacred by the army, shot to pieces by cannons, old people, babies. I could feel their spirits telling me to do it. Everybody at Wounded Knee could feel the presence of the ghosts of those who had been killed, their bodies lying in that ditch, right under our feet. So I rounded up as many people as I could get hold of, with the help of Wallace Black Elk. We were going to dance for the sake of the spirits. For our own sakes.

I spoke to the people. Somebody taped it, so my words are not lost: "Tomorrow, we're going to ghost dance. For eighty-three years it has never been danced. When they killed our people here so long ago, it was said that the nation's hoop was broken. We'll make the sacred hoop whole again. We're going to dance, whether it rains or snows. Whether the land is muddy or covered with snow, the spirit will come traveling. There'll be no rest, no intermission, no coffee break. During the day, we're not going to eat or drink water. We'll unite together as one tribe through the language of the Great Spirit. We're not going to divide. We're going to be brothers and sisters. Whether you're Mohawk, or Cheyenne, we'll be as one.

"We will hold hands. If one of you gets into the power, if he's in a trance, if he falls down inside the ring, let him. If somebody goes into convulsions, let him. Don't get scared. The spirit will be the doctor. If anything happens like that, hold hands, keep dancing. There will be no drum. The earth will be our drum. Our feet will do the drumming. There's a song I'm going to sing, my grandfather's song. The clouds will be dreams. They'll go into your minds. You will see visions. We will elevate ourselves from this world to another. From there we can see Tunkashila.

"We're going to remember our brothers who were killed by

the white man, and you will see your brothers, your relations who have died. You will see them. The ghost dance spirit will appear. The sacred pipe is going to be there. The fire is going to be there. The sage is going to be there. Indian tobacco is going to be there. It starts physically and goes into spirituality. And then you will get into the power. It's going to start here, at Wounded Knee, and it will continue. We are going to unite as brothers and sisters. We will ghost dance. Everybody has heard about the ghost dance, but nobody has ever seen it. It was something the United States government had forbidden—no ghost dance, no sun dance, no Indian religion. That hoop has not been broken. We will dance for the future generations.

"I don't have to instruct you. After you get into the circle the spirit will tell you, give you the power to speak. We're all going to speak another language all of a sudden, because we dance in a sacred way. We're going to bring everybody together with his eagle bone whistle. I want to see a vision tomorrow. We'll all be blessed in the Indian way. This hoop has not been broken.

"This is a vision of four dimensions. Nobody can stop us. An old man should direct this dance, but there's no elder here who knows how to do this. So I guess it's up to me, because this dance has been in my family for four generations. This sacred stick will travel from tribe to tribe. We will eat sacred food. You'll hear the buffalo, hear their voices coming up through Mother Earth. Then the buffalo could come back. You'll know how the Indian has been born. There will be spiritual knowledge.

"We have a medicine bag. We'll make ghost shirts and medicine bundles. We'll wear eagle feathers. We'll wrap ourselves in upside-down American flags like the ghost dancers of old. We'll paint the shirts—yellow for the thunder, red for AIM, flowers for the yuwipi, stars, half-moons, eagles, magpies, designs like that. I'll wear a breechcloth, won't wear white man's pants. But it's up to you what you wear. The women should wear shawls. We'll have the sacred tree there, the evergreen, the tree of life.

"We need a young girl, a virgin, representing Ptesan Win, the

White Buffalo Woman. She will fill the pipe and take it to Mother Earth. There is going to be an altar there. The virgin will light the peace pipe and she'll let Mother Earth smoke. She'll let the smoke rise to the four winds of the earth and up to Tunkashila, the Great Spirit. The ghosts are going to smoke. Our dead relatives are going to respond to this.

"I follow my great-grandfather's way. He performed the ghost dance. He warned Chief Big Foot not to come through here with his people, because a dream had foretold him that death was waiting for them. And this happened. They were all killed, by the quick-firing cannons and by the Seventh Cavalry, Custer's old regiment. They were avenging themselves for having been beaten by us, avenging themselves on women and children. Today, here at Wounded Knee, the white man is again all around us, with his armored cars and heavy machine guns. His planes and helicopters are circling above us. Like Big Foot's people we might be killed here. If we die we'll be buried here on this sacred ground. That's where I want to be buried. First, put me on a scaffold in a blanket, and then put me in the earth here. Whether we're going to die or not, we're going to dance!"

Many of those who danced with me at Wounded Knee knew nothing about the old ways and ceremonies. They were Indians, but they had lived all their lives in the white man's big cities, or they came from tribes where the missionaries had destroyed their old religion. Many had never been in a sweat lodge. So before dancing we had to have a sweat, and some of them found it hard to take the heat.

I ran this ghost dance the way my father, Henry, and Uncle Dick Fool Bull had described it to me. My father was fourteen years old when Jerome, the first Crow Dog, died. So he still remembered much of it, and also what he learned from his own father, John. Uncle Dick Fool Bull died in 1975. He witnessed the ghost dance as a teenager.

We began with the sweat bath, one sweat for the men and one for the women. We rubbed our bodies with sage and sweet grass. We prepared the dance circle. We put the evergreen, the tree of life, in the middle. We put tobacco ties and cloth offerings on it. We used sacred red face paint. We used magpie feathers. Every dancer wore an eagle feather in his hair. We danced in a circle, holding hands, from right to left, starting slowly and then going faster and faster, sometimes with arms upraised. We danced in the ravine where so many of our women and children had been killed by the Seventh Cavalry. It was cold. The grass was brown. There was frost on it. In some places there were snow patches. On and off it snowed. We had the young girl representing Ptesan Win standing in the circle, holding the pipe. She should have had an elk horn bow and four arrows with bone points to shoot toward the clouds in the four directions, but we did not have such a bow. I wished that I had the sacred stick my great-grandfather used when he was the dance leader so long ago, but that is now in the museum in Pierre, the state capital. It has two buffalo horns on it, bending downward, forming a moon crescent. The handle is made of wood, but you could not burn it, no matter how hard you tried. I will get that stick back someday.

The earth trembled. I felt the ghosts dancing beneath the ground. And some of the dancers fell down in a trance, fell down like dead, receiving visions. So, at Wounded Knee, with a cold wind blowing, we reeducated ourselves. We had about thirty dancers. Many were barefoot, in the old ghost dance way, even though there was snow on the ground.

Wounded Knee gave knowledge to the people. Wounded Knee is the spirit that knows the red man. It is an identity you can stand on. I felt good. I felt proud. I had brought something back to my people that had been lost for almost a century.

At Wounded Knee I brought the ghost dance to the American Indian Movement. A year later, in May of 1974, I brought it back to my own people. I put it on at the place where we Crow Dogs have gone on vision quests for generations, where we have our vision pit. Nature has split the Crow Dog allotment land into two parts—a high and a low one. At the bottom, near the Little White

River, my father had his house, which burned down some twenty years ago. This is where we hold our sun dance every summer. To get to the high part you have to cross a little stream. There is no bridge, just a large tree trunk to get over as best you can, and then there is a very steep footpath to the top of the hill. Up there is a large flat place covered with grass, with pine and cedar trees all around it. This place is very beautiful and very sacred. Nobody ever goes there but some animals, for whom this is a shelter where they are safe. It is this spot I chose for my ghost dance. This time I was happy to have my father there and old Uncle Dick Fool Bull to instruct me and the dancers and to teach us some of the ancient ghost dance songs.

This dance was not advertised. It was supposed to be only for us Rosebud Sioux, but somehow, through the "moccasin telegraph," which always spreads the news among Indians in an almost mysterious way, the word got around, and many native people came to dance from as far away as Canada, Alaska, and Mexico. A Navajo man came, and a young mother and her daughter from a Northwest Coast fishing tribe. Two Mexican Indians came in their loose Huichol and Nahua outfits.

Before the dance I gave everybody medicine in the form of a special kind of tea. Everybody put on ghost outfits. Some wore upside-down American flags. Everybody wore a small medicine bundle made for this day. I had on a yellow buckskin shirt and leggings. I had an eagle head tied to the back of my head. I wore the old Crow Dog wotawe—a shield showing the two arrows and the two bullets. My father wore a buffalo horn headdress. He had his face painted. Then, in a long line, walking Indian file, we went up on the hill. On the hilltop my father had prepared the fire and the sweat lodge. He had put up a tipi. The dancers formed a circle on the grass and sat on the ground. My father, Henry, talked to them for a long time, telling them how our family had been connected to this ceremony right from the beginning. He instructed them in what to do. Then I took over. The dance began. We were holding one another's hands and moving, making the sacred hoop.

Some of the dancers went into the power. One teenage girl got into a trance. Two women fell down, lying there unconscious for a while, having visions. I doctored them and fanned them off with an eagle wing. When one of these women came to, she said that in her vision she had reexperienced the killing of our women and children at Wounded Knee. This woman wore the upside-down stars and stripes, just as those did who were massacred by Custer's cavalry. At the end of the dance a snooper plane came out of nowhere and flew in circles above us. What did the pilot look for? All he could see was some forty unarmed Indians, including women and some children, dancing and holding hands in the middle of the lonely prairie. I could not understand this. But then a whole flock of eagles came circling over us. They seemed to fly in some sort of formation. The eagles made the plane fly away. So our dance had a good ending.

fourteen

A HOT LINE TO THE GREAT SPIRIT

Oyate yanka po
channupa wa wakan
yuha chewaki yelo he
oyate yanipikta cha
lechi mu welo.

People, behold me.
There is a pipe that is sacred,
therefore I pray with it.
Our nation will live,
that is why I do this.

Pipe song

The most sacred thing for us Lakota is the chanupa, the holy pipe. The pipe and the Indian go together. They cannot be separated. The pipe lifted up in prayer forms a link between man and Tunkashila. It's a spiritual bridge to the Great Spirit. With the pipe I can communicate with Tunkashila, the Grandfather Spirit, whom we also call Wakan Tanka, the great sacredness. With the pipe I let my mind fly through the air. The sacred pipe is a smoke signal to Tunkashila. The pipe is not a thing. It is alive. You can feel its power as you hold it, power from Ptesan Win, the White Buffalo Woman, who brought this great gift to us. Within the pipe dwells the power of Wakan Tanka, male and female power. Man is the stem; woman is the bowl. At Wounded Knee I lifted up my pipe for survival, not for survival of us who had come to that place, but for the survival of all our Indian people.

When I speak of the pipe I speak with an ancient knowledge that lies within me. I was born before my father. By this I mean that my spirit was born hundreds of years ago. What my ancestors left, whatever the white man has not destroyed, I pick up and continue on. A man without a country, that's Mr. Indian, but our spiritual country is still there, thanks to the pipe.

I had a vision. It came from the morning star, a star whisper. I heard this voice saying, "Any understanding you ask from the morning star shall be granted you, but ask with the sacred things, the drum, the sacred tobacco, the sacred sweet grass, and, above all, with the sacred pipe." Our dead sleep not. They tell me what I want to know. I have the power to see through things. I have only limited vision with the eyes I have in my head, but with my spiritual eyes I can see across oceans. The pipe is here to unite us, to remove the fences people put up against one another. Putting up fences is the white man's way. He invented the barbed wire, the barbed wire of the heart. The pipe is a fence remover. Sitting in a circle, smoking it the right way, all barriers disappear. Walls crumble.

The pipe is us. Inyan sha, the red pipestone, is our flesh and blood. The stem is our spine, the bowl our head, the smoke rising from it is Tunkashila's breath. There is an old story handed down from grandparent to grandchild, generation after generation. It is the story of a great flood that carried everything before it. The people fled to the top of high mountains, but even there the rising waters swept over them. Their flesh and blood turned to stone, the red pipestone. Only one young woman survived. An eagle carried her to the top of a tree on the highest cliff above the water. The young woman had twins, a boy and a girl, the eagle's children. These twins are the ancestors of our Lakota nation. The sacred red stone occurs at only one spot in the whole world, at a quarry in western Minnesota. In the old days this was a sacred ground, not only to the Sioux but to many other tribes who came there to get the red stone for their pipes. At that place even bitter enemies became friends, digging the stone side by side. Among whites the stone is known as catlinite, after the painter George Catlin, the first white man to visit the quarry, way back in 1837. The sacred stone forms a long band sandwiched between layers of other kinds of rock. I have been there many times to dig out the inyan sha. There is little of it left and one must dig deeper and deeper to get at it, even dig under the water that covers the quarry's bottom.

Pipes for ceremonial use often have their stems beautifully decorated with porcupine quillwork. Sometimes shiny green mallard feathers are tied to it. Some pipes have an eagle feather dangling from them, because the eagle saved the young woman from drowning during the great flood and in this way made human beings survive, and also because the eagle is the grandest and wisest of birds and Tunkashila's messenger. The pipe bowl is called pahu, meaning head bone. They call the stem ihupa, handle, or sinte, the tail. The mouthpiece is called oyape, and the spot where the stem joins the bowl is oagle, the holding place. Pipes are often very plain, elbow shaped for just the pleasure of smoking, or T-shaped for ceremonial use. Some old bowls were carved in the shape of a horse, a buffalo, or even a human being. Some bowls are inlaid with lead designs. Some are made of black stone—shale, steatite, or calcite. My uncle old George Eagle Elk used to make black bowl pipes. Pipes of all shapes and materials are found in the thousand-year-old tombs of the ancient Mound Builders and in the equally old ruins of southwestern pueblos. Throughout human history, wherever there were Indians there were pipes.

Pipes are kept in special bags called chantojuha, heart bags, because the pipe stands at the heart of our existence. Usually fringed, the pipe bags are beautifully decorated with beadwork and quillwork. When pipes are not being smoked, the bowl and stem are kept separate. They are just too powerful to be joined together for any length of time. Together with the pipe a man may also keep a poker, ichasloka, for tamping down the tobacco in the bowl. It is often also beautifully decorated. Sometimes as a tamper they use a wooden skewer with which a friend has pierced himself during the sun dance.

Chanshasha, the tobacco used for smoking the pipe, is also sacred. It is not like the stuff in a white man's cigarette that gives you lung cancer and makes you an addict, something used only to make you feel good. It contains no nicotine. Chanshasha is made from the inner bark of a dogwood or red osier dogwood, which grows along the Little White River, right near our place. Some tribes use red willow bark, but we prefer the dogwood. Sometimes we mix it with sweet-smelling herbs, such as chanli ichahiye, snakeroot, which keeps poisonous snakes away. We also mix our tobacco with arrowroot. Some people say that what we are smoking is kinnickinick, but that is not a Lakota word but one used by northeastern tribes.

The pipe should always be treated with great respect, even awe. Never walk in front of people who are smoking it. Never step over it. A pipe should never be lent out. No menstruating woman should come near the pipe, because at that time her power fights with the power of the pipe. When she is not on her moon, a woman can smoke the pipe during a ceremony. Hold the pipe with the bowl in the left hand and the stem in the right, across your chest, not sticking way out. With the pipe in your hand you cannot lie; you can speak only the truth. When you load up the pipe with tobacco, you pray, you sing the pipe-filling song. You must smoke it in the right way, always going clockwise from one person to the next and everybody taking four puffs, because four is the sacred number. That's why we sing,

Channupa kile wakan yelo   This pipe is sacred,
tanyan yuzo yo.   hold it in a good way.

As the pipe goes around, every puff is a prayer. As you inhale the smoke, all humankind smokes with you. Your breath mingles with the breath of all other living beings. The spirit is in the pipe. *It is there.* Smoking in a circle you hear voices coming out of nowhere. Spirits may appear and talk to you, and they speak every language in the world. There is a purpose and a reason for using the pipe this way, the way Tunkashila wants it. The pipe is like a human being, it is not a thing. It is our flesh and blood. Without the pipe there can be no ceremony. It stands at the center of all our seven sacred rites. It unites us and makes us one. Smoking in a circle we renew the sacred hoop of the nation. The pipe breaks down the concrete walls that separate us. With the pipe you must concentrate, think only good thoughts, and pray for understanding.

April 16, 1968, was the most awesome day of my life. That day I was allowed to behold, to touch, and to pray with the Ptehinchala Huhu Chanupa, the Buffalo Calf Pipe. It is the most holy thing we Lakota possess. Maybe this is the most sacred object for all the red nations on this continent. This is the pipe that Ptesan Win, the White Buffalo Woman, brought to our people so long ago. Some say this pipe is eight hundred years old, some say it's a thousand years. The pipe was there when the Lakota people were born, when understanding was given to the human being, when the holy woman with this pipe taught our people how to live in a sacred manner.

For many generations the Calf Pipe was kept by the Elk Head family. From them it passed to the Looking Horses. Arvol Looking Horse is at this time the pipe keeper. On that day in 1968, I was allowed by my father and other elders and spiritual men to travel to Eagle Butte, where the sacred bundle in which the pipe is kept was to be opened. This happens only on very special occasions, maybe not even once in twenty years or even within one's lifetime. So then we traveled more than a hundred miles to Eagle Butte, to the Greengrass community on the Cheyenne River reservation, one of several Sioux reservations in South Dakota. The people there are mainly Minneconjou, one of our seven Lakota tribes. There was my father, Henry, and myself, and one of my grandpas, Old Man Little Dog. He was eighty-seven years old and didn't do much of anything anymore, but he said that he had to be there to pray with the Calf Pipe. The others in our group were Abel Stone, Joe Black Tomahawk, Laura Tomahawk, John

Williams, Noah Eagle Deer, Joe Eagle Elk, Uncle Moses Big Crow, and Jeff LaBuff Baker. We all met at the house of Stanley and Celia Looking Horse. Stanley had just named his son, Arvol, as the keeper of the Calf Pipe. He was a young boy then, even younger than myself. The old Looking Horses were like a strange horse that shies off when you come near it. By this I mean that they kept to themselves, away from white folks, living in the old Indian way.

We purified ourselves. We prayed. We walked barefoot to the shed where the pipe bundle was kept at that time. There were twelve of us. We put up an altar. We had a ceremony. We smoked up the bundle with sweet grass. We made offerings of tobacco ties, colored cloth, and Bull Durham. Then, at about five o'clock in the afternoon, we started to unwrap the bundle. I was trembling and breathing hard. I started to weep. I felt the power coming out of the bundle, a power so strong it scared me. I sensed the presence of spirits. All of us experienced this.

First we untied the frayed strings holding together an old army canvas. Then came another old canvas. Then what we call a crazy blanket, with designs all mixed up. Then came an ancient star quilt. Then a buffalo hide and next a deer hide of great age. Then some old Hudson's Bay trade cloth, then some four direction materials of different colors. Thus we unwrapped the bundle, layer by layer. Within, we came upon a ball of some eight hundred tobacco ties, some eagle feathers so old that almost only the quills remained. We found also some small round pieces of skin with hair on them. I believe that these were human scalps. There were also two flat pieces of carved bone like the ones they used in the old days to handle glowing coals from the fire during ceremonies. And, finally, there was the Ptehinchala Huhu Chanupa, together with an ancient tribal red stone pipe, also sacred, but not as sacred as the holy Calf Pipe. After we had unwrapped the bundle, my father went outside and started a fire. Inside the house we smoked up the room with sage and sweet grass. The twelve of us were privileged to pray with the Calf Pipe and to touch it. We could not smoke it. It is too old for that. It is brittle with age and very fragile. It has to be handled with the greatest of care. Its stem is made from a buffalo calf's legbone. We were allowed to smoke the companion pipe with the red stone bowl.

I have no words to describe the great power of the Calf Pipe. As I touched it I felt its heart beating. Power flowed up my arms as, very lightly, I put my hands upon it. The power flowed into me like ocean waves. It overwhelmed me. I was crying; I felt as if I were enfolded by a black cloud. Outside there was thunder and lightning. It lit up the house. We all felt as if the lightning was coming from the inside of the room. I heard the pipe speaking. It was Tunkashila's voice: "This pipe I am giving you—for life, for good understanding." Tears were streaming down my face. I sobbed, "Tunkashila, we hear you." We all sat still for a long time without moving or talking.

My father and Joe Eagle Elk tied up the pipes and rewrapped them. Arvol Looking Horse picked up the bundle and took it to the place where it was kept. We followed him. We walked four times around the place. Then we went back inside the house and ate. Arvol told me that there were designs on the pipe, wakan designs, which change from time to time in a magical manner. I told Arvol, "You have a great sacredness here, the soul of the nation. With it the people will follow you. Pass it on to the next generation. It is a great responsibility. You carry a heavy burden."

Often I have gone hungry. Often I have been in trouble. But always the pipe was there to help me. It is the one thing they can never take away from us.

Friend,
to you I pass the pipe first.
Around the circle I pass it to you,

around this circle to begin the day.
Around the circle to complete the hoop,
the hoop of the four directions.
I lift up the pipe to the spirit.
I smoke with the Great Mystery.
It is good.

fifteen

SOUL KEEPING

Treat this soul well.
Treat it lovingly.
Give sacred food
to the soul you are keeping.
Because this soul is wakan.
It is not dead.
It is alive.

                    Henry Crow Dog

We have seven sacred ceremonies given to us by Ptesan
Win, the White Buffalo Woman:

Inipi—the sweat lodge
Hanblecheya—the vision quest
Wiwanyank wachipi—the sun dance
Ishnati alowanpi—making a girl into a woman
Hunka kagapi—making relatives
Tapa wakayapi—throwing the ball
Nagi uhapi—soul keeping

I have already talked about the vision quest and the
sweat lodge. These two ceremonies have come back
strong. And the sun dance, too, is getting stronger. Every
summer more and more people come to Crow Dog's
Paradise to dance, to pierce, to suffer in the sacred way.

All over the Lakota reservations they are sun dancing now. But the other four sacred rituals are hardly being performed anymore. Now that some of the old spiritual men have died, I think I am the only one left who can run these ceremonies in the right way. People don't ask anymore to have these ceremonies performed for them. It seems to me that there is only a handful of people left who want them done. Some people in our tribe have not even heard of the ball-throwing ritual or the women's puberty ceremony. This is sad, because these sacred rites bound us to one another, kept our families together, and preserved a way of life that now is disappearing. The ceremonies were given us for a purpose. I still perform them. I want them to live. Yuwipi is not one of the seven rituals. It is as old as the others, maybe even older, but it was not inspired by a vision from the White Buffalo Woman, but by the rock spirit. The ghost dance and peyote are also not part of our ancient seven rites. They came to us from other tribes some hundred years ago.

Nagi uhapi, the keeping of the soul, is a very important ceremony. For many generations our people have been keeping the soul of someone they loved who died. In former times they lived with nagi, the soul, the spirit, the shadow, the essence, the ghost of him who passed away. So the soul knows them and understands them.

If you miss a dear one, the soul can be kept for four years. Most people keep it for only one year, but it should be four. You start the soul keeping by having a holy man cut off a strand of hair from the head of the one you loved. Before cutting off the lock of hair he purifies the knife with sweet grass. The smoke makes a hoop around the whole earth and is breathed in by every living being. The holy man makes three motions as if he were cutting it, then the fourth time he does it. You wrap the hair in red trade cloth. The eyahapa, the crier, or herald, as the whites call him, goes around and weeps over the dead one's spirit. And everybody shows sadness, everybody cries. The name for the spirit keeper is wanagi yuhapi. Usually he is the dead one's father. He has a cottonwood stick and ties the spirit bundle to it; they call it wichaske. After four days the keeper takes three sticks and forms them like a tipi and ties the whole bundle to that. This is the wanagi tipi, the soul's home. He smokes and cedars it up with wachanga. This is for the spirit to live in. The spirit keeper and his family behave as if somebody alive dwells inside the spirit lodge. For them the soul is alive. They show respect and have only good thoughts. They act friendly toward everyone. They take the soul tipi inside their home when the weather is bad, when it rains or snows. They have a special wooden dish to feed the soul.

There is something else they keep separately—the dead person's navel cord. The umbilical cord was put in a beaded or quilled pouch in the shape of a lizard or turtle at the time the child was born. This chegpagnaka, the navel bundle, is made in the shape of a lizard, because this little creature can flatten itself on the ground and play dead, but it is alive and can run off once the danger has passed. So that means telanunwela, dead but alive. Sometimes they make the pouch in the shape of a turtle, because turtles stand for long life. A turtle's heart will keep on beating long after the animal itself has died. This navel cord bundle is tied to a child's cradle board. An exact duplicate of this lizard or turtle pouch is made, but there is no navel cord in it. This one they hang up in a tree to fool the evil spirits. They think the umbilical cord is up there and vent their anger on the empty pouch without doing harm to the child. The umbilical cord, the chekpata, is the vein of the divine human being. Before you finally release the soul from the keeping, put the chegpagnaka away in a spot that only the soul keeper knows. Then the soul will come back to visit there.

You have to keep a soul in a sacred way. You have to remember constantly the one who died. You have to walk in a sacred manner. You have to love in the old traditional way. You don't socialize. You don't make speeches. You don't tell people what to do. You don't hack, and spit, and scratch yourself. You live out in the woods. Every bit of the time you keep a soul you must do things right. You watch your language. You are careful how to talk to people. In public you wear dark, simple clothes. You don't show off. There must be no fighting, no using of a knife while a soul is being kept. The keeper must pray often and smoke the pipe. He should stay much of the time by himself, close to the spirit bundle.

In the old days, when many people kept souls, there were no bad spirits, no wakan sicha, the missionaries' devil. Crow Dog and his people had the knowledge and understanding for this ceremony. Many people don't understand that anymore. In the ancient days people lived to a very old age. Death was not always around, stepping on your heels. People didn't die from drunken driving, from AIDS, from crack, from all those white man's diseases. You didn't die before your time. Life was hard but natural and in many ways better than now. The soul was among the people all the time. You saw that spirit with the eye that's in your heart. The old people used to talk to that spirit. They could feel its presence. Once in a while, when they slept, the spirit showed itself in their dreams. My dad and I were the only ones left to perform this ceremony. And I am still performing it, inside the tipi and outside it. Inside the tipi we speak with the soul, within the hearth fire and within the mind. Sometimes that soul talk is not very clear, so you have to interpret it spiritually. The soul keeper has to be generous. He has to invite many people and feed the hungry and give many gifts. He has to give away many of his possessions to the poor. People respect the man who keeps a soul; they look up to him as to a chief.

In the old days, when a soul was bundled up and put into the ghost tipi, its physical body was put up on a scaffold or a tree. It was given back to nature, to the earth and the wind and the birds, to the sacred four directions of the universe. But the soul lived on in its keeper's charge. We Crow Dogs always had a burial tree, putting the bodies of our dead in the crook of one of the branches. Our relations the Two Strikes, the Iron Shells, the

Hollow Horn Bears all had their own burial trees. That's why the mountains and hills are sacred, because the burial trees were up there. You were not supposed to go near these places. We never crossed the ancient burial grounds. Now you have those cemeteries and have to put your dead ones there. But I still bury some relations wherever I see fit.

At one time, about a hundred years ago, the missionaries and government people forbade us to own ghosts and souls. But we kept doing it in secret. The white man could order people around, but he could not command a ghost to obey him. He can't enforce his law upon a soul.

There comes a time when you have to let go, when you have to release the soul. After four years, or even after one. The soul finally wants to be free to go to the spirit land, just as a child becomes an adult and leaves its parents. That does not mean that the bond is broken. The time comes to tell the soul, "Takoja, today you will go. This is the moment. Tunkashila, have pity on this soul." The releasing is a fulfillment. It is a great thing. The soul keeper does not do this. It is done by the ataya itanchan, the universal everything chief. This medicine man runs the releasing ceremony. He puts on his best rawhide outfit. The soul keeper and his wife do the same. In this way you honor the hokshi chantkiya, the beloved departing one. There is holy food—papa, wasna, wojapi—as the soul is fed for the last time. The ataya itanchan sets up the spirit post, called wanagi glepi, made from the sacred cottonwood. At the top of the post is painted a human face. And the post is clothed with a beautiful girl's dress or boy's outfit. It is put up inside the tipi and the women hug it and cry over it. You place the special wooden dish with the food before the wanagi glepi. The holy man lights his pipe with a glowing buffalo chip, a dried patty of buffalo dung. Everyone sings over the soul. They smoke. The soul keeper speaks to the spirit post figure that represents the departing spirit: "Takoja, grandchild, see your people standing around you for the last time. Now we let you go out of the tipi. With visible breath you will walk. We loved you. Now we must part, but your lock of hair we shall keep forever."

The moment the wanagi wapahta, the spirit bundle, is brought out of the tipi the soul is released and everybody is happy. The soul keeper gives away everything he owns to the poor; he does not worry about tomorrow. The soul travels along the Tachanku, the Milky Way, to the spirit world. As the soul has been freed, so also the spirit keeper has been set free. He and his wife can now resume a normal life. They have fulfilled their task.

I want the generations to continue the sacred ways. Ceremonies such as soul keeping come from the springs of generations of our Lakota people. I have run this ceremony. I have acted the part of the ataya itanchan. I have done this. Hechetu. This ceremony will not be forgotten.

sixteen

BECOMING A WOMAN

The Sun created woman power.
He used lightning to make a bridge
from the moon to the earth.
Woman walked on that bridge.
She is forever connected to the moon.

                    Leonard Crow Dog

When a woman is on her moon time she has sacred power. Her power at that time is so strong that it overcomes a medicine man's power. If a woman on her moon should be present at a ceremony, that ceremony would be ineffective. If a menstruating woman should be present at a curing ritual, the sick person wouldn't get well. This is power from the moon.

When a girl has her first period her father gives a feast in honor of her entering into womanhood. This is one of the seven sacred rites. It is called ishnati Iowanpi, meaning "singing over the first moon time." When a girl experiences this for her first time, she wraps up her moon flow and puts it up high in a wild plum tree where the coyotes and evil spirits cannot get at it. If a coyote should eat it, this animal would get an evil power over the girl. If a bad person with some magic knowledge should get hold of it, he could make a love medicine from it to get power over a certain woman. So you hide this.

In the old days a woman used to stay alone in a tipi for four days, with female relatives feeding her. The word for menstruating, ishnati, means dwelling alone. We don't do this anymore, but we are still very strict about a woman on her moon time not participating in a ceremony or being anywhere near a sun dance. Formerly, when a girl was "dwelling alone" for the first time, her mother or some other wise older woman spent much time with her in the moon time tipi. She was taught everything she needed to know about being a woman, such as how to purify herself after her monthly period, what to expect upon becoming a wife and mother, and how to bead and how to do porcupine quillwork. I think this passing on of woman wisdom from mother to daughter in a solemn, ceremonial way is very important. The white man's system has taken away a mother's power to instruct her daughter in the right way to live and given it to the teacher, the missionary, the social worker, the bureaucrat. In the same way they have taken over much of what a father should do raising his son. The old ceremonies held the families together. So I am trying to be a guitar—the people are the strings while I try to be the tune that unites us.

When a girl's four days of dwelling apart are over, the ishna ta awi cha lowan ceremony is performed. It is also a tatanka lowanpi, a buffalo ceremony, because this sacred animal is the protector of young womanhood. You need a new tipi, made ready for the ceremony, and a new, beautifully beaded buckskin dress for the girl. You also need the following:

> a wooden bowl, chokecherries, an eagle plume, sage, sweet grass, dry cottonwood sticks, a drum, the pipe, chanshasha (native tobacco), a buffalo skull for an altar, food and presents for the guests.

The girl is seated at the chatku, the place of honor, in back of the tipi. Between the chatku and the fire place is a mound of earth representing Unchi, Grandmother Earth. A wichasha wakan, a spiritual man, performs the ceremony. He has prayed earlier for a vision and, during the ceremony, reveals and interprets it. He tells the girl what her mother already has told her: "You are no longer a child. You are a woman now, capable of becoming a mother." The girl still wears her hair loose, like a child's, rather like mourning the passing of her childhood. Now her hair is braided like that of a grown-up woman and the wichasha wakan paints a red stripe along the line where her hair parts in the middle. He tells her not to sit like a child, with her legs stretched out or tucked under her chin, but to sit modestly, with her legs to one side. He tells her that when getting up she should do this gracefully, not push herself up with two hands.

In the days of my grandfather and great-grandfather, the spiritual man performing the ritual wore a buffalo headdress with horns and a buffalo tail on his back. He bellowed and snorted like a buffalo and behaved like a buffalo bull during the rutting season. This symbolized the close relationship between the Lakota people and the buffalo, the bond made by the White Buffalo Woman binding us together. The medicine man nudged the girl lightly while her mother put sage in her daughter's lap and under her arms to ward him off. This symbolized that the girl would soon be old enough to get married and bear children.

Today we do not do it this way. Maybe we should do it exactly as it was done a hundred years ago, but somehow our ceremonies have been watered down. Fewer and fewer fathers want to have a special feast to honor their daughters' first moon time. I still perform a meaningful ceremony for this. I want my children to have a legend.

I try to keep much of the old ishnati alowanpi when I perform it. I burn dry cottonwood sticks to please the buffalo spirit and to chase away evil spirits, such as Anung Ite, the double-faced woman. I sprinkle sweet grass on the fire. I cedar the girl. I make red cloth offerings to the buffalo. I fill my special wooden bowl with water mixed with chokecherries and give it to the girl to drink. Sometimes I use a turtle shell for this. After that the father drinks and then the bowl goes around clockwise and everybody takes a sip. This chokecherry drink represents the color red—the color of the buffalo, the color of our blood. I have a drum going. I sing a song to go with this ritual and all the women join in. Then we smoke the pipe. Finally I have the girl escorted out of the tipi—no longer a winchinchala, but a full-fledged winyan. After that we have a giveaway.

There is another ceremony that is done when a girl reaches womanhood. It is called tapa wakayapi, meaning "throwing the ball." It also is one of the seven sacred rites and likewise it is a buffalo ceremony. We have a legend of how it started. Long ago a man had a vision sent to him by Ptesan Win. In it he saw a buffalo calf changing itself into a human girl. She had in her hand a ball made of buffalo skin stuffed with buffalo hair and she threw it up into the air toward a small herd of buffalo and, immediately, these, too, turned themselves into humans. The man who received this vision understood that he was to start a new ceremony, and so the tapa wakayapi was born.

This ceremony is hardly ever done now. As in the ishnati lowanpi, the girl is instructed in the duties of womanhood. She gets a beautiful new buckskin outfit. She is given a buffalo skin ball painted red to represent the universe. She is brought into the midst of the people who have come to be part of this ceremony. These people form groups standing at the corners of the sacred four directions. The girl throws the ball first toward the west, then toward the north, the east, and the south. After someone catches the ball he throws it back to the girl. Every time the ball is caught, the girl's father gives away a horse in the girl's honor. Having these rites performed after a girl's first moon can make even a rich man very poor.

I performed this ceremony for my daughters Ina and Bernadette when they became twelve years old. I still have the tapa luta, the red ball, handed down in the Crow Dog family from generation to generation. I did it at the rising of a new moon, but I performed it somewhat differently from the way it was done in the old days. I had an elderly person throw the ball for the girls at a buffalo robe. If the ball hits the left side of the robe, the girl's first child will be a girl. If it hits the right side, it will be a boy. If it hits in the middle, it will be chekpapi, twins. I gave the girls holy food—wasna, chankpa (chokecherries), corn, wojapi. I burned sage in a turtle shell and, with my eagle wing, fanned the smoke over them. And, naturally, I gave away things. The ball that I have, I am told, was made from the skin of an unborn buffalo calf, a calf fetus.

All our people, whether traditional or not, are still very strict about a woman on her period not coming into a ceremony or even being near it, because her power at this time is so overwhelming. But this power is not, as in some other cultures, unclean. On the contrary, the power is sacred. Once a woman gets to an age when she no longer has her monthly time, she not only can participate in all ceremonies but can become a medicine woman.

In 1964, I went to Allen, South Dakota, to perform a ceremony. There I met a medicine woman named Bessie Good Road. She had a little altar and she used a buffalo skull in all her ceremonies. And always a buffalo came into her meetings. You could see him like a shadow. She used the buffalo spiritual power. She invited me to help her and I took my drum and sang for her. I had never met a medicine woman before. I was twenty-two years old then. Every time the buffalo spirit moved his legs I saw lightning. Every time the buffalo talked you saw a little flame. When the buffalo swung his tail it made a flaming circle. Bessie told me, "Nephew, someday I won't be here anymore. I want to leave this for my son, for my people to stand on. We are losing things, sacred things, but to this place the buffalo spirit still comes."

That we look upon a woman's moon time as sacred is shown by our legend of We Ota Wichasha, the Blood Clot Boy. So how was this first man born? We Ota Wichasha was born from the Sun and from the woman. This woman was all alone on the earth after it had been created. She was the only human being in the whole world. She was beautiful and no man had touched her. Then she met a spirit, a power from the sun, the moon, and the winds, a shadow of the generations, a buffalo spirit. And it worked on her so that she began to bleed after a woman's nature cycle. And she took yellow bark powder and rabbit fur and put it between her thighs to stop the flow and to contain it. But a tiny drop of her moon blood fell to the earth. And the woman heard a voice talking to her: "Respect the sacred cycle of the earth and respect the sacred cycle of your moon time. From your blood a boy, a man, will grow and start the generations. You will be blessed by takushskanskan, the power that moves and quickens. And I will give you peta owihankeshni, the fire without end. I will strike the earth with lightning, which will turn into wahin, into flint. And you will strike two flints together and the spark will kindle dry weeds, very small and thin. In this way you will light the flame of generations."

And mashtinchala, the rabbit, came across the little clot of blood and kicked it into life through the power that moves. The blood clot turned into a human boy, who grew up to be We Ota Wichasha, the first male of the Lakota tribe. This is the way the story was told to me by my father and by two holy men, Frank Good Lance and Jesse White Lance, after a ceremony at a sun dance held at Corn Creek when I was a young boy. They also told me that the woman's monthly cycle was given to her by the moon and by Mother Earth, who also has such a cycle, bringing forth the green, growing things.

Henry Crow Dog and his granddaughter Colleen making a fire for the sweat lodge.

Henry Crow Dog in the sweat lodge, 1969.

Leonard Crow Dog in the sweat lodge.

Mary Gertrude Crow Dog and
friend cooking for a feast.

Mary Gertrude Crow Dog
making moccasins.

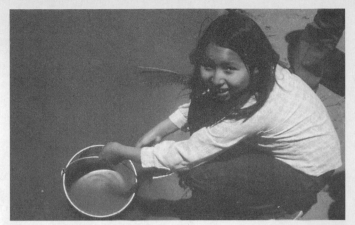

İna Crow Dog getting water.

Sioux hoop dancer.

Henry Crow Dog with pipe.

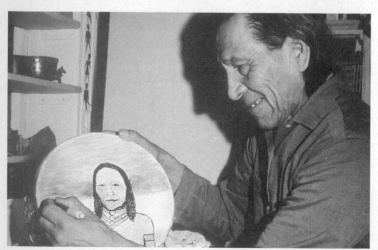

Henry Crow Dog painting a drum.

Leonard Crow Dog dressed as road man for a peyote meeting.

Leonard Crow Dog during a peyote meeting.

Leonard Crow Dog with a courting flute.

Buffalo ceremony to cure Ina Crow Dog.

Leonard Crow Dog with a buffalo skull for the sun dance.

Leonard Crow Dog sun dancing.

Leonard Crow Dog at Wounded Knee sun dance, 1971.

Sun dancer with sage wreath at Wounded Knee, 1971.

Sun dance at Crow Dog's Paradise, 1971.

Sun dance piercing at Crow Dog's Paradise, 1971.

Leonard Crow Dog entering vision pit at the Rosebud Sioux Reservation for a vision quest, 1972.

Leonard Crow Dog and friend in front of the BIA building, Washington, D.C., November 1972.

Russell Means speaking during the takeover of the BIA building, Washington, D.C., November 1972.

Floyd Young Horse during the takeover of the BIA building, Washington, D.C., November 1972.

Woman being arrested during the protest in Custer, South Dakota, February 1973.

Wallace Black Elk praying at Wounded Knee..

Wounded Knee, 1973.

Dennis Banks at Wounded Knee, 1973.

Leonard Crow Dog in jail talking to his son Pedro (Rip Torn at right).

Revival of the ghost dance, May 1974.

Leroy Keams ghost dancing.

Crow Dog's Paradise, 1974.

Mary Gertrude Crow Dog in the old house, 1974.

Leonard Crow Dog in the interior of the Crow Dog home, 1981.

Henry Crow Dog, 1981.

Leonard Crow Dog with his children, 1989.

seventeen

THEY WILL DIE FOR
EACH OTHER

Le hunka   This honored one
echa   behold
wakantu kin   you who are above
          Hunka song

Finally, I am going to speak of the hunka lowanpi, the relation-making ceremony. Some call it the "They are waving
horsetails over each other" ritual. At times two people
want to make a bond between them, a bond stronger than
the bond between parent and child, a bond stronger than
any physical bond could ever be. In that case they have a
hunka ceremony. When two people are bound by this ceremony they share everything. They will share their last
morsel of food. They will care for each other unto death.
They will die for each other.

We have been a relation-making tribe from the very
beginning. All our ceremonies, a sweat or a vision quest,
end with the words "mitakuye oyasin"—"all my relations"—and that means every living being on this earth,
down to the tiniest bug or flower. Everything that lives is
related. The hunka lowanpi is a part of this life philosophy.

The hunka lowanpi is very old. I was told that about
two hundred years ago Bull Bear put all the elements of
this ceremony together. I learned to perform it from the

old people. They were natural professors, natural historians, word-of-mouth scientists. As in most other ceremonies, you need a holy man, a wichasha wakan, to perform the hunka lowanpi. Usually, when you require the help of such a man you send him a loaded pipe, but for this ceremony you sent a bag made from a buffalo calf's bladder, filled with tobacco offerings. If he opened the bag it meant that he would perform the ceremony. If he did not, you had to find another holy man to do it. We do not do it exactly this way anymore. For one thing, a bag made from an unborn buffalo calf's bladder is hard to come by. But I still perform the hunka lowanpi, in my own traditional way.

For the hunka ritual you set up a ceremonial double tipi— that is, two tipis joined together. You cover the ground inside the tipi with sage. This sacred herb makes good spirits come in and chases bad spirits away. You also need two staffs with hair from a horse's tail dangling from them. The strands of hair are painted red. These wands are called hunka chanupa, meaning hunka pipes, but they are really wooden wands. They represent the White Buffalo Woman. You also need a stick on which a perfect ear of corn is stuck. We are not corn planters, but maybe a long time ago, when we were still living near the Great Lakes, we raised corn. This plant represents survival and Mother Earth. You also need eagle plumes and two wagmuha, two rattles, made from a buffalo's scrotum and painted red, as well as two dried buffalo chips and glowing coals to light the pipe. You need red face paint, sweet grass, Indian tobacco, a pipe rack, and the pipe itself. Finally you need a buffalo skull for an altar. All these things have to be smoked up with sweet grass.

The tipi's door looks toward the sunrise. Opposite, at the west side, in back of the tipi, is the seat of honor. From there the holy man conducts the ceremony. In front of him is an altar made of earth smoothed with an eagle wing or wooden staff. The wichasha wakan has some helpers near him. On his left sits the ate hunka, the older of the two people making the bond. All the relatives of the two hunka are there, the women on the left, the men on the right. There are usually some hunka present, those who have "made relations" before. Also there are two drummers.

In the old days they pretended that the mihunka, the younger person, was a captive. Somebody would say, "I think there is an enemy nearby. Let's kill him!" Then some men would "capture" the mihunka and bring him into the tipi. Someone would then say, "Maybe somebody wants to rescue this captive by adopting him." The ate hunka stood up and said, "I will adopt this one as my mihunka. I will save him. I adopt him as my brother." Or he might adopt him as his son.

Adoptions of captives happened in real life. Around 1857 the Lakota were at war with the Hohé, the Assiniboin. The Lakota came across a small party of Hohé and killed them all, except a young boy about eleven or twelve years old, and they were about to kill him, too. This young boy was brave. He stood his ground and did not cry. He had a little bow, more a toy than a weapon. He aimed his arrows at our warriors. At this moment Sitting Bull came riding up. He cried, "This boy is too brave to kill. Don't shoot him! I'll adopt him as my brother!" They took the Hohé boy back to camp and there they had a ceremony in which the Hohé boy became Sitting Bull's mihunka. His name was Jumping Bull. In every one of Sitting Bull's battles Jumping Bull fought at his side. When, many years later, some forty tribal police members surrounded Sitting Bull's one-room log cabin to arrest and kill the great chief, there was a big shootout. When this fight ended, six of the tribal police members and six of Sitting Bull's friends were lying dead on the ground, among them Jumping Bull, who went to the spirit world with his ate hunka. He died like a hunka should, faithful to the end. So, adopting a captive is one of our customs.

Inside the tipi the mihunka sits next to his ate hunka. Two helpers then wave the two wands with the strands of horsehair over them. This wand waving, called hunkakazopi, is a chief part of the hunka lowanpi. Some old people told me that this symbol-izes the capture of the mihunka. It also stands for strength and power. The horsetails mean that the two hunka will always have fast horses. An eagle plume fastened in the mihunka's hair stands for bravery. They also wave the stick with the corn over the two hunkapi. The wichasha wakan then paints their faces with red stripes, leading down from the forehead to the chin. By these stripes the spirits will know and respect them.

The wichasha wakan goes to the buffalo skull altar. The skull's eye sockets are stuffed with balls of sage. The skull is painted with designs according to the holy man's visions. He approaches the skull howling like a wolf. He smokes up the skull with sweet sage. The buffalo spirit also comes to the skull. His presence is felt by all. The holy man burns sacred tobacco and blows the smoke into the skull's nostrils. The drums and the rattles are going. Hunka songs are being sung. One of the older hunka who have come to take part in this ceremony stands up and makes a speech, instructing the two new hunka in their duties. He might tell them, "Your hunka's friends are your friends. His enemies are your enemies. Should he become a captive you must not rest until you have freed him. Should he die in battle you must avenge him. You must never be stingy. You must always be generous."

Toward the end of the ceremony the holy man covers the two hunkapi with a large buffalo robe. When the robe is lifted, it will be seen that the two are tied to each other with rawhide thongs. The left arm of the ate hunka is tied to the right arm of the mihunka. In the same way their legs are tied together. The holy man tells them, "You are now tied together forever. You are inseparable. You are as one." There is a rack in the tipi with roasted buffalo meat. The mihunka cuts a chunk off and puts it in his mouth. The holy man says, "I am hungry, but I have no food." The mihunka takes meat from his mouth and gives it to the holy man. The holy man says, "I am cold, but I have nothing with which to cover myself." The mihunka gives him the buffalo robe. The holy man says, "I am naked, but I have no clothes." The mihunka gives him his beautiful decorated buckskin shirt. The holy man says,

"My feet are sore and bleeding because I have no moccasins." The mihunka takes off his moccasins and leggings and hands them over. In this way the wichasha wakan is rewarded for running the ceremony. The mihunka is now stripped down to his breechcloth. He cuts up the rest of the meat and distributes it among those present. The mihunka keeps the horsetail wand and the corn stick. If the mihunka is a woman, she does not strip but just gives presents. At the end of the ceremony there is a feast and a big giveaway.

You start out with your friendship with the land and then you understand the meaning of the hunka ceremony. You have to get along with yourself before you can get along with others. That is hard. It means peace, wolakota. It means choosing a relation rather than inheriting one. The whole tiyospaye is involved, the whole "extended family," as the white man calls it. So we made the sacred four directions at the center of our lives. Our ceremonies represent the whole life cycle—birth, growing up, parenthood, and death. And then it begins all over again. It represents the hoop without end. We remember things from way back, all the way to our beginnings. We pass it on from generation to generation. Some people have forgotten it. But no matter what, there will always be one man or woman to keep the flame going, a tiny glowing spark deep underneath the ashes, and all of a sudden it will flare up and there will be the sacred fire again that is never extinguished. We have to take care of that light. Let there always be a person who wants the flowers and the rocks to tell him their secrets, who keeps the old people's wisdom in his heart sack. So many ceremonies have been buried, wiped away like chalk from a blackboard. The horse dance used to bring rain and heal sick minds, but it has not been performed in more than fifty years. They say that there is no one left who knows how to run it. But I know. My father knew, his father told him. Two old holy men told me. This dance is written on my heart. Someday I will bring it back. Our ancient sacred rites, we are not just part of it, we are all of it.

eighteen

I GAVE MYSELF TO
THE MOVEMENT

AIM is the new warrior class of this
century, bound by the bond of the drum,
who vote with their bodies
instead of their mouths;
their business is hope.

Dennis Banks

It was like in the days of the ghost dance. There was a
whispering in the air, a faint drumbeat, a hoof beat. It
became a roar carried by the four winds: "A nation is
coming, the eagle brought the message." What was coming called itself AIM, the American Indian Movement.

White people call me a medicine man or spiritual
leader. They think that my job is just to pray and to perform ceremonies. But that's only part of it. A medicine
man lives among his people. He has to experience life, all
of it. He must be higher than an eagle and, sometimes,
lower than a worm. He exists for the people and he has to
fight for them if necessary. He must even turn himself into
a politician if a politician is what his people need.

The American Indian Movement is something new,
but it is also something very old. It was born when the
white man killed the first Indian and stole some of his
land. AIM was founded inside a Minnesota prison by
young men who had been abused, mistreated, and

starved in boarding schools, orphanages, and foster homes, who had been taken away from loving parents whom white bureaucrats called unfit because their homes had no electricity or indoor plumbing. When they came out of these foster homes and boarding schools they were angry, and because they were angry they got into trouble and wound up in a penitentiary. A group of these men, including Dennis Banks and Clyde Bellecourt, began talking inside prison walls. They were all Ojibway born on various Minnesota reservations. Out of these talks an idea was born. After their release they founded an Indian civil rights organization. During one of their first meetings in Saint Paul somebody proposed that they call themselves Concerned Indian Americans, but abbreviated that would have been CIA. Then one woman said, "You men always aim to do this or to do that, why don't you call yourselves AIM, the American Indian Movement?" After that nothing was ever the same again.

AIM was an organization of Indians living in big-city ghettos. Most of them no longer spoke their tribal languages. Many had never seen an Indian ceremony performed. They started out the right way, keeping Indians from drinking, protecting them from police brutality, founding an Indian Way School for Native kids, demonstrating against racism and injustice. But for over a year we on the reservation didn't know about them.

Even so, I was already involved in the struggle. I want to say up front that I am not against the white man as a person, but I am against his system, under which I am forced to live. So from early on I fought against it. I try to educate my people. I am like a magnet, I pull the people to me, pull them together. I went to the fullbloods who live way out on the prairie and in the hills, the neglected and forgotten folks living in tar paper shacks without indoor plumbing.

I told them, "Listen, I'm speaking to you. I want to tell what is happening to you and to your lives. I'm concerned for you. I've seen how much hardship you've endured. I don't want you to be left out. I don't want to see you in old folks' homes. I don't want to see you poor and hungry. You are the real Indians, the real Lakota, the backbone of the nation. You know the language and the ways of our people, but your voice has not been heard. We must stop letting the government and the tribal council talk for you. We must stop letting them tell you how to run your lives. I will talk to you in our language so you can understand. We'll be talking about our land, because we are its caretakers. I'm talking to you, elders, to you, grandfathers and grandmothers, who have the wisdom. We must plant a seed and we must watch it grow.

"You are my people. I'll stand by you. The carpet of the universal earth is still here for us. It's a web of sunrises and only we traditionals can walk on this web. And we must never accept money for the Paha Sapa, our sacred Black Hills. That's our Earth. She wears Wakan Tanka's ornaments and jewels—the pines, the aspens, the cottonwoods. The Black Hills are not for sale. The government stole them from us. Now they want to ease their bad conscience by paying us a little money. No! The Hills, the home of the sacred thunderbirds, are not for sale."

The BIA—the Bureau of Indian Affairs—is better than it was twenty years ago; it now has some real honest-to-goodness Indians at the top. But at the time I'm talking about it represented all that was wrong with the government's Indian policy. So I told the people, "We are not the BIA's wards anymore. Enough, enough, enough!"

I also tried to educate the white people. I told them, "Hey, white America, listen to me. Before you came here we had no lawyers, no penitentiaries, no foster homes, no old age homes, no mental institutions, no psychiatric clinics, no taxes, no TV, no telephones. We had no crime or madness or drugs. Look at these wonderful things you brought us. You call it 'civilization,' but we had a culture long before you came. You call us 'Indians' because a stupid and greedy man called Columbus thought he was in India when he landed here. He did not discover America. We had been here for tens of thousands of years. We are the landlords and one day we'll come to collect the rent." When I was young I was afraid to talk in front of a white man, but I'm not that way anymore.

The white man is very clever, but our elders are wise. There's a big difference between cleverness and wisdom. Our elders have an orbit mind. We had a religion and history before Columbus arrived. The Great Spirit planted us here and planetized us. They used to call us "hostile" and "unregenerate." Now they call us "militants." I guess I am a militant, a militant on behalf of the tree, the earth, the river, all living things. The white man does not respect Mother Earth. He has a barbed wire mind. We first have to cut through this wire before we can begin to talk to each other.

We were nursed at the breast, not at the bottle. You gave us the cow for a mother and also the condom. We don't need it. We are not overpopulated. Thanks to you we are underpopulated, victims of genocide. You have a Holocaust Museum in Washington to remind us of a genocide that happened far away in Europe. What about having a museum about the holocaust that happened right here, the Native American holocaust? We used to put our dead in the burial tree, to give their bodies to the winds and the universe. We are not allowed to do this anymore. We must plant them six feet underground in a casket. But Crazy Horse was not buried in a casket. Beneath our reservations lie coal, oil, uranium, gold, silver, all the elements. It should make us the richest people in the world, but we are the poorest. There are more than three thousand counties in the United States and out of all of them the county covering Pine Ridge, the Oglala Sioux reservation, is the poorest, and my own Rosebud reservation isn't far behind.

There are thirty million blacks and fewer than two million of us. African-Americans live in big cities and have a lot of voting power, forming one big power bloc. We are divided into some three hundred tribes scattered all over the continent. If we want to talk to one another we have to do it in English. We live far from the centers of power where decisions are made. So we cannot make our influence felt.

Whites say not to blame them, they aren't involved. It's their ancestors who did wrong. But they should be involved. They are living on our land. We are still third-class citizens. We are still invisible. Indians are in jail. Indians are starving. You should take some responsibility, not for what was, but for what *is*. We can't put all of you back on the *Mayflower*. So we've got to live with one another as best we can. I look upon my white friends who have for so long supported me as brothers and sisters. I don't look at the color of their skin. Many young wasichus have come to Crow Dog's Paradise, often staying for weeks or months. I feed them and give them shelter. There are many good, understanding white men and women. The only trouble is, there's not enough of them.

In 1970 a man came to Crow Dog's place. His name was Dennis Banks. He was an Ojibway from the Leech Lake reservation in Minnesota and a co-founder of AIM. He knocked at our door. My dad opened it and invited him in. Dennis said, "I've come because you people have got something that we city Indians lost. We have an Indian organization that is doing fine, but it needs not only a political philosophy but also a spiritual meaning in order to be complete. That is why I have come."

My father asked him, "Have you ever gone on a vision quest?" Dennis said no.

My father asked, "Are you a sun dancer?" Dennis said no.

My father asked, "Have you ever purified yourself in a sweat lodge?" And again Dennis said no.

My father told him, "Then I don't know why you have come." Dennis said, "I live close to Pipestone. I can make red stone pipes."

My father said, "Then we have something to talk about."

My mother fried up some meat and brewed some coffee. They all had something to eat. Then my father and Dennis talked for a long time. After that my dad took Dennis in back of our place where we have our sweat lodge. It was just the skeleton of the lodge, the little dome of willow sticks. It was winter and there was a lot of snow on the ground. My father had Dennis shovel away the snow inside and around the lodge. He made Dennis chop some wood. They made a fire and heated the rocks in it. The buffalo skull was already there. My dad brought some tarps and blankets to cover up the lodge. He had a sweat with Dennis and purified him. It made Dennis into a new kind of man. My dad told him, "Come again. We have lots to talk about."

Dennis left and came back with Clyde Bellecourt, another of the AIM founders. They and Dad became good friends. Finally I met Dennis Banks. He told me about AIM and what it stood for. This is what I had been waiting for. After listening to Dennis I really believed that the American Indian Movement could bring about a rebirth of our people. I believed it could unite all the Native Americans in the United States.

Later I got a telegram to go to Rapid City and meet all the AIM leaders. Dennis was there, and Russell Means, Lee Brightman, and Clyde Bellecourt. I talked to them for a very long time. I spoke to them as a spiritual man. They asked me what I thought about the Black Hills and the government offering us some chickenfeed money in exchange for the sacred land they had stolen from us. I said that we'd never accept money for our land. Dennis agreed and said that AIM and all the tribes would take a stand.

Then I went to Denver to meet some more AIM leaders—Vern Bellecourt, Clyde's brother, Eddie Benton, John Trudell, and Stan Holder. Dennis Banks told me that AIM had enough political leaders, but they needed spiritual guidance. He asked me to be AIM's medicine man. I answered, "I will give myself to the movement."

When the traditional Lakota and the city militants got together, that was the moment AIM took off. Suddenly men wore their hair long or in braids. They threw away their neckties. Everybody started wearing bead or bone chokers. They began wearing ribbon shirts. They wore Levi jackets with AIM patches and buttons reading, INDIAN POWER or INDIAN AND PROUD. They had eagle feathers tied to their hair or stuck into their hatbands. We became warriors again. In 1970, Dennis Banks, Russell Means, and Clyde Bellecourt pledged to pierce themselves in the sun dance. In 1971, at Pine Ridge, they offered their pain to the people. The American Indian Movement spread like wildfire.

On a Saturday night, in February of 1972, at Gordon, Nebraska, close to the Pine Ridge reservation, a couple of rednecks grabbed fifty-one-year-old Raymond Yellow Thunder, an Oglala Sioux, and dragged him into an American Legion hall that was hooked up to a bar. There, before a crowd of drunken, grinning cowboys and cowgirls, they stripped Raymond naked from the waist down and forced him to dance at gunpoint. They beat and kicked him. They had nothing personally against Raymond. They didn't even know him. They just wanted to have themselves some fun. They stuffed him into the trunk of a car and he died. The men who had grabbed him first, a pair of brothers called Hare, were arrested, charged with second-degree manslaughter, and released without bail. Second-degree manslaughter meant that the murderers would not serve a single hour in jail.

I had known Raymond Yellow Thunder since 1959. At that time we both worked on farms in Scotts Bluff, Nebraska. He was a humble and kind man. He did not drink. He worked hard for as little as eighty cents an hour. He had no enemies, only friends. He had no car and I used to drive him where he wanted to go. He was from the Pine Ridge reservation and had been killed for no reason. What were we going to do? How could we get justice? Raymond's relatives went to the police, to the FBI, to the BIA, and to the tribal council for help. Nobody gave a damn. Then we called the American Indian Movement for help. A man called Severt Young Bear, a representative of the Porcupine community, who had some AIM friends, called Russell Means. Virgil Kills Right called Dennis Banks. The whole Yellow Thunder family asked AIM to come in. I called everyone I could think of. So there was the war cry: "We're going to Gordon!"

Dennis Banks called for a thousand people to join the march. Sixteen thousand came. A caravan of more than two hundred cars drove to Gordon. Members of fifty-one tribes were represented. It was the biggest Native American civil rights march ever. It was like a thunderstorm, a hurricane blowing across Nebraska. Before we set out we had a big meeting at Porcupine, on the Pine Ridge reservation. The main question was this: Should we go armed or without arms? Russ Means stood up and said, "This is a serious matter. We have a lot of people involved here who are not prepared for what might be coming down on us. Gordon police and white vigilantes could be lying in wait for us. There could be a bloodbath. We could get killed. This is a matter for our spiritual leader, Crow Dog, to decide. I am asking him now to perform a ceremony for us."

So I put on a yuwipi ceremony that night. The spirits entered the ceremony and told me that we should go unarmed, that our spiritual power would be greater than any guns. They also told me to use sacred gopher dust, the kind that made Crazy Horse bulletproof. So in the morning I sprinkled gopher dust over our leaders—Dennis Banks, Russell Means, Ron Petite, Clyde and Vernon Bellecourt. I cedared them. I fanned them off with my eagle wing. We smoked the pipe. And before we started out we organized an AIM chapter at Porcupine. We got one hundred seventy-two new members. We called the Justice Department and the governor of Nebraska to let them know we were coming. Besides having some one hundred fifty cars starting from Porcupine alone, we got hold of a Greyhound charter bus, which joined the caravan. That bus was crammed full to overflowing. And so we went to Gordon.

We went to that town not just for Raymond Yellow Thunder, but for all Native Americans in this country. We went there as one big family. We went there with the drum. I told the people, "The thunder power is in that drum, the wind of the eagle wing. The drum represents the sacred hoop." And we went there with a new song. It was made up by a fourteen-year-old boy. Some say he was an Ojibway, others say he was a Lakota. This song spoke in all the Indian languages. Soon every Indian knew it and they were singing it in every tribe. And like the ghost dancers of 1890, we came with American flags flying upside down as a sign of distress and a cry for justice.

Russell Means, Dennis Banks, and I were the first to enter Gordon. The sheriff's deputies, the state troopers, and the FBI were waiting for us. They had riot guns, but they didn't make a move. They were as meek as lambs. They were scared of us. The whole town was scared. We hardly saw any people on the streets. The stores were closed and locked. As we marched up Broadway, a handful of Indians and whites were there to support us. A half a dozen rednecks threw beer cans and firecrackers at us and then ran like hell. Russell, Dennis, and I led the march to City Hall. Yellow Thunder's relatives walked behind us.

We took over City Hall. Dennis Banks set up shop in the mayor's office. We had microphones and loudspeakers and held rallies. We made our demands. We made the mayor, the state attorney, and other officials come to us and negotiate. We had Raymond Yellow Thunder's body dug up to document the cruelties done to him. We forced them to bring the Hare brothers up on murder charges. (They were later convicted and put in jail. They did not stay there long enough, but a short time was better than no time.) We forced them to charge the Hare brothers for his death. We also forced the mayor to dismiss Gordon's chief of police. There were at that time cops in Gordon who harassed young Indian women; their victims were too scared and embarrassed to complain. We got a promise that Indian teenagers would no longer be thrown in with adult prisoners for a misdemeanor. We set up a special phone chain so that whenever an Indian was mistreated or discriminated against, word would get around fast so that action could be taken. We sensitized the white community and let them know that from now on they would be held responsible for what they did. Finally we set up an AIM chapter in Gordon. We had been in that city for about a week. It was a great victory.

They brought Raymond Yellow Thunder's body back to Porcupine, where he had been raised among his Oglala people.

His relatives asked me to bury him. So I filled the pipe. I put the staff right in front of the sacred ground. We smoked the pipe. We used sacred gopher dust, we used red face paint, we used spiritual power. Before we gave Raymond back to Mother Earth we faced toward the west, the north, the east, and the south. I lifted the pipe up toward the sky and then pointed it down toward the earth. When the body was going down into the ground we sang the AIM song. One of our elders chanted a special song in honor of Yellow Thunder, Crazy Horse, Sitting Bull, Big Foot, and all of our great chiefs of long ago who had been killed by the white man. We prayed, using ancient, sacred words.

I explained why I buried Raymond Yellow Thunder six feet underground. I said, "I'd rather put our dead brother on a funeral scaffold or a sacred tree for the wind and the eagle to take care of him, but then some anthropologists could come and take his body for whatever purpose. I have to bury him deep where they can't steal his body. It will go back to the earth, but his soul will stay with us forever." I put an eagle plume with him to be the flower of the bloom of the universe, of the earth and the sky. One man asked me why I didn't bless the body with water. I told him that the first thunder, the first rain to hit the earth, would bless his body. Then he asked why I didn't put a cross on Yellow Thunder's grave. I said, "Our cross is equal, of the same length everywhere. It stands for the sacred four directions. But the white man's cross is a cross of injustice and inequality. That's why the bottom part is long and the top is short. This cross represents the suppression of Indian religion." So I buried our brother in a ceremonial way.

We had made a big first step in getting justice for Raymond Yellow Thunder. We could build on this foundation. AIM and the Lakota people together had won this victory. It was the beginning of a new Indian nation.

nineteen

A HELL OF A
SMOKE SIGNAL

We want to be Indian,
We want to be red,
We want to be free,
Or we want to be dead.
          Anonymous Native American who
                      committed suicide

The years from 1960 to 1975 were the years when things happened, when Indians began to wear their hair long again and throw away their neckties.

In 1960 the American Indian Youth Council was founded by Vine Deloria, a Lakota, and Clyde Warrior, Mel Thom, Shirley Witt, and Herb Blatchford. This was a forerunner of AIM and a big step for Native American rights. In 1964 began the war for Indian fishing rights at Frank's Landing, in Washington State. The leaders there were Sid Milss and, later, Hank Adams, who both joined the struggle at Wounded Knee in 1973. They were holding fish-ins and there was a lot of violence on the part of the state troopers.

Things were happening all over. In 1967 Bob Burnette, a friend of mine and twice chairman of our tribe, took twenty-one Rosebud men and women to New York in order to break through the Buckskin Curtain and join Dr. Martin Luther King's peace march. Bob was what the whites called a moderate Indian leader, but he broke a lot of ground for us. My dad, Chief Lame Deer, and I were part of this group. Henry and Lame Deer stood on the platform next to Dr. King. Later we all had dinner at Richard Erdoes's place. That's how I met the friend who is helping me write this book. Later we went to Harlem to meet up with some of the Black Power leaders. Lame Deer joked and told Stokely Carmichael, "Indian kills his enemy, white man skins his friend. What do you do?" Stokely laughed and said, "We eat them." This march was a breakthrough. Our tribe got on the map.

In 1969 some three hundred Native Americans, calling themselves Indian of All Tribes, took over Alcatraz Island. Their leader was Richard Oaks, a Mohawk, who was later murdered by a white racist.

In 1970, on the three hundred and fiftieth anniversary of the landing of the Pilgrims, a group of AIM members led by Russell Means boarded the *Mayflower II* and hoisted an AIM flag on her mast. They later buried Plymouth Rock under a truckload of sand. Russ told the press that Indians were "an endangered species." Throughout these years we staged rallies, confrontations, marches, and protests.

Everywhere Indians were waking up to the danger of becoming extinct as the result of the government's "termination policy." Under this plan Native Americans would give up their reservations and release the government from all obligations to the tribes. In return every Indian would get a few thousand dollars and from then on be on his own, free to become a tax-paying soda jerk or garbage collector. For the money they could buy themselves a new car or washing machine. When these had turned into junk, the Indian would be left with no land, no money, and no federal protection. We would simply die out like the dinosaur or the dodo bird. We had to fight that.

Everywhere our old hunting and fishing rights were being taken away from us. Tribal people who lived by hunting and fishing were told to take out licenses like white sportsmen—"good for ten trout or one deer." Under such laws our people would have starved to death. So this became part of the struggle too.

And our people were remembering our brothers who had been murdered—Norman Little Brave, Richard Oaks, Raymond Yellow Thunder, and Timothy Iron Bear unjustly executed in the electric chair in 1949. We also remembered the kids who hanged themselves in jail or who died drunk out of despair.

The time was right for the next big step. In August 1972, during the sun dance at Crow Dog's Paradise, Bob Burnette started talking to the people. He announced that the broken treaties would no longer be ignored. All the tribes had to march like a human wave, like Martin Luther King's people did. He began organizing what he called the Trail of Broken Treaties. The marches on Gordon and Alcatraz and the fish-ins had been ignored by the media. Most white people had never heard of them. Bob promised that the Trail of Broken Treaties would be known to the whole world. It would open the eyes and the ears of America. Bob went to New York to organize the march in the East, while Reuben Snake, a Winnebago from Nebraska, did the same in the West and Midwest. Both are dead now, but what they did will not be forgotten. About a dozen Native American organizations promised to participate. Caravans would start out from Los Angeles, San Francisco, Seattle, Rapid City, and Denver. They would stop at sacred sites where Indians had been massacred, such as Wounded Knee and Sand Creek, where ceremonies would be held and prayers said. This was to be a spiritual march. Each caravan would be led by a medicine man. Drums would be beaten day and night to remind America of the three hundred treaties that had been broken by the government. Some caravans would meet in Minneapolis, where the main group of AIM members would join them. There the name of the march was to be changed to *Trail of Broken Treaties and Pan–American Native Quest for Justice.*

Twenty points or demands would be presented to the government. Bob Burnette told the people, "We must be on our best behavior. No drugs or alcohol will be permitted. And no rough stuff. Anybody who violates these rules will be expelled. The old, the sick, the children, the poorest and weakest who cannot march, will be with us in our thoughts. This must be the greatest moment in our history." The Indians would come in friendship, hoping to be welcomed in friendship. Tribal leaders would visit the senators and congressmen from their states. There would be cultural events—fry bread for the senators, Indian fancy dancing for the public.

But it did not quite work out that way. The Trail of Broken Treaties arrived in Washington, D.C., on November 2, 1972. I was there not only as AIM's spiritual leader but also as our tribe's medicine man. We were tired and hungry. We had been promised food and places to stay, but the only food was provided in a hurry by a black community organization. Without them there would have been nothing. We were herded into the basement of a huge abandoned church. There was no heat, but there were rats.

From the start the government insulted us. I was supposed to hold a spiritual ceremony at Arlington National Cemetery at the grave of Ira Hayes, a Pima Indian who was the hero of Iwo Jima, where he had won the Congressional Medal of Honor for raising the American flag over Mount Suribachi. Ira Hayes had been without a job, poor and forgotten, when he had drowned in a ditch, having gotten drunk to forget his misery. I was told that I would not be allowed to remember him with a ceremony because this would be a "political activity," which could not be permitted at Arlington. We were also told that President Nixon would not meet with us. Louis Bruce, the commissioner of Indian Affairs, who himself was a Native American, was ordered under no circumstances to help us in any way, and especially not to help us with funds. That was of course one of our chief complaints—that the head of the BIA had no power to act on behalf of the Indian people, because the BIA was a part of the Department of the Interior, and the secretary of the Interior and his deputies were cracking the whip over the Bureau of Indian Affairs. One of our twenty demands was to take BIA out from under Interior and make it a department by itself, with its head a member of the cabinet. The deputy secretary of the Interior, Harrison Loesch, had promised to support us in every way and then had gone back on his word.

The Indians marched to the Bureau of Indian Affairs Building and there the moderate leaders lost it. There was a lot of anger, especially among the young people, and the AIM leaders took over the leadership of the Trail of Broken Treaties. Dennis Banks, Russell Means, and Clyde and Vernon Bellecourt became the spokesmen of the Trail. The marchers drifted into the building and flopped down wherever there was a sofa, an easy chair, or a carpet to lie on. The people filled up all the rooms and offices to get some rest. They sat on the marble staircase. They leaned against the walls. There was a cafeteria in the basement and the women started making coffee. Nobody, not even the AIM leaders, had planned to take over the building. It just happened, because the government broke its word to provide accommodations. Bob Burnette became a surplus leader. He supported the takeover once it had happened, but the leadership had slipped out of his hands. This was sad, because the Trail had been his idea, but events just stampeded over him.

Soon the police arrived, surrounded the building, and threatened to storm it if we did not leave. Nobody left. Some armed gangs came into the building and started cracking heads with their nightsticks. They didn't stay long. Some left in such a hurry that they left their nightsticks behind. More caravans arrived and joined us. There were about a thousand Indians inside the building. Somebody set up a big drum in the auditorium and began singing the AIM song. I performed a ceremony and blessed the crowd with sage. Because the police threatened to attack us, some young men painted their faces for war. They started to arm themselves. They found fishing rods and rebars and made spears out of them. They broke off table and chair legs and made them into clubs. They fastened knives, letter openers, and scissors to them and made the chair legs into tomahawks. They found some bows and arrows in the gift shop and some of the warriors took them. Some Vietnam vets made Molotov cocktails out of light bulbs, breaking off the screw-in parts and filling the bulbs up with gasoline. They tore up some rags and used them as wicks. Some young kids piled up two dozen typewriters on the roof, ready to hurl them on the heads of anybody who wanted to mess with us. Some riot squad guys busted windows and tried to sneak into the building. They were discovered and kicked out. In the meantime, negotiations went on at the nearby Department of the Interior. Loesch told us that the department was not in the housing business and that our occupation was unlawful. In the end we were told that we could stay until the next morning. Thus started a pattern—negotiations going hand in hand with threats.

On Friday, November 3, a marshal appeared with a court order for us: GET OUT OR ELSE! He was scared. He waved a white handkerchief and cried, "I come in peace!" We told him, "Come and get us!" Every day we got a court order to get out by six P.M. or force would be used. We left them in no doubt that we would defend ourselves even if we had to die for it.

We had some support. Louis Bruce stayed one night in the building, though he knew that he would be fired for it. LaDonna Harris, a Kiowa-Comanche and wife of Senator Fred Harris, also stayed overnight. Some black leaders, including Stokely Carmichael, came to lend support. The Reverend McIntyre, with a group of followers, paraded out in front of the building, singing "Onward, Christian Soldiers." Nobody knew what they had come for. We set up a tipi on the lawn in front of the building and formed a line of security behind it.

We settled in for a long siege. All the Lakota were on the second floor. I took over one office for the Crow Dog family and relatives. We stacked up chairs and tables against the walls so that we could sleep on the floor. Even so the room was crammed. Room 219 housed the Rosebud delegation. Down the hall were the

Iroquois, under the Onondaga chief Oren Lyons. Every tribe found some spot to stay, because this was a very big building. Every day these various groups talked over what complaints to present to the government. Once a day hundreds of us assembled in the huge auditorium to listen to what the leaders had to say.

Every day, sometimes twice, the police piled up in front of the building and threatened to storm it. And every time they backed down in the end. This was election week. The town was full of press and foreign correspondents. A heap of dead Indians would not have looked good on TV.

Negotiations went on and on. We had our twenty demands. They had chiefly to do with the government's recognizing the old, broken treaties, particularly the 1869 Treaty of Fort Laramie, giving back to the tribes a hundred million acres stolen from us, letting us address a joint session of Congress, repealing the Menominee and Klamath termination acts, abolishing the BIA, protecting Indian religion, and recognizing tribal sovereignty. For making our demands, the secretary of the Interior called us a "splinter group of radical blackmailers."

Hank Adams, one of the fishing rights leaders, did a lot of negotiating for us. He had the ability to be tough without letting his anger show. He was always calm and in control. Our women also were strong speakers. One of our best speakers was an elderly lady named Martha Grass. She shook her fist in the deputy secretary of the Interior's face. In one speech she said, "If I don't get what I'm asking for, this building will have to come down. Why should they have these beautiful offices and sit behind these shiny desks and be comfortable and not do a damn thing for us? I work for a living. I have to earn it. Why don't we make them earn theirs? We got nothing in this Department of the Interior but crooks and liars. Up here they'll steal you blind. They sure as hell did. They stole the whole country. They stole the air, the grass, whatever they could get their hands on. We have to get back what we can the best way we know. We are the grassroots people. We are tired of all this!"

We occupied the building for a week. In the end the government agreed to "seriously consider" our twenty-point proposal and promised that we would have an answer soon. They distributed some sixty thousand dollars among us, for gas money and bus fare home. It was a bribe to get rid of us. We left the building with a truckload of documents proving the government's wrongdoings as far as Native Americans were concerned.

After a few months we got the answer to our demands. The government called them "impracticable." But we did not go away empty-handed. One thousand, five hundred Native Americans had traveled the Trail of Broken Treaties, representing some two hundred tribes. It was the greatest gathering of Indians in the nation's capital. AIM had made its mark on the white man's mind. We were a different kind of Indian now. We had won a victory.

twenty

THE TOWN WITH THE
GUNSMOKE FLAVOR

We have taken the lead in
determining our destinies,
and even though we have made mistakes,
we have done so on our own accord
without the white man's guidelines.
AIM spells self-determination and
re-identity and supports any Indian man,
woman, or child in the struggle.

Dennis Banks

Being AIM's spiritual leader caused problems for me.
Before, I had been one of several medicine men in our
Rosebud tribe. Now it seemed that I was the medicine
man for every Indian in the country. That was hard, especially for my family. Crow Dog's Paradise became a sort of
AIM settlement. People were camping out everywhere.
Folks dropped in at all hours, day and night. Guests had
to be fed. They slept anywhere they could find a place to
plant their bodies. They slept in my dad and mom's
house, which Dad had built himself out of odds and
ends—tree trunks, car windows, whatever. They slept in
my family's house just a few yards away, a red-painted
"transitional" house, the kind the tribe put up for us
Rosebud people. The floors of both houses often were
covered with sleeping figures. You had no place to put

your feet. The transitional house was not solidly built. It seemed to fall apart with the wear and tear of so many visitors. Young white people, hippies, and flower children camped out on the Paradise, trying to find something they had lost, some spiritual belief, and they stayed, and stayed, and stayed.

People came to the medicine man for help, for spiritual as well as material assistance. I was expected to provide. As long as I was the medicine man just for some Rosebud people, I could do it. Now it seemed the whole world was coming to me for advice, consolation, doctoring, money, food. So what was I supposed to do? I had to hustle. In between all my other tasks, I traveled, always with my whole family. I raised money by giving lectures on Native American culture, even though my English at that time was pretty bad. Richard Erdoes got me to do a TV commercial. They needed a Native American who could ride a horse and do war whoops. They had an Apache outfit ready for me to wear, but I told them I had my own Sioux outfit. They let me use that. They took me way out to a place on Long Island. For three days I galloped all over the landscape, screaming out war whoops. I got so hoarse I could hardly talk. They paid me one hundred sixty-eight dollars, which was very disappointing, but six months later I got a check for six thousand dollars, for "residuals." That was more money than I had ever seen in my life. I hoped to get maybe a well out of it, because at that time we still got our water from the Little White River in a bucket. Or maybe I could have gotten a second-hand pickup truck.

We had a four-day giveaway feast, and so many people came to me for help that on the last day I had only five dollars left. But that was okay. That's what medicine men are for. I always had something to give to those who needed it, though sometimes all I had left was a bag of potatoes or a pound of hamburger meat.

In the meantime things had gotten bad in South Dakota, especially at Pine Ridge. The tribal president was a half-blood named Dick Wilson, who ran the tribe like a dictator and won elections by fraud. The U.S. Justice Department later issued a twenty-eight-page report saying, "Almost one third of all votes cast appear to have been in some manner improper." Wilson dealt out all the chief tribal jobs to his relatives. Besides having his hand-picked tribal police he misused federal funds to hire a private army of killers, who beat up, and even murdered, those who were against him. He fired his own elected vice-president, David Long, for "condoning publicly the American Indian Movement." This was against tribal law. Long told a reporter, "Wilson is influencing the council in a violent way to keep the people quiet. He is seeking power. I have bullet holes in my window and eight horses shot."

Wilson had condemned the Trail of Broken Treaties as a trail of hoodlums, commies, and radicals. He suspended free speech and the right to assemble peacefully on the reservation. When Russell Means, a tribally enrolled member of the Pine Ridge Oglala tribe, ran against him for tribal president, he had his tribal court sign a restraining order prohibiting Means from setting foot on the reservation. He had a poster in his office reading REWARD! RUSSELL MEANS' BRAIDS $50. RUSSELL MEANS' HEAD $50. RUSSELL MEANS' ENTIRE BODY, PICKLED, $1,000. When Russell went on the rez anyway, Wilson had his goons beat him with their billy clubs; Russ was lucky to get away with only a cracked skull. Nobody was safe. The goons had high-powered rifles with armor-piercing bullets. The full-bloods got together a group calling themselves Oglala Sioux Civil Rights Organization (OSCRO). The leaders were Eugene White Hawk, Vern Long, and Pedro Bissonette. Pedro was my true friend. He was later brutally murdered by the goons.

OSCRO handed out petitions to impeach and get rid of Wilson. But people were afraid to sign them, because those who did were worked over by the goons. They fired guns into people's homes. They threatened to hurt Indian children. By the middle of 1972 there was a civil war situation on the rez. Members of OSCRO and AIM were shot at. In spite of all this, the government supported Wilson, because he was *their* goon, their stooge, who had given away eighty thousand acres of tribal land as a gift to the National Park system.

At the end of 1972 and the beginning of 1973, AIM had come in force to Rapid City to demonstrate, educate, and sensitize the white people there. AIM called South Dakota "the most racist state in the Union, and Rapid City the most racist town in the state." In Rapid, Indians were discriminated against in every way. They were made to feel unwelcome in stores, restaurants, and bars. They were called all kinds of names and beaten up. If they got any jobs at all they were paid less than whites.

Conditions were worst at a place called Sioux Addition, three miles out of town. This was a kind of apartheid slum the city had set aside to get rid of its Indian population. Sioux Addition was a jumble of more than a hundred shacks and rusting trailers without running water or sanitation. The fire department would never come in there. It was a place of neglect and despair.

At that time Ron Petite was executive director of the Sioux Indian Emergency Rehabilitation Center in Rapid City. He was very worried about Indian veterans who were being mistreated and could not get the services they were entitled to by law. Instead of an open door they got the back of the hand. Ron Petite called on AIM for help. So, many reservation people and about two hundred AIM members from all over came to Rapid City to clean up the situation. Dennis Banks, Russell Means, and the Bellecourts were in charge of the operation. I was there, too, as the protest's spiritual leader. Most of us stayed at the Mother Butler Center, a Catholic church hall, which became our headquarters. There were three thousand Indians living in and around Rapid City, and we were going to deal with their grievances. Dennis Banks declared a freeze on the whole city. He said, "We will shut the whole business district down on account of the discrimination and mistreatment of Indian veterans. We'll literally chain up the doors of the big business enterprises, federal agencies, and local community service centers." We boycotted Northwestern Bell Telephone, Black Hills Power and Light, Kmart, Piggly Wiggly, Dunkin' Donuts, Sooper Dooper, and the law enforcement agencies. We put up posters: WELCOME TO THE

MOST RACIST STATE IN THE U.S.A. and SEE SOUTH DAKOTA LAST. Dennis tried to train the people in nonviolent tactics, giving orders by blowing a whistle, but he gave it up soon, because young AIM kids weren't good at being drilled.

I was resting at Mother Butler's when someone came to warn me that the town was about to blow up. A Pine Ridge man had brought the news that still another Lakota, Wesley Bad Heart Bull, had been killed by a white man and that the murderer had been charged with only involuntary manslaughter, which meant that he would go free. Without waiting for any leaders to tell them what to do, all the young AIMs went down into the streets. The real trouble started when an Indian went into a bar crammed with white customers. One of them threw a glass of whiskey in the Indian's face. A real battle began. These saloons had always been places of humiliation for us. So now the young Indians did a thorough job on them. Whites and Indians fought each other with fists, bottles, ashtrays, bung starters, whatever they could get their hands on. The police went amok and arrested every Indian in sight. The mayor ordered a bus and a fire truck to be used as extra paddy wagons. Hundreds were arrested and wound up in the Pennington county jail. I myself knew the jail from the inside. Being a South Dakota Sioux, you couldn't avoid it. Not a single white man was arrested.

I led some one hundred fifty Indians to protest in front of the jail. We were faced by a line of police in full riot gear. We had a drum and were singing and chanting. Then we went to the courthouse and did the same. The situation was dangerous. Anything could have happened. Bloodshed was averted when Dennis Banks created a "demilitarized zone" between wasichus and Native Americans, but Rapid City was just a warm-up for what took place immediately after—the confrontation at Custer.

It started with a murder on January 20, 1973, at Bill's Bar, in a place called Buffalo Gap at the edge of the Black Hills. The town got its name from being on an old buffalo trail at a spot where the hills opened up to make a passage. Buffalo Gap and the bar look like a set from a western movie. It was a Saturday night, and there was a big crowd at Bill's Bar, mostly white cowboys and ranchers from Hot Springs, Hermosa, and Custer. In the bar was also a young Lakota named Wesley Bad Heart Bull, his mother, Sarah, and a friend, Robert High Eagle. Wesley was only twenty years old. The bar's owner had told Wesley several times that he did not want him around, but Wesley had come anyway. Why should a white man tell him that he couldn't have a drink in there? It was the only bar for miles around. Also in the bar was Darald Schmitz, a thirty-year-old air force vet who ran a gas station in Custer. Schmitz made some racist remarks about Wesley, and Wesley answered back. They had had words before that, and Schmitz had threatened several times that someday he'd kill "that son-of-a-bitch Indian." The next morning, Sunday, January 21, Wesley Bad Heart Bull was lying in the street near the bar with a knife stuck in his chest. He died on the way to the hospital at Hot Springs.

Sarah and High Eagle had seen Schmitz with a knife in his hand, leaving the bar after Wesley. Schmitz himself boasted of "having got myself an Injun." The white bartender said that Wesley had attacked Schmitz. High Eagle said that the stabbing had been unprovoked. Schmitz was arrested on a charge of second-degree manslaughter, the smallest charge they could use. He was taken to Custer and there released on bail.

The news spread fast that another Lakota had been killed by a white man, almost exactly a year after the murder of Raymond Yellow Thunder. People from Rosebud and Pine Ridge went to Custer to see that justice be done. They asked AIM for help. It was a coincidence that so many AIM people were already in Rapid City for the protests. Rapid is only about an hour's drive from Custer. We hated that city already for its name. It is deep inside our sacred Black Hills, stolen by the government in violation of the Fort Laramie Treaty after gold had been discovered in the hills. On February 6, we formed a caravan of more than thirty cars out of Rapid City to drive the forty-five miles to Custer and join the Indians already there. It was snowing and it was cold, six or seven degrees above zero. We got there in the early afternoon.

About two hundred of us, AIM and reservation people, assembled before the courthouse, an old stone building with a white wooden porch. Wesley's mother, Sarah, was there too. At the start, things were peaceful. We had made up a delegation of five to speak to the DA, Hobart Gates, and the sheriff, Ernest Pepin. Dennis Banks, Russell Means, and I were part of the delegation. Bob High Eagle was already there as a witness, but the DA told Bob that he believed Darald Schmitz's version of what happened. It was going to be the same old story—a white man who had killed an Indian would go free.

As word of this got out, there was a big howl of protest from the crowd at the steps of the courthouse. Some twenty-five Indians forced the door and got in. During the scuffle that followed, law enforcement shoved a young boy down the porch steps. The sheriff ordered the courthouse cleared. About two dozen highway patrolmen had been hiding on the second floor. They now came down on us, swinging their long clubs. They wore red jackets, gray pants, and fancy golden helmets. They were armed with shotguns, rifles, and nightsticks. The sheriff and his deputy had huge six-shooters. They drove us out of the building with their clubs and tear gas. I busted a window on the first floor and jumped out. Dennis jumped after me. Outside, nobody was smiling. Russell was down on the ground, dazed, clubbed, bleeding, handcuffed. Sarah Bad Heart Bull, who tried to get in and talk to the DA, was stopped by a highway patrolman. He grabbed her from behind, put a nightstick across her throat and, using both hands, was almost choking her to death. Her jacket was gone, her glasses smashed. The police used more tear gas, smoke bombs, and firehoses on us. Some of the elders told the sheriff that we hadn't come here to riot, we only wanted to be heard. But it was no use. There was fighting in front of the courthouse and all along Main Street. Some kids were trashing two patrol cars. Others were chucking rocks, bottles, and Molotov cocktails through the courthouse windows. A crowd of young people tried to storm the building. Two guys came running up and poured gas all over the steps and door. One patrolman pointed his shotgun at them, screaming, "If you set a match to this I'll shoot to kill!" A dozen of our girls were making the wichaglaka—the high-pitched, trembling brave-heart cry that gets the blood pumping in your veins. Someone tossed a match and the front of the courthouse caught fire. A gas station was in flames. Then some of the AIM boys set the chamber of commerce on fire. The police had two fire trucks going but couldn't prevent it from burning to the ground. The police and highway patrol were all over us. I saw two of them dragging a young girl along the ground. It was twenty below zero and they had ripped most of her clothes off. Ashes and snowflakes were swirling around them. I saw a middle-aged Indian lying beaten unconscious on the ground, like a heap of rags. The billboard WELCOME TO CUSTER, THE TOWN WITH THE GUN SMOKE FLAVOR went up in flames. Stores along Main Street were torched and wrecked. I saw brothers and sisters spread-eagled against a wall, being frisked and handcuffed. The sheriff was saying to Russell, who was still handcuffed, "We were waiting for you AIM sons of bitches. We knew you were coming. You were looking for trouble and you got it!" Russell told him, "If we had wanted to have a war here, we wouldn't have brought our women and children."

Forty-one Indian men and women were arrested and charged, among them Sarah Bad Heart Bull. She was later tried for rioting and attempted arson, and served five months in the penitentiary. Her son's killer did not serve a single hour.

twenty-one

THE SIEGE

"Bury my heart at Wounded Knee."
They might bury more than
just our hearts here.
There are three hundred bodies
buried up there, buried in 1890.
They could bury some more soon in
that place unless the marshals stop firing.
                    Wounded Knee occupier

On February 27, 1973, started the biggest event in Indian
history during this century—the seventy-one-day occupation of Chankpe Opi, Wounded Knee. This place has great
meaning for me because my great-grandfather Jerome,
the first Crow Dog, was a ghost dancer. At the time they
massacred our people there, in the ravines along
Wounded Knee Creek, his own band was dancing deep
inside the Badlands not so far away. He and his people
also had been surrounded by the soldiers, and would
have been killed if Crow Dog had not had an inspiration,
given to him in a vision, through which he could save his
dancers. In 1973 our close relative and member of our
clan, Uncle Dick Fool Bull, was still living, close to ninety
years old, and he was a survivor of what had happened
back in 1890. He was the last flute maker and player in
our tribe, and he told me his story many times. I still have
on tape what he told me in 1968.

"I'll tell you what I remember about the trouble, the terrible trouble. I was born in Indian Territory, in 1883, I think. I'm not sure, really. They didn't have a census in them days. They didn't have birth records like they have today. There was the ghost dance going on, in 1890. We happened to be in Rosebud, camping under guard—soldiers, cavalry, cannons. They rounded up all the fathers and grandfathers and made sure they didn't mix up with the hostile bunch—that's what they called the ghost dancers, 'hostiles.'

"My father was hauling freight with an ox team from Valentine, Nebraska. He went there in the morning and camped there overnight and then came back to Rosebud and unloaded. Sometimes he used horses, hauling rations, flour and stuff like that, for the government. Rosebud had been an agency, a reservation, for some time.

"Things were bad up north at Standing Rock. They killed Sitting Bull and his men for ghost dancing. Everybody was scared. My father and my uncles got a twenty-day pass to haul freight to Pine Ridge Agency. After twenty days the police would send them back. Pine Ridge was just a few buildings then, a couple of offices and the stockade. The tipis were all pushed together and crowded, and they were guarded day and night. But some of the people got away in the night to join the ghost dancers in the Badlands.

"We camped near Wounded Knee. We went there with a team and covered wagon. My father was a medicine man and as kids we had learned the ghost dance and the ghost dance songs. It was winter and very cold. There was a little snow on the ground, here and there. Other people were camping near us. The soldiers said that if we gave them our bows and arrows, our knives and guns, they would let us visit our friends. So the men stood around in a circle and piled up their weapons. Even the women's awls, which they used for sewing, they called them weapons too. But the last guy, an old man, he had a blanket around him, and he had an old carbine under it and wouldn't give it up. And the sergeant, or lieutenant, or whatever he was, almost had us killed over it.

"A little ways off, at Wounded Knee, they had trenches dug for reinforcements, you know, and quick-fire guns, big ones, pointing at Big Foot's band of Minneconjou from all around. In the morning I was playing with my cousins when I heard the cannons, the quick-fires. Everybody was scared and hollering, 'War is on! War is on!' And the women started weeping: 'They are killing our people!' Everybody was running around: 'What shall we do?' I heard the gunshots, the cannons, the rifle fire. Then it was still for a while. I guess they had already killed most of them. But it started all over again, shooting, shooting, shooting. That's when the soldiers went down into the ravine, killing the women and children who were hiding in there, killing mothers with babies on their breasts. I don't know how many they killed there or how many were in that camp. They left them to lie there, I guess, overnight. The next morning they were digging the grave, a long ditch, and they had mule teams and wagons, and so they took the frozen bodies and just piled them in the wagons and took them to that ditch and threw them in there. When they had them all in there, they took shovels and covered them up. When it was safe, my father, my uncles, and cousins went there. I saw it all."

The second Wounded Knee happened just three weeks after Custer. At Pine Ridge the goons were running wild. Things had gotten to where the people just could not endure it any longer. Nobody was safe, not even women and children. The goon squad beat up people every day. They shot into windows. Houses were firebombed. There were murders that never got investigated. So the elders, the traditionals, the AIM followers and the OSCRO people, and all the medicine men called on AIM for help, and AIM answered the call.

Pedro Bissonette and his OSCRO people were holding a get-rid-of-Wilson powwow at Calico, six miles north of Pine Ridge. So AIM went there to meet with the Oglala people. The chiefs were there and all the medicine men and a lot of strong-hearted women. There was a big crowd, about three or four times as many as we had in the AIM caravan out of Rapid City. It looked peaceful. People were drinking coffee. Kids were playing ball. Then everybody crowded into the community hall. The place was crammed, but only two AIM leaders took part in this meeting, Dennis Banks and Russell Means. I was glad that the two most respected and oldest medicine men, Pete Catches and Frank Fools Crow, were there too. It seemed as if all the main speakers were women. One of the women said, "We're going to make a stand. We're going to Wounded Knee and make our stand there. If you men want to hold back, we women will do it. If we're going to die, then we'll die there!"

As soon as Wounded Knee was mentioned, I got very serious. Everybody did. Wounded Knee was our most sacred site. To be standing up there would be the greatest thing we could do. Why hadn't the leaders thought of this? One of our women had shown the way. So you see, the occupation of Wounded Knee wasn't planned. It came about naturally, as the spirit inspired the woman. So we took off to meet our destiny.

Someone started worrying about roadblocks. Wilson and his goons had been watching us. They reported by radio, telephone, teletype, and walkie-talkie on our every step. And they *were* waiting for us, all got up in their riot gear. Wilson was happy. He had told his men, "The AIMs want to be martyrs. Let's accommodate them!"

We drove right through Pine Ridge, the whole caravan of fifty-four cars crammed with people. We roared right by them. We saw them standing on the roof of the tribal council building. It was all lit up. We saw Wilson standing there, open-mouthed. We passed some goons on the road. They were bug-eyed. They didn't catch on. It didn't occur to any of them where we were headed. We got to the Knee after nightfall.

Standing on that hill where so many of our people were buried in a common grave, standing there in that cold darkness under the stars, I felt tears running down my face. I can't describe what I felt. I heard the voices of the long-dead ghost dancers crying out to us. Their ghosts were all around. They had been waiting for us for a long time. They had known that we were coming. They were standing with us on that hill. It was the night of all nights.

A wind was playing with the eagle feathers some had stuck in their hair or hatbands. I heard birds. Toward morning I saw two magpies in the ravine. They were black and white, standing for night and day. Magpies are sacred to the ghost dancers, who have pictures of magpies painted on their ghost dance shirts. Maybe, I thought, these birds wanted to tell us that the long night was over for Native Americans and that for us a new day was dawning. Coyotes were whooping. I took it all for a good sign.

At first we tried to take stock of the situation. People were milling around the white-painted Sacred Heart Church, the "museum," and Gildersleeve's trading post with its garish sign: WOUNDED KNEE MASSACRE, NATIONAL HISTORIC SITE. TRADING POST, AUTHENTIC INDIAN ARTS AND CRAFTS. SEE THE MASS BURIAL GRAVE, VISIT THE MUSEUM. CURIOS FOR SALE. GAS, OIL. ALL CREDIT CARDS ACCEPTED.

The trading post was the biggest building in "downtown" Wounded Knee. It was a combination general store, cafeteria, food market, curio shop, and pawn shop. It had a gas station with pumps and neon lights in front. It had started as a little peddler's store and then had been added on and on until it was now a million-dollar emporium. The place on earth most sacred to us had been turned into a tourist trap. So now the people were taking it over, liberating cigarettes and food. A few people who were cold took some clothes. I told people not to take anything, but they did it anyhow. They were saying, "Gildersleeve has robbed us and overcharged us for years and years. We are only getting a little back of what is owing to us. We are the ones who made them rich."

There were about three hundred of us occupiers. We had people from many tribes. Navajo, Cheyenne, Crow. Arapaho and

Shoshone. We had Oto, Potawatomi, Sac and Fox, Ojibway, Kiowa, and Hopi. There were North Dakota and Northwest Coast Indians, too. Also Blackfeet and members of New York State tribes, Onondaga and Mohawk, one single beautiful Shinnecock lady from Long Island. We were joined by some Apache and Cherokee. Altogether we had close to fifty tribes at the Knee. Among our warriors were Charles and Robert Yellow Bird, who claimed to be descendants of either General George Armstrong Custer or his brother, Tom Custer, who had repeatedly forced themselves upon a Cheyenne woman prisoner who later married a Lakota. The thought of what had happened to their great-grandmother made them extra-militant. The leaders stood in front of the church, speaking to the people. Russell Means said, "I am ready to die right here. I'm not going to die in some barroom brawl, I'm not going to die in some car wreck on the side of a lonely road on the rez because I've been drinking to escape the oppression of white society. I'm not going to die walking through Pine Ridge because Wilson's goons think I should be killed. That's not the way I am going to die. I am going to die for my treaty rights, right here if necessary."

Dennis Banks spoke: "This is not an AIM action, it's an all-Indian action. They can't do anything worse than kill us. The feds will be coming soon. Be prepared to defend this position with your life! What is at stake here at Wounded Knee is not just the lives of a few hundred Indian people, but our whole Indian way of life."

I told the people, "Our movement began when the Great Spirit organized the creation. The sacred altar is this hemisphere, this earth we're standing on, this Wounded Knee. They massacred us here, our women and children. We want to massacre only the white man's attitudes. I am not afraid to die. If I die here I will go where Crazy Horse and Sitting Bull are."

The first thing we did was establish a defense perimeter, at the start only around the top of the hill, around the church and the cemetery. We dug a trench and put up a low wall made of cinderblocks, sandbags, and sacks of masonry cement. Later we widened the perimeter to include all of "downtown." Downtown was where we lived, and cooked, and ate, and had our meetings. It was made up of about ten buildings: the trading post, which we turned into our community center; the post office; the clinic; a low wooden house across from the trading post, which had running water and heat; the museum, which became the security center; and another wooden building, where some people slept. Overlooking downtown, about two hundred yards to the north, the Sacred Heart Church was used to house people. We established a kitchen in the basement. Toward the east were two small churches and the minister's house. We put some seventy people in there. Wounded Knee was the hub of four roads, coming from Porcupine, Manderson, Pine Ridge, and Denby. The whole area around the Knee is rolling prairie with grass-covered hills. Way in the distance are patches of pine. It looks as if there is little cover for a man to hide. You can see far. But there are all kinds of little gullies and ravines that we could use to sneak in and out.

It was decided that I was not only to give spiritual guidance, but that I would also doctor the wounded and handle all gunshot cases. Wallace Black Elk, a Rosebud Sioux like myself, was the other medicine man. He had come with his wife, Grace. We both performed ceremonies. Stan Holder was named head of security and Bob Free would be our engineer in charge of electricity, the gas pumps, and all other equipment. Lorelei Decora was put in charge of the hospital. We lost little time getting organized.

We counted our weapons. We had twenty-six firearms, mostly hunting rifles, .22s and 30-30s, 12- and 16-gauge shotguns. Some had been liberated from the trading post. We also had maybe a dozen handguns. We had no high-powered rifles. There was only one automatic weapon, an AK-47. It belonged to Bobby Onco, a brother from Oklahoma and a Vietnam vet, who had brought it home as a war souvenir. Only one in ten was armed. One young kid had brought a modern hunting bow and arrows. One guy had an old Italian World War I rifle but could find no bullets to fit it.

Ammo was a big problem. We piled up what little we had on the altar of the church and Dennis or Stan Holder rationed it out. That was all we had to challenge the greatest power on earth.

The feds, as we found out during the long siege, had armed personnel carriers (APCs), heavily armored tracked vehicles, like tanks. They had M-60-, 50-, and 30-caliber machine guns, aerial illumination flares, trip wire flares, M-16 automatic rifles, searchlights, fancy starlight and infrared night scopes, M-79 grenade launchers, and rockets to launch CS tear gas. They had three helicopters to watch us, and several times we were buzzed by low-flying phantom jets. They had mobile field communication systems. We had all this coming down on us.

We took stock of our food supplies. We had taken a lot of food, mostly in cans, from the trading post and stored it in the church basement. But we had no idea how long it would have to last. Some thought we would occupy the Knee for only a few days. I thought it could last for a month. As it turned out, the siege lasted for seventy-one days. The feds, of course, tried to stop supplies from coming in. Dennis announced that we would eat horses, dogs, cats, rats, and even dirt before we'd let the government starve us out.

Inside the church was an altar with a plaster cast Jesus, Virgin Mary, and Saint Joseph. Vases with paper flowers stood at each end. Some of our people slept in that church, so there was drumming, singing, and dancing—a spiritual dance. The priest came running. He seemed dazed and in shock. He asked us why we were doing "a heathen dance, a defilement" in a sacred place. A woman asked him what his church was doing here in *our* sacred place. "It was sacred long before you came. Those people who died here, whose bodies were thrown on top of one another, they weren't Catholics. They believed in the Great Spirit, the pipe, and the ghost dance. They weren't baptized. And you built a church over them and put a cross here. You made this a place to make money from the tourists who come to see where all those Indians were killed."

It did not take long for the feds and the goons to arrive. We could feel them surrounding us. They were setting up roadblocks. A pickup full of goons drove up, and they fired some shots at us. A few of our young guys shot back. Some shot out some street lights to make us less visible. The war had started.

At sunup the next morning, February 27, we were already surrounded by two hundred fifty marshals and the FBI, with the goons hovering around the edges like jackals. Planes were flying overhead to keep tabs on us. Some of our men fired at them to keep them at a distance. We could see APCs moving back and forth on the ridge about a mile off. Some reporters sneaked in through the federal lines. Carter Camp told me later that if it hadn't been for the presence of the press, the government would have moved in and slaughtered us as they did in 1890.

An FBI big shot, Joseph Trimbach, came up under a white flag to "negotiate." He wanted to negotiate our surrender. We wanted to negotiate issues. He told us that he wasn't there to bargain. He was authorized to offer only one thing: safe-conduct to BIA headquarters in Pine Ridge for further talks. Otherwise the feds would take Wounded Knee by storm. I refused. Russell gave him a choice: Either negotiate with us for meaningful results or kill us right here. So there was a stand-off. We put up a tipi in no-man's-land between the church and the feds' roadblock, to have talks on neutral ground.

There were some white people living in the village, and we didn't quite know what to do with them. The feds called them hostages, but they really were nothing of that kind. Some did not want to leave. Those who wanted to go did so, and the feds picked them up at the roadblock.

It became clear that we were in for a long war. We put up our own roadblock, placing a row of old burned-out cars across the road. Then we built bunkers. Bob Free started a big yellow digging machine with a large front scoop, a sort of bulldozer. He and his crew dug twelve bunkers, made an apartment house out of the trading post, dug latrines, put up wooden privies, kept the juice going, repaired cars, and operated the forklift. When the juice got weak he made a rule that the only electricity we would use was for the freezers to store meat, to keep the pumps going, and to keep the three most important lights burning. And that was enforced. He also had a sanitary squad picking up garbage, digging trenches, and burying the trash in them. When gas was low, journalists, doctors, and lawyers coming in cars, whenever the feds allowed them through, often let us syphon off some of their gas.

After a while Bob Free had a confrontation with some of our leaders. He told them, "Things have gone to your head. Your noses are stuck up in the air. You want only to talk to the media. You guys better get your act together. Spend some hours a day with the people doing bunker duty. Spend an hour, now and then, digging slit trenches. Collect garbage. We're all Indians here. There's nothing here like a higher-class Indian for the media and a lower-class Indian doing the work." And with that, Bob resigned.

They couldn't persuade him to change his mind. So they elected me chief engineer as well as their medicine man. Russell Means just told me to take over. I continued with the bunkers. I made them four feet deep and put logs and sandbags on top of them. The women made the bags out of old jackets and things like that. I taught them to make zipguns and small bombs out of battery acid. I learned these things a long time before from a cousin who was talented that way. I used Coke bottles and light bulbs for bombs. What I did was to put fifteen hundred of those on one fuse all the way around, connected to a battery, so when you touched two wires together they would make a spark and set them off. That was part of our defense system. We had a few hundred pounds of coal, and I had some of the boys pound that up for charcoal, and we used that with battery acid for our bombs. Dennis Banks and I took forty people to dig up the ground and pretend we were planting mines. We also put up a stovepipe and spread the word that we had a trench mortar. That kept the feds at a distance.

We had a dozen bunkers. There was the Red Cloud Bunker toward Pine Ridge, the Black Elk Bunker near the Sacred Heart Church, the Little Bighorn Bunker on the Big Foot Trail by the creek, the Sitting Bull Bunker on the Denby road, the Coyote Bunker manned by Navajo, the Crow's Nest Bunker near the clinic opposite the trading post. The northernmost bunker was the Hawkeye, the southernmost the Little California Bunker. We also set up the Last Stand roadblock up on Manderson road, near the tribal housing project. Carter Camp and Sid Mills distributed the men in the bunkers so that every two hours we changed the guard and another team took over. We had men out patrolling on shifts too. Sweat lodge fires were going most of the time. Wallace Black Elk took care of them. Every evening the guys on security purified themselves in the sweat lodge, taking turns. Sometimes they had sweats during the wee hours of the night.

The feds had their own bunkers. The main one was Red Arrow on the Denby road, which served as their headquarters. They had the whole area crisscrossed with trip wires. When somebody tried to sneak in and stumbled on one of those wires a flare went up, turning night into day. They also had sharpshooters out there with infrared sniper scopes, and attack dogs. Even so, they never could seal the area off. People got in and out with supplies all the time. Sometimes parties were guided in by Severt Young Bear or Oscar Bear Runner. They knew the land and could tell where they were going by the moon and the stars. People walked ten or fifteen miles from the drop-off points with their heavy packs. Some walked in their socks through the snow, making as little noise as possible. They knew all the little gullies and washes to come in unseen. The feds called this AIM's Ho Chi Minh Trail. It was these backpackers who kept us alive.

Our clinic was just a two-room, one-story building. One room was supposed to be the surgery room, and I was the surgeon.

The clinic was run by Lorelei Decora, who is now a nurse at the Rosebud tribal hospital. Madonna Gilbert was her main assistant. Both were Lakota women. Every week a team of one or two white doctors or medics came into Wounded Knee to help. This was arranged by the National Council of Churches. The doctors were closely searched before the feds let them in. They were run through a nationwide computer check on their credentials. The FBI rummaged through their things piece by piece and messed them up. These MDs had to go through a real hassle until they were allowed inside the perimeter. A volunteer team usually stayed for a week and then was relieved by another. Dr. Pat Kelly had heard on the radio that doctors were needed at the Knee, and so he came out of Seattle with a team, and also medicines and food. Kelly told me, "I am a veteran from Nam, and the things I've seen here, the tracers, the flares, the government burning off all the cover down to the last shrub to be able to watch for people coming in, the APCs—it's identical to what I experienced in Vietnam. Every night it's like an incredible flashback to Da Nang."

During firefights, with thousands of rounds coming in, the medics made up first aid kits and waited, ready to go in, to help the wounded and bring them out. They also made stretchers. The medics and nurses worried about Indians walking around in the open, ignoring the bullets zipping by them. They worried about folks living in flimsy trailers and shacks, with slugs coming in through the walls. They worried about women standing in line to go to the toilets, joking while the bullets flew around them. It usually took the nurses and doctors three days to adjust to the situation. After that they no longer bothered with ducking and running for shelter, and went about their business like the rest of us.

Taking care of sanitary conditions was also the work of the medical team. They used lime to fill in pits where waste had been dumped to prevent disease. Carla Blakey, a Saulteaux Indian from Canada, turned an old garage into a four-way women's toilet. There were always four or five women standing in line there, and after every firefight the medics came running, yelling, "Everybody all right? Anybody need tranquilizers?" Carla said to me, "Imagine a place where you gotta have tranquilizers to go to the can!"

I doctored people with Indian herbs. They are from the earth and we are from the earth. They work better than the white man's wonder drugs. Operating was up to me. For this I used my pocket knife, my prayers, and taopi tawote, wound medicine. I also used an herb that numbs the flesh so that you don't feel anything. One of the men I operated on was Rocky Madrid, a Chicano medic. There had been a firefight, and Rocky and Owen Luck, who had been a helicopter medic in Vietnam, started to run to the front with their first aid kits to see if anybody needed help. Suddenly there were tracers zinging around them. Rocky was hit in the stomach by a tumbling bullet that ricocheted. It was a miracle he didn't get his guts blown out and could walk himself to the hospital. The bullet was stuck in the muscle. I dug it out with my knife. Chuck Downing, a white doctor, sewed up the wound. Rocky didn't feel a thing. I fanned him off with sage and three days later he was walking around as good as new. Rocky Madrid was senselessly shot. When he was hit there were enough flares overhead that you could have read a newspaper by the light they gave off, and he wore a large red cross on a white armband. The feds were machine-gunning the whole area, they just opened up and sprayed everything. On the day of the airlift they fired on a man carrying a large white flag walking alongside a wounded Indian being carried on a stretcher.

I fixed up one wounded warrior, Milo Goings, who was shot in the knee. To take the bullet out I used a piercing knife, but first I used porcupine quills and a medicine, red wood, to make it numb. I put the red wood there, and after it had its effect, I took the bullet out. Then I used deer sinew to sew it up. One kid was wounded with an M-16 bullet in the wrist, just under the thumb. So I made a cut and pulled the bullet out with tweezers. Then I used the same medicine on it. I didn't sew him up. I just wrapped the hand up, and in about two weeks he could use it again. Two Shoes got shot just under the ball of the foot, so I did the same thing, numbed him, cut it open, took the bullet out, and used that wound medicine. These medicines are powerful. To stop bleeding I use fine gopher dust. It stops the blood every time.

Almost right from the beginning, there was serious fighting. There were a lot of automatic weapons, and every sixth shot was a tracer bullet. It looked like long strings of lightning bugs. Things became serious as we settled in for a long standoff.

twenty-two

A GOOD DAY TO DIE

Obviously, somebody is going
to die at Wounded Knee and
if those guys do die, well,
that's the way the ball bounces.

Dick Wilson

It was crazy the way the government treated us. One day there was a firefight; the next day we were negotiating. Sometimes there was negotiating and shooting at the same time. One day the roadblocks were up, the next they were down. The feds would shoot somebody and then fly him out in a helicopter to the hospital in Rapid City. The FBI armed the goons and worked closely with them, but the marshals would have nothing to do with "those murderous drunken bums." The feds would curse us over the radio and the next moment chat and joke with us. Our bunkers were communicating with Red Arrow all the time. Witko wasichu, crazy white men, was all we could say. We could not figure them out.

The media were as fast getting into Wounded Knee as the feds. At first the FBI refused to let the press in, but some fifteen reporters made it past the perimeter anyhow. Later the press was admitted sometimes and refused entrance on other days. Here again it was hard to figure out what the government's policy was. Some of the media were against us. They wrote that Wounded Knee was a "guerrilla theater offering blood and pageantry." One reporter called us a "bunch of publicity seeking militants," another called what we were doing a "cannily orchestrated news event." Most of the journalists were friendly and rooted for us, because we gave them something to write about. The press used us and we used the press. As Carter Camp put it, "As long as we are good Boy Scouts behaving ourselves, nobody gives a shit. But as soon as we're waving guns, the media come running. If it takes waving guns to get our grievances before the public, then that's what we have to do." Wounded Knee was reported by TV, radio, and newspapers all over the world. All of the AIM leaders "had a good mouth." They were powerful speakers who could draw wonderful word pictures.

On March 1, Senators James Abourezk and George McGovern came to talk to us. Because Abourezk was sympathetic to us, his son's house at Wanblee, on the Pine Ridge reservation, was firebombed. McGovern was not pro-AIM. He said he had not much time for us, he had to get back to Rapid to change into a clean shirt. Russell said, "He's worried about his shirt. We're worried about seeing another sun rise." We had a lot of church support. John Adams, a Methodist, Paul Boe, a Lutheran, and Father Garvey, of South Dakota, did much to help us. A team of lawyers formed the Wounded Knee Legal Defense-Offense Committee, WKLDOC for short. We pronounced it "Wickledock." The committee consisted of Bill Kunstler, from New York; Beverly Axelrod, who had defended Eldridge Cleaver; Ken Tilsen, from Minneapolis; Mark Lane, who had his own ideas about the Kennedy assassination; and Ramon Roubideaux, a local Lakota attorney. Later Bruce Ellison joined the team. They had a lot of paralegal help.

On March 3, the government sent in Colonel Volney Warner, chief of staff of the 82nd Airborne, to see whether the regular army would be needed to make an end of us. Warner turned out to be good for us. He changed the FBI order from "shoot to kill" to "shoot to wound," and then to "do not shoot at all." He reported that the Indians weren't going to harm anyone. He thought that it was unlawful to use the army in a local domestic conflict. He told the marshals, "You guys are good only for handing out subpoenas. You aren't worth shit as fighting men." He said he would be only too glad to let the Airborne loose upon the goons. In the end the FBI, the marshals, and the goons hated Warner more than they hated us. Without Warner I could not have written this book. I would be dead.

On March 6, the feds' spokesman, Erickson, told us to come out and surrender, or else. He tried to scare us by ordering us to send all women and children out of Wounded Knee before darkness fell on March 8. But he didn't impress us. Dennis asked the women whether they wanted to leave. Not one of them did. Carter Camp told the feds, "I know we can't whip the whole United States, but we'll sell our lives as dear as we can." We ran up an AIM flag on the church steeple. I painted the faces of our warriors with sacred red paint. Some of the people remembered Crazy Horse's old war cry, "It's a good day to die!" Then the government backed down and negotiations started all over again. They led to nothing.

On the morning of March 11, four postal inspectors, guided by two ranchers, drove into the village "to inspect the post office in the trading post." That's what they said. They were government agents armed with handguns and handcuffs. They carried fancy badges like the FBI. They were stopped and disarmed by our security. They were, of course, not interested in finding out how the mail service functioned during the siege. They had come to spy. Security brought them to the museum and put their pistols, handcuffs, and badges on a table. I served them coffee and scrambled eggs and gave them a half-hour lecture on Indian history and why we had taken over the place. Then I had them escorted back to the federal lines. For this I was later tried and convicted as an accessory preventing federal officers from performing their assignments.

March 11 was also the day on which we proclaimed the Independent Oglala Nation under the 1868 Treaty of Fort Laramie that the government had broken. We declared Wounded Knee a liberated country and offered Oglala citizenship to everybody who was there with us. Dennis said, "This is no longer a perimeter, it's a border." We issued visas to members of the press. Russell Means declared, "If any foreign country, especially the United States, tries to enter the village, it will be considered an act of war and treated accordingly. Spies entering the village will be treated as spies anywhere." The Six Nations of the Iroquois at once recognized the Independent Oglala Nation and sent a delegation to support us, led by Chief Oren Lyons of the Onondaga. So we established what Dennis called a provisional government. One of our women said, "I'm weeping with joy that we are a nation again, a tiny nation in a small space, but it's a beginning. We don't need a tribal council, we don't need the BIA, we don't need the Reorganization Act of 1934. We're standing on the Treaty of Fort Laramie."

In the meantime we tried to establish a routine of daily living. The women were cooking as long as there was food. They made blankets out of old skirts. They made mittens out of old sweaters, with trigger fingers on them. They made socks out of sleeves and headgear with holes for eyes, nose, and mouth. This was for the guys in the bunkers. The women would go down to the bunkers to see if the men needed coffee, blankets, or ammo. Every time a flare went up, the guys would yell, "Hit the floor!" but no one bothered. The women were really strong. During one firefight, one woman held off several marshals with an old six-shooter while everybody else got away. She was real good with a gun.

For the first three weeks we had enough food. After that it was rice and beans, and then not even that. At first we ate a lot of fry bread, and that was okay, but the women ran out of shortening, flour, and baking powder. When we ran out of coffee, sugar, and cigarettes, things got real bad. Without coffee and cigarettes even the greatest warrior can't get it together anymore. It's a question of how long you can stand up on an empty stomach.

One white rancher donated a steer to us. That wasn't enough to last more than three hundred hungry people seventy-one days. So we took to liberating cattle. We called them slow elk. Dennis Banks sent a few young guys out to bring back a fat cow. They brought back an ancient skinny bull. It took eleven bullets to kill the poor beast. None of those great warriors knew how to butcher it. One of the white journalists had to do it.

The occupation was based on Indian religion. The sweat lodges were going twenty-four hours a day and we had yuwipi ceremonies almost every night and even a few peyote meetings. When things got really bad, men and women made flesh offerings. The leaders went so far as to pierce their chests as in the sun dance, thinking that their pain could help the people through spiritual power. Our medicine was strong. As an Indian you don't divide life into little boxes: A—politics, B—education, C—religion, and so on. It is all one, it is life. You break it up, white man's style, and it becomes just a jigsaw puzzle without meaning. I put on the ghost dance for four days and I felt that the bodies in their mass grave were dancing with us. Whenever negotiations went on inside the no-man's-land tipi, Wallace Black Elk or I was there with the sacred pipe and our eagle bone whistle, smoking in a circle, cedaring the government negotiators as well as our own people. The feds were impressed, I think, but did not know what to make of it. We were not on the same wavelength.

Then the situation became ugly. Even when there was a ceasefire, Dick Wilson maintained that he and his people weren't bound by any concessions the government made. He was angry at the government for being too easy on us. He was angry at the marshals for not blowing us away. He was angry at us for being Indians. He issued proclamations that read, in part, "What is happening at Wounded Knee is all part of a long-range plan of the Communist party. Disrupt the normal function of society. Demand the resignation of key officials. Demand the resignation of the head of state. To combat this we are organizing an all-out volunteer army of patriots. We need able-bodied men over 18 years of age. We are requesting General Chesty Puller, United States Marine Corps, to take command."

He continued, "Fellow patriots, we need you. Come in and sign up. We will organize and train you, and when the federal government has yielded, conceded, and appeased, we will march into Wounded Knee and kill tokas, wasichus, hasapas, and spiolas. They want to be martyrs? We will make it another Little Bighorn." In short, he called on his goons to kill all non-Sioux Indians, whites, blacks, and Hispanics.

On April 5, we signed an agreement with Kent Frizzel, the government negotiator. The White House big shots would not come to the Knee to talk with us, but we would send a delegation to Washington to meet with them there. So we smoked the pipe together. I told Frizzel, "Many hundred years ago the white man and Indians smoked the pipe. Now, today, we smoke the pipe again. Before we smoke, I will blow the eagle bone whistle that has been given to the Indian people. At this time, Great Spirit, there are many, many things that we ask for. Many, many days we've been here at Wounded Knee, at this sacred altar, the sacred circle. At this time, Grandfather, I ask you to take care of my Indian people, my red man."

The agreement called for both sides to disarm. On the same day we would lay down our arms, the feds would withdraw the APCs and the marshals, and the FBI would go home. In the meantime our delegation took off for Washington. It consisted of Russell Means, Chief Tom Bad Cob, our Sioux lawyer, Ramon Roubideaux, Judy Bridwell, and myself. The talks in Washington came to nothing. Nixon would not see us, and talks with his underlings were just hot air.

On April 11, while I was in Washington, Mary Ellen Moore gave birth under fire to a little boy. The people took it as a good sign. They held the newborn baby up for all to see. The people wept and sang the AIM song. Dennis Banks said, "We've been reinforced by a little warrior." A few days later I managed to sneak back into Wounded Knee.

In the beginning, the feds had let some food and medical supplies through, but as the ring tightened, they tried to starve us out. They got a court order that made it illegal to bring supplies to us. Supporters on the outside organized an airlift. The first, which took place early in April, delivered four hundred pounds of food into Wounded Knee: rice, dried beans, powdered milk, oatmeal, yeast, flour, baking soda, bandages, antibiotics, vitamins, some clothing, and, most welcome, coffee and cigarettes. The machine was a single-engine plane piloted by a Vietnam vet. The co-pilot and navigator was also a Nam vet. It was all over in no time. We knew the plane was coming, so we rushed up and unloaded the plane in minutes. It took off bobbing and weaving to throw the feds off their aim and to prevent them from reading the numbers painted on the underside.

The big airdrop happened on April 17. It was made up of three planes, each carrying four parachutes with duffel bags full of supplies tied together. The cargo doors had been taken off for quick action. Each plane had a "kicker" who kicked out the bundles with the chutes on them. The planes flew in at first light. They knew that this time the feds would be waiting for them, so they did the mission when most of them would be sleeping.

Although the drop was successful, this turned out to be one of our saddest days. As the food was being distributed, Eddy Whitewater was walking back to his house with his little children when, suddenly, a helicopter was hovering above them. A sniper in the copter started shooting at them. So the guys in the bunkers began shooting back to protect the people moving on the ground and to keep the copter at a distance. That started the biggest firefight up to then. Frank Clearwater, a Cherokee brother from North Carolina, was resting inside the church, getting a little sleep after having walked all night with his pregnant wife, Morning Star, to join us. A bullet came crashing through the wall and hit him in the back of his head. Clearwater did not have any weapons and did not plan to use any. The medics were notified that he was badly wounded, but could not get to him for an hour because of the heavy fire. Finally three women just ran up the hill, zigzagging through the line of fire, and dashed into the church. They put him on a blanket and got him down to the clinic at a dead run, with the bullets flicking up dust at their feet. Even though they had Red Cross armbands and were waving a white flag, they were fired on all the way down. It took hours before the shooting died down enough for Clearwater to be carried to the roadblock, from where the feds took him in a copter to the hospital in Rapid City. His wife went to the roadblock to be with him in Rapid but was arrested and put in jail.

Clearwater died on April 25. The Independent Oglala Nation offered a plot of land inside the perimeter, but Wilson would not let his body into Pine Ridge because Clearwater was not an Oglala. (Of course, there are many whites buried all over the reservation.) Clearwater was part Cherokee and part Apache, he was a Native American. He had every right to be buried at the place where he had given his life for his people. We mourned for him for four days inside the Knee and I made a tape to be smuggled out to be played at his funeral.

I said, "Early this morning our brother Frank Clearwater left us for another world. I never thought they would try to kill us here. We at Wounded Knee are mourning. We are red men, fighting for our rights. So, brothers and sisters of our tribes throughout this continent, pray for Clearwater's spirit. He was here only twelve hours. They massacred him. I use 'massacred' because our dead brother was not armed. He carried no gun. He was not in a bunker, he was inside a church. So all of you everywhere who believe in the Indian ways, you must pray for him. You must pray for the people at Wounded Knee."

I had said that if Clearwater could not be buried at the Knee, he should be put to rest on Crow Dog land. And so his body was taken from Rapid City to Rosebud. The hearse had to cross Pine Ridge, and everywhere the goons and the FBI had put up roadblocks. Everybody was checked out. They let through only the widow and the hearse. Everybody else, Indians and whites, was turned back.

Finally, Clearwater came to Crow Dog's Paradise. The casket stayed at my dad's house for a day. During the night my father ran a Native American Church ceremony for Clearwater. They came out of the ceremony just as the sun was rising, painting the valley red. They put the casket on a pickup truck and drove it to a grassy hill near our vision pit. More than a hundred people followed on foot. They formed a circle around the grave. My father was there with his pipe, saying prayers in Lakota. The people sang the AIM song as the body was laid to rest. I think Clearwater's spirit likes it there. From the grave he can see the Little White River and pine-covered hills.

At the Knee the fight continued. April 26 saw the biggest shoot-out of the whole siege. It was started by the goons who fired at the feds' position. This provoked the marshals and FBI to open on us with automatic weapons. The night was lit up by flares and crisscrossed with tracer bullets. The shooting went on and on. The next day I learned that Buddy Lamont had been killed. I had always known inside of me that a Lakota friend of mine would lose his life, but the news still hit me hard. Lawrence "Buddy" Lamont was an Oglala from Pine Ridge, a marine and a Vietnam veteran. He was thirty-one years old. He had been shot through the heart and died instantly. Buddy was an only son. He received his honorable discharge in the mail just at about the time he was hit. Buddy was shot early in the morning close to his Last Stand bunker. A sniper from one of the feds' positions had pinned him down. He jumped up, trying to draw fire so that he could locate the sniper and shoot back, and was hit.

Buddy had known that he was not to come out of the Knee alive. Maybe a spirit told him. Maybe the owl had called him. He had told friends, "If something happens to me I want to stay at Wounded Knee. Don't make any fuss over me. Just bury me in my bunker." Buddy's mother was Agnes Lamont, whose grandparents had been with Crazy Horse at the Custer battle. Some of her ancestors had been massacred at Wounded Knee in 1890. Buddy's sister, Lou Bean, was one of our strongest women.

Wilson could not stop Buddy from being buried at Wounded Knee; he was a tribally enrolled member of the Oglala tribe, and his being buried there was part of an agreement we made with the feds. With the sacred pipe in my hand I chanted the prayers over him in our Lakota language.

Wallace Black Elk also spoke at the graveside: "This boy was murdered by the United States government. He served in Vietnam, he fought for them. And then they shot him, right through the heart. So this is the total judgment. The government will have to face these two boys, Buddy Lamont and Frank Clearwater, when the time comes. Before the spirit, these two boys will be standing there."

Buddy Lamont is buried close to that long trench containing the bones of Chief Big Foot and the three hundred ghost dancers, men, women, and children. He is there with the spirits. His burial took place two days before the long siege ended. Later a headstone was put up over his grave. It bears his army serial number and the name of his unit. It also says, "Two thousand came here to Wounded Knee, one stayed."

The end was near. On April 29, the trading post burned down together with everything in it. A kerosene lamp had fallen over and set fire to the place. Nothing but black ashes remained. The electricity was gone, the food was gone, our ammo was nearly gone. The earth was scorched. The women and children were at the point of total exhaustion. Most of the press had left; they were now more interested in Watergate. There was a steady trickle of brothers walking out during the night with their weapons in order to escape arrest when the end came. Some of the leaders were no longer there. Russell Means had been prevented from returning after we had been in Washington, where Nixon had refused to see us. Dennis Banks managed to walk out at the last moment. An agreement was signed. We would have to lay down our arms, surrender, and submit to arrest. In return the government made promises that meant little and were not kept.

Stan Holder told me that people wept when the agreement

was signed. They knew it was just another treaty that would be broken. Forty people walked out during the last night. They tried to get through where nobody ever went because the area was too open, but they set off a trip wire flare. Some marshals opened up on them and did not even wait for them to hit the ground. I still can't figure out why nobody was hurt. They all made it to Porcupine and from there scattered themselves to wherever they had a home. I was glad for them.

I could have walked out with the others without any trouble, but I had signed that agreement. I couldn't walk out on my words. Stand Down happened on Friday, May 8, 1973. On that day one hundred forty-six men and women laid down their arms and surrendered. Not a shot was fired. All was quiet. The feds took down our four-color AIM flag and raised the American flag. A marshal made some kind of a victory speech. With a helicopter whirling overhead, the marshals and FBI in full battle dress swarmed all over the place looking for booby traps and holdouts. They thought some of us were hiding in the ruins. The feds rummaged through the debris. Finally a loud voice came over the loudspeaker: "Gentlemen, the village of Wounded Knee is secured."

The feds lined us up for processing. Everybody was questioned, searched, and fingerprinted. Wallace Black Elk told them that he was a medicine man. They slammed him against the side of a car, ripped his headband off, and took away his medicine bundle and sacred things. Carter Camp and I were the last ones to be helicoptered out. I was handcuffed and the cuffs fastened to a waist chain. My legs and feet were also chained. Trussed up like this I was the last of the "hostiles" to leave the Knee. We never got our Black Hills back, the Treaty of Fort Laramie was not honored, nor did the government recognize us as an independent nation. And yet I think that this was the greatest moment in my life and that our seventy-one-day stand was the greatest deed done by Native Americans in this century.

twenty-three

THE BIG RAID

They won't let Indians like me live.
That's all right. I don't want to
grow up an old woman.

Annie Mae Aquash

Of the Wounded Knee of 1973 nothing is left. Of the Sacred Heart church, only the square hole that was once the basement remains. The trading post, the museum, the wooden house that was our clinic, the gas station—all are gone. Patches around what had been the perimeter are today just black scorched earth where nothing will ever grow again. The only thing left was Gildersleeve's huge, open, rusting safe, full of buzzing wasps. But that, too, disappeared a short time ago. It is as if the government has wiped out every indication that Indians made a stand there. But Wounded Knee lives on in our hearts.

After having been taken in a copter, chained and handcuffed, to Rapid City and the Pennington county jail, I was released. I went back to Crow Dog's Paradise, but that was not the end.

A short time later, after the sun dance, Mary Ellen Moore moved in with me together with her little boy. We were married Indian style, not in a church but with a blanket around our shoulders, holding onto the pipe.

The three years following Wounded Knee were years

of fear, fighting, and tension, the bloodiest years in my experience. At Pine Ridge, as long as Wilson was in charge, it was murder, pure and simple. At Rosebud it was mostly a matter of endless harassment and surveillance.

Someone put the number of persons killed by Wilson's goons at more than one hundred. Others thought the number was higher. But nobody really knows, because most of the acts of violence were never investigated. In June 1973, Clarence Cross and his brother, Vernal, were shot by tribal police while sleeping in their car. Clarence died. Vernal survived a bullet wound and was arrested for "assaulting the BIA police."

In late summer, goons were firing M-16s through the windows of the Little Bear family home, shooting out the eye of seven-year-old Mary Ann.

At about the same time, Helen Red Feather was attacked and arrested for "being an AIM sympathizer." The goons kicked her in the side and belly, although she told them that she was three months pregnant.

In early October, Aloysius Long Soldier was shot to death at Kyle by unknown goons. He was known to be working for the impeachment of Dick Wilson.

On October 17, 1973, my friend the Oglala civil rights leader Pedro Bissonette was provoked by a man at White Clay, Nebraska, who made racist remarks and shoved him around. Pedro knocked the man down. This gave the BIA cops the opportunity to stop him at a roadblock, where he was killed with a shotgun blast. The cops claimed that Pedro had reached for his gun while resisting arrest.

Pedro's sister-in-law, Jeanette Bissonette, a mother of six, was shot and killed by a sniper's bullet as she changed a tire on an isolated road.

Matthew King, a respected elder and tribal interpreter, had twenty rounds fired into his house. He called it a miracle that he wasn't hit.

My sister's stepdaughter, Jancita Eagle Deer, was found dead on the highway. Her death was ruled a traffic accident. Like so many other Indian women, she had had abusive encounters with white authority; however, instead of keeping quiet, before her death AIM had helped Jancita publicize her experience. My sister Delphine Eagle Deer wanted to continue to pursue Jancita's accusations. She was found beaten to death on an icy road.

Russell Means had gone to visit friends on the Standing Rock reservation in North Dakota. He had applied there for a job as director of a youth ranch for kids with problems. Russ was in a caravan of three cars that was stopped at the Cannonball River by BIA police. Russell got out of his car to ask what they wanted and was shot in the back. The shot pierced one of his kidneys, but he survived.

On January 17, 1975, Dick Wilson was easily defeated in an election for tribal president by Al Trimble, a good man who tried to clean up the reservation. But Wilson was in office until April, when the new administration took over. So he had three months to let his goons avenge his loss. The village of Wanblee had voted heavily for Trimble. On the evening of January 31, the goons unleashed a reign of terror at Wanblee, shooting into and fire-bombing people's houses. They ambushed the car driven by the tribal lawyer, Byron DeSersa, a Wilson opponent, and sprayed the car with automatic guns. DeSersa's leg was ripped up by the bullets. Prompt medical aid could have saved him, but he was left to die in a ditch.

One of the last victims was Annie Mae Aquash, whose body was found in a snow-filled ravine near Wanblee. The FBI reported that their autopsy concluded that she died of exposure. They then had her buried in an unmarked grave. AIM and Annie Mae's relatives insisted that she be exhumed and a second autopsy be performed. The doctor found that the FBI had cut off her hands to send them to Washington for fingerprinting. He also found a .38-caliber bullet lodged in her skull.

On June 26, 1975, occurred the big shoot-out at Oglala, on the Pine Ridge reservation, during which two FBI agents and one

Indian were shot and killed. Oglala, in the northwest corner of the reservation, is a small village of mostly traditional full-bloods. The goons were especially hard on them. The people there asked AIM for help and protection. Harry and Celia Jumping Bull had their place nearby, together with some relatives—three houses, a barn, some sheds, and a little way off an old cabin. Harry donated five acres of his land and the cabin for Dennis Banks to set up an AIM camp. Dennis moved into the cabin together with his wife, Kamook, and their baby daughter, Tashina Wanblee Win, Eagle Shawl Woman. Kamook is a Lakota woman from Pine Ridge. The camp, along White Clay Creek, was made up of some twenty to thirty-five people—Lakota, Navajo, Inuit, Klallam, and Coeur d'Alenes. On the day of the shoot-out, Dennis Banks and Kamook were away on business. In Dennis's absence the people in the camp looked up to Leonard Peltier as their leader. Peltier was from Turtle Mountain, North Dakota, part Sioux and part Ojibway. He was active in AIM and had been involved in a number of confrontations with the police and FBI.

By this time things had come to such a pass that any little incident could set off an explosion. The reservation was swarming with goons, tribal police, FBI, and swat teams.

The way the shoot-out happened had to be a setup. There is no other way to explain it. The feds were determined to wipe out the AIM camp. They had a media blitz going, preparing the minds of white people for what was to come. They said the camp was made up of a bunch of heavily armed renegades who had built bunkers. There were no bunkers, just an old root cellar. The feds talked about "fortifications and entrenchments." These existed only in their imagination. Attorney General Janklow said, "The best thing to do with an AIM member is to put a gun to his head and pull the trigger."

On the evening of June 25, two FBI agents drove up to the Jumping Bull place. They went into people's homes without warrants, saying they were looking for a kid, Jimmy Eagle, who, they said, had stolen a pair of old cowboy boots. Now, to come into that place, at that time, looking for a pair of stolen boots was crazy. The feds, of course, had other reasons. They wanted to provoke the Indians to a fight so that the FBI would have grounds for going in there and making an end of that camp. The agents were watched by some members of the AIM camp, looking down from the top of a ridge. It made the agents uneasy and they drove away. During the night there were heavy storms, thundering and lightning, as if some spirits were trying to warn the people.

On the morning of June 26, two FBI cars drove up to the camp. They were driven by special agents Ron Williams and Jack Coler. What was bound to happen, happened. It doesn't matter now who fired the first shot, the agents or the AIM men. The agents had gotten themselves into a situation they could not handle. They were screaming into their two-way radios to their back-up cars: "We're drawing fire! Come quick or we're dead men!" But their back-ups didn't come. When the firing finally stopped, Coler and Williams were lying dead near their cars. Later, the body of an Indian, Joe Stuntz, was found in a mud puddle, where the feds had dumped him. In no time the whole area was swarming with agents and police. People afterward could never figure out how they arrived so quickly on the scene. They had to have been ready for this confrontation. The death of a human, whether Indian or white, is a tragedy, but I have a strange feeling that Coler and Williams were set up by their own people as a sacrifice, to have a reason to make an end of AIM.

The whole crowd of agents, tribal police, and goons formed a ring around the area, searching the gullies and ravines for AIM members. It seemed they covered every foot of ground so thoroughly that not even a mouse could have gotten through, but somehow the people from the camp, led by Leonard Peltier, cut their way through during the night, finding shelter and a hiding place wherever they went, in Pine Ridge, Rosebud, and as far away as the Cheyenne River reservation.

Peltier and most men in his group were sun dancers. Peltier had first danced and pierced the year before. That meant he would have to sun dance three more years, because you make your vow for four years in a row. According to the traditional Lakota way, I had to let Peltier come to Crow Dog's Paradise to fulfill his vow. The FBI knew that he was there, and they did not like it. They did not like me or my father, either, for letting him dance at our place. A report from an FBI informer, released years later under the Freedom of Information Act, is heavily censored, but what is left reads, "[Name deleted] advised August 1, 1975, that Leonard Peltier is at Crow Dog's Paradise staying at the residence of Leonard Crow Dog's mother. [Name deleted] saw Leonard Peltier evening of July 31, 1975, and day of August 1, 1975, at this location [name of location blacked out]. That there are approximately 300 to 350 people at Crow Dog's Paradise participating at the 'Sun Dance,' an Indian religious ceremony sanctioned by the National Council of Churches and other religious groups, and the fact that there are 300 to 350 persons at Crow Dog's makes it inadvisable to arrest Peltier at Crow Dog's. There is a good chance a gun fight could break out, thus endangering the lives of innocent people. Further, it is felt that a raid at Crow Dog's at this time could be interpreted as interfering with a religious ceremony. [More lines deleted.]"

Informers also spread the rumor that during the four days of the dance we discussed plans to blow up churches, FBI headquarters, and the state capitol. This was particularly implausible because the National Council of Churches and the Methodist, Lutheran, and Catholic Churches had helped us with food and medicines at Wounded Knee and were still supporting us at the time. Anyhow, the FBI was waiting for a better time to come to Crow Dog's Paradise.

There was a man called Robert Beck living on the rez. He was not a tribally enrolled Lakota, he was probably not even Indian. He was an alcoholic and a man of violence. On July 28, 1975, Beck got some bootleg liquor and was drinking heavily. He invited my nephew Andrew Stuart, son of a Native American Church road man, to go "hunting" with him. They picked up two girls, Virginia and June Elk Looks Back, and went up into the hills south of Crow Dog's Paradise. There, in the hours before dawn, Andrew was shot and killed with a bullet through his forehead. The rifle that fired the shot belonged to Beck. There was blood all over his car. The girl Andrew was with came running down onto the road, screaming with terror. She was run over by a car but recovered. The case was never investigated. Beck called it a "hunting accident." He never went before a grand jury or faced trial.

As a kid, Beck had done time in a reformatory. In 1974 he had driven past my place and fired a rifle at me. According to the Rosebud tribal police, Beck was arrested seven times in 1975 alone for acts of violence. He entered people's homes; he fired into their houses. He used force entering my sister's home, firing at her. He was arrested by the tribal police but he just grinned: "I'm immune from arrest. You can't hold me. All I have to do is make one phone call." And he was right. No matter what crimes he committed he always remained free to commit some more. Much later he murdered a peaceful man by the name of No Moccasin in front of witnesses. He was convicted for this crime and sent to jail, but that was after the FBI had no further use for him.

On September 2, 1975, Beck was seen driving around with some FBI agents. In the evening he drove to Parmelee, about twenty-five miles from Crow Dog's Paradise. There he and a side-kick, Bill McCloskey, without provocation, started a fight with my sixteen-year-old nephew, Frank Running, and beat him up badly. When Frank arrived at our place a little later, there was blood all over him and he was in shock.

On the same night we were celebrating my father's birthday. All the men purified themselves in the sweat lodge. Then we had a yuwipi ceremony. After that we went to bed. At one-thirty A.M. a car came crashing through two wooden gates at the entrance to Crow Dog's Paradise. The car drove about one hundred fifty feet into our land, coming to a stop in the yard between my and my father's houses. The driver was Beck. With him was McCloskey and their two women, all drunk. In the car they had two cases of bootleg beer and a bottle of lemon vodka. Beck and McCloskey came out of the car spoiling for a fight. Frankie ran out of the house to see what was going on and they began beating him for the second time. Then my security came running, Coke Millard and my brother-in-law, Frankie's father. They got into a fight and Coke cracked McCloskey's jaw. The whole fight lasted maybe five minutes, then Beck and McCloskey drove off. I arrived on the scene after they were gone.

Now, most of the Pine Ridge murders were never investigated. At Rosebud there are drunken fights every weekend, with bloody noses and teeth knocked out, and such things are handled in tribal court with a fine and a night in the drunk tank—if there is a complaint. But that cracked jaw of McCloskey's, a case of self-defense against violent trespassers, got Beck a federal warrant for assault and battery against everybody who had been at our place, and the warrant was issued within twenty-four hours. That gave the feds the excuse for their Omaha Beach–style raid, which cost me two years of my life.

They came to Crow Dog's Paradise at dawn on September 5, 1975—one hundred eighty-five of them, FBI, marshals, and SWAT teams. They came in full battle dress, with flak vests. They came with helicopters, heavily tracked vehicles, trucks, and even rubber boats "to prevent the Indians from escaping across the Little White River." Some even came down the hill under an artificial smokescreen. I woke up when I heard a shout: "This is the FBI! Come out with your hands up or we'll shoot!" Some agents smashed the windows of my house and climbed in. Others broke down the doors. They dragged me out of bed. I was sleeping in the nude but they would not let me dress. They pushed me down on the floor and held an M-16 to my head. They put plastic handcuffs on me, the kind that tighten with every movement and cut off your circulation. They put M-16s to my wife's head. They dragged three-year-old Pedro from under his blanket and threw him against the wall. He was crying. Mary wanted to go to him and comfort him but the feds would not let her. One FBI kept asking me again and again who shot those agents, who shot Coler and Williams. I told him I didn't know. I was in Cedar Rapids, Iowa, at the time. They kept on: "Where's Peltier? We know he's around here somewhere. You're hiding him." When I said, truthfully, that he wasn't here, they dragged me by the hair out of the house and tied me to a tree. I still was naked. There were women and children around, weeping. Some of the women were only half dressed. They searched even the children. My wife tried to bring me some clothes, but the feds wouldn't let anyone come near me. Choppers were landing and taking off in my yard. The feds were wrecking houses, tipis, and cars. They shot my old horse, Big Red, out of sheer meanness. He had been the kids' pet. My dad tried to bring me my pipe, but the feds stopped him. They looked into my beaded pipe bag, saying, "There might be a gun in it." I told them that I was a medicine man and allowed no weapons in my place, but they paid no attention. My wife asked them to show her their search warrants. They did not have any, only blank arrest orders against John Doe and Jane Doe. As usual, we had people staying at the Paradise, and wherever I looked I saw men and boys tied to trees. There wasn't one tree without somebody tied to it.

And what happened at my place happened down the road, a half mile away, at my sister Dinah's place. She and her husband, Al, had their kids there, Frankie and little Colleen, and several guests. The feds brought all of those they arrested at my sister's place over to the Paradise, where they put us all in squad cars and took us to Pierre, the state capital.

At Pierre they put me into jail, awaiting trial. They cooked up three phony charges against me. Much later I found out the reason for the big raid. An informer had told the FBI that Peltier was hiding on my place. They searched the Paradise and miles around with choppers, dogs, and rows of men, but they didn't find him—for the simple reason that he wasn't there. Because the FBI goofed I had to go through three trials and spend time in jail.

But I think, regardless of Peltier, they would have found a way to put me away, because as a spiritual medicine man I was a greater danger to them than our political leaders.

My mother, who was in her seventies at the time, watched the whole thing. "They were looking for Peltier, but he wasn't there. He wasn't anywhere near Rosebud. Because they couldn't find Peltier, they took my boy. That was a very bad day for us and for Rosebud."

twenty-four

WHITE MAN'S JUSTICE

In 1492 there were eight million
Indians in this country.
Today there is only one million.
Where are the grandchildren of
those eight million? Where are the
murderers of Buddy Lamont,
Raymond Yellow Thunder,
Chief Crazy Horse, and the
women of Sand Creek?
Let the truth be known.
Who are the criminals?
Who should be on trial?

Stan Holder

After Wounded Knee, the word went out from the FBI to the Justice Department and the courts: Prosecute, prosecute, prosecute! No matter if you can't get a conviction, prosecute! If one AIM leader is acquitted on one charge, try him for another. Don't dismiss cases that are weak or not worth the effort. Keep AIM in court all the time. Keep them busy so they can't do their civil rights campaigns. Prosecute not only the big guys, but also the foot soldiers, the little people.

Out of every hundred Indian civil rights cases, only seven led to convictions. It did not matter that it jammed up the courts and wasted the taxpayers' money, just as long as it kept us involved in trial after trial and ate up our supporters' money. No case was too insignificant.

Some prosecutors went to any length to get a conviction against AIM defendants. In the trial of Dennis Banks and Russell Means in Saint Paul, Minnesota, the prosecutor put on the stand a witness who swore falsely under oath to have seen Dennis and Russell do certain things at Wounded Knee, when at the time this witness had been a thousand miles away in California. When the judge, Frederick Nichol, found out about this, he exploded in anger. For an hour and a half he told the prosecutor and the FBI what he thought of them. He said that all his life he had believed in the FBI and the American system of justice, until this moment.

In his decision, Judge Nichol found sufficient evidence of further governmental misconduct to push him 'over the brink' of dismissal: (1) the prosecutor's offering and failing to correct obviously false testimony; (2) seemingly intentional deception of the court as to the possibility of a witness's involvement in a rape incident; (3) the deliberate deception or grossly negligent conduct of the prosecutor in eliciting testimony which was directly contradicted by a document in the prosecutor's possession but which he had failed to furnish; (4) the attempt to conceal the extent of military involvement at Wounded Knee; and (5) the reasons given to the media by the prosecutor for refusing to proceed with eleven jurors after one juror had become ill. Judge Nichol dismissed all charges, finding the administration of justice had been "tainted" by "serious" prosecutorial "misconduct." He said, "I am forced to the conclusion that the prosecutor in this trial had something other than attaining justice foremost in its mind. . . . This case was not prosecuted in good faith or the spirit of justice. The waters of justice have been polluted."

The first of my three trials took place before the shoot-out at Pine Ridge and before the big raid on Crow Dog's Paradise. This was the case involving the four postal inspectors who had come to spy on us at Wounded Knee. The trial was a heyoka deal, a clown theater. I could not believe that this sort of "doing justice" could happen in America. It would have been funny if they had not found us guilty.

The prosecutor was R. D. Hurd, who had been criticized by Judge Nichol for his misconduct in the Banks-Means case. Instead he was named "prosecutor of the year." The charge against Carter Camp, Stan Holder, and myself was "aiding and abetting in preventing federal officers from exercising their functions, and robbery." Preventing them from exercising their functions meant that our security had stopped them from spying on us. Robbery meant that their guns had been taken away. We were tried simply because we had been in the museum when the postal inspectors were brought in. The prosecution said that being present there made us as guilty as the young guys who had stopped the agents at the roadblock. All three of us had asked to be tried together with Dennis and Russ before Judge Nichol in Saint Paul. This was denied us. The government wanted to have as many trials going on as possible, at different times and places. We were tried two years after the event. This denied us our constitutional right to a speedy trial.

The judge in this case was Edward "Speedy Eddie" McManus. He rushed the jury selection through in one day, giving our lawyers a deadline of five o'clock to finish their questioning. This did not give them enough time to find out whether some of the jurors were racist or prejudiced. We found out when one of the jurors threw a fit when I swore on the pipe instead of on the Bible. All the jurors were white.

Our first objection was that our trial was a case of "selective prosecution." By this we meant that AIM members opposed to the government's policies were prosecuted for trivial reasons, whereas in the case of Wilson and his goons, the government chose *not* to prosecute the arson, aggravated assault, and murder. In June 1974, while negotiations were going on about a plea bargain that would have resulted in the dismissal of most Wounded Knee–related charges, the FBI wrote the attorney general an "action memorandum":

> In order for the FBI to be effective in both the intelligence and criminal fields in curbing the militant activities of AIM, it is imperative for the Federal Government to discharge its responsibility of vigorous prosecution in U.S. District Courts for criminal offenses in violation of federal statutes. To do otherwise would encourage AIM and its sympathizers to believe they may engage in militant activities both on and off Indian reservations with impunity. In view of the above, it is requested that this Bureau be advised by letter concerning any contemplated decision to limit prosecution in the non-leadership Wounded Knee cases and the reasons therefor. It is further requested this Bureau be given the opportunity to respond and express our views prior to final determination to exchange a few guilty pleas of some defendants for the dismissal of prosecution against numerous other defendants because to limit the prosecution of these cases would severely affect our operations.

This, of course, was against the rule that "the government may not prosecute for the purpose of deterring people from exercising their right to protest of official misconduct and petition for redress of grievances."

We got nowhere with this. So they violated our right to equal protection under the law. We suffered from a double standard of justice from the beginning.

Immediately after their release at Wounded Knee, the postal inspectors were questioned for hours by the FBI. They testified before a grand jury. At that time they had nothing bad to say against me, Carter, or Stan. They didn't know me. They didn't even know my name. They didn't know that Crow Dog existed or that he was AIM's medicine man. I was just a person who had given them breakfast and a lecture. They were shown a stack of photographs of people involved in Custer and Wounded Knee, including myself. But none of them could identify me from the photographs.

The witnesses against us were three of the four postal inspectors—Graham, Schneider, and Hanson. Jack Hanson spoke the truth. He said over and over again, and he also wrote, "Crow Dog gave us a dialogue and then left without having taken any part in the kidnapping, robbery, or release." This was true enough, except that there was no kidnapping. The inspectors were simply stopped and detained for, maybe, an hour and a half.

The biggest problem was Graham. Before the trial he had made four conflicting reports. Now, on the stand, he suddenly testified that I had asked security to "search the inspectors' crotches for hidden radios and microphones." We had to laugh. Even the prosecutor said he "was surprised by this allegation." My lawyer asked him how he knew it was me. Graham said he recognized me because he had seen a picture of me in a newspaper together with Russell Means when we were part of an AIM delegation in Washington, D.C. The defense proved that there was no such picture. Then Graham said that he knew me because the FBI had pointed me out to him. He testified that I had asked him for the keys to his car. Schneider later said, "Not for the car keys but for the keys to a briefcase inside the car, and it was Stan Holder, not Crow Dog." Schneider also testified that I was one of those who had stopped the inspectors *outside* the museum, and that I had told him that he was a "prisoner of war." He said the FBI had shown him the picture of a man at the roadblock and told him that it was Crow Dog. The picture was not shown to the defense. Had they shown it to us we could easily have proved that the man in the picture was not me. One of the inspectors said that my lecture lasted twelve minutes, another said it had been forty-five minutes, Hanson called it a half hour. And so it went. They all said different things.

Finally the case went to the jury on a charge of aiding and abetting. With no deliberation or discussion, they found us guilty.

On August 5, 1975, I went to Cedar Rapids, Iowa, for sentencing. My family and friends came to be with me. The courtroom was dark and gloomy, with heavy wood paneling. Everybody was searched before going in. They spread-eagled my seven-year-old daughter Ina and ran a metal detector over her. They ran the detector over little Pedro's diaper. I wore my hair loose and unadorned. I carried my pipe. The courtroom was full of my Indian supporters and white racists who wanted to see us taken off to jail.

Then there was a hitch. Stan and Carter did not show up for the sentencing. Somebody said he'd heard on the radio that Dennis Banks had not shown up for his sentencing at Custer and jumped bail. I guess they didn't trust the American justice system. At any rate, they had me.

Our prosecutor, R. D. Hurd, told the court, "Crow Dog is a danger to the American way of life. He must be put away." He begged the court not to let me out on parole. He talked about the humiliation of the postal inspectors who had to stand with their hands on their heads when they were caught spying. He said, "I don't care, and I submit to you that it doesn't make any difference if conditions on the reservations are good or bad. I don't care if the 1868 Treaty of Fort Laramie was violated or not by the United States." Hurd went on and on. He told the jury that Wounded Knee "strikes at the very heart of the ability to maintain law and order." He said that Crow Dog's being a medicine man was immaterial. He said, "Crow Dog is not a peaceful man."

Ken Tilsen spoke on my behalf. He said, "I know my client to be innocent of these charges and the prosecution knows he is innocent." He said Hurd "lies to and deceives the court."

The judge said, "The guilt of the defendant is established by the jury's verdict." He pronounced me guilty of aiding and abetting, of interfering with federal officers, of robbery. He called Wounded Knee "a violent insurrection going beyond the nonviolent approach to injustice." He then sentenced me to three years for "interference" and eight years for "robbery"—that is, taking away the agents' guns.

But this was Iowa, not South Dakota. Judge McManus went

on, saying that I was "a borderline case" because I was a spiritual leader. He cited the many letters he had received supporting me. And it was my first offense. He suspended the sentence and put me on five years' probation. And so I walked out an almost free man.

Outside the courthouse my sister Dinah sang a brave-heart song and put sacred red face paint on my cheeks and forehead. The press surrounded me, holding microphones to my face. I said, "We Indians have been in suspended sentence for three hundred years. We were here long before the wasichus came with their courthouses and jailhouses. We will be here after all their courthouses and jailhouses have crumbled to dust."

My troubles were not over. I knew that the government would not rest until it had me behind bars. Waiting for my next trials, I had a Native American Church meeting. I talked to the Great Spirit: "Grandfather, this is me. This is how I pray to you, so that I could be with my people. In the future, Grandfather, I am going into another trial. Grandfather, don't let me be in the penitentiary. My Indian people need me. I want my Lakota people to learn the old Indian ways. I want to teach them. Grandfather, bless my nephew who is taking care of the fire for us. Bless my other nephew, who is going to do the cedaring. Bless my drummer. Grandfather, for many generations people came here to this place to pray. Our ancestors' moccasin trails are still here. Let them be recognized by the United States government. Grandfather, I ask you, I ask the great Creator, the earth maker, don't let them take me away. Mitakuye oyasin."

I was first to be tried for having defended my home when Beck and McCloskey came, claiming to be looking for Leonard Peltier. The trial took place in Pierre. The presiding judge was Robert Merhige, whose court was in Richmond, Virginia. The government probably picked Merhige because he knew nothing about the situation of Indians on the reservations, or about AIM, or about me and my background. The government had instructed him to run several AIM-connected federal cases as quickly as possible, and he did. He tried a case against Russell Means in the same courtroom, on the same day, as my case. The prosecutor again was R. D. Hurd. There seemed to be no way to evade him. He had become the government's special anti-AIM prosecutor.

My lawyer, Dan Taylor, arrived on the scene when my trial had been going on for some time. I had been given a court-appointed lawyer by the name of Srtska, who had been the campaign manager for state attorney general, later governor, Bill Janklow, who had run on an anti-Indian, anti-AIM platform. In his campaign speeches Janklow often said that he would put AIM members behind bars above ground, but that he preferred to see them six feet underground. Srtska had made no investigations on my behalf; he just advised me to plead guilty. I spoke English very badly at the time, did not understand the language of the law, and often had trouble following the proceedings. I was not given an interpreter.

Dan Taylor rescued me from Srtska, but he was given no time to familiarize himself with my case, no time to go to Rosebud to interview witnesses. He asked for a continuance, and the judge gave him forty-eight hours. Dan protested that he had not even been notified and that he needed time to prepare my defense. The judge said the court-appointed lawyer had been given enough time to prepare the case. The defense was not allowed to question would-be jurors. An all-white jury, mostly ranchers, was selected within one hour. The trial lasted only one afternoon. The jury found me and Coke Millard guilty. Sentencing would take place the next morning, November 30, 1975.

The next morning, the judge made the point that although I was not myself physically involved in the fight, because I was a leader and a medicine man with influence on young people I should have prevented it. He sentenced me to five years. I was immediately dragged off in chains and handcuffs without even a chance to say good-bye to my family and friends.

The government still wasn't satisfied. They wanted to make sure that I would go to prison for a long time. So they filed another charge against me. On the morning of March 25, 1975, my wife, Mary, and I had driven to Pierre on some business. We got back about eleven-thirty P.M. and found the house full of strangers—two young white women and an unkempt vagrant-type man. Mary went into the kitchen to cook something for us to eat and I went across to my mom's for a moment. When I returned, Mary was busy at the stove. The man put an arm around Mary and grabbed her in front. I hit him. He hit me back and split my lip. There was a chain from a chainsaw hanging on the wall. He grabbed it and came at me with it. I held onto his arm so that he couldn't use the chain, but it cut my hand. At that moment some of my friends came in. They gave him a few good whacks and threw him and his friends out of the house. We heard a car starting and thought that was the end of it.

It was not. The raggedy man's name was Royer "Woody" Pfersick, and he brought a charge against me for aggravated assault and battery.

The trial was held in January 1976, in Rapid City, South Dakota. I was then doing time at Lewisburg Penitentiary in Pennsylvania for the Beck-McCloskey case. I was flown to Rapid City to meet with Dan Taylor. I waited in the good old Pennington county jail.

At court we again had Judge Robert Merhige and R. D. Hurd. There was no voir dire. Because the judge was in a hurry, he questioned the jurors himself: "Are you prejudiced against Indians? You're not? Fine. You're in. Please take a seat."

The witnesses against me were the two girls and Pfersick himself. At first I didn't recognize him. He wore a nice new suit and a necktie with an American flag design. His hair had been neatly cut. The first thing we learned was that the prosecution's witnesses had been given immunity for any crimes they might have committed before coming uninvited to my home and since. That made me believe that they had been given this immunity in return for testifying against me.

Dan Taylor asked for a continuance so that we could get our

witnesses together. He explained that they had no phones and lived way out on the prairie. The judge said we had had enough time to subpoena them and get them to Rapid City. Dan pointed out that our witnesses had no mailboxes or mail service and were very hard to reach, especially in winter. Merhige denied the motion. He did not know the situation on the reservations. He lived in Richmond, Virginia.

Pfersick testified that I had hurt him with the chainsaw chain. He said that I had beaten him with a tomahawk. This was a serious accusation, but I had to laugh. There had not been any tomahawks on the reservation for more than a hundred years. The two women seemed embarrassed to testify. One of them said, "Crow Dog is a good man, a peaceful man. He didn't start it."

During the recess, Dan Taylor was happy. He assured me that not even an all-white jury in South Dakota could find me guilty on this cockamamie evidence. I told him, "Another five years."

After the recess came Mary, my only Indian eyewitness. She told a simple story: "This man made a crude pass at me. He tried to touch my breasts. He grabbed the chainsaw chain from the wall and swung it at Leonard. It cut Leonard's hand."

Then it was Hurd's turn. He showed the jury a color photograph of Pfersick, saying it was taken after I had beaten him up. Hurd showed that there was blood on Pfersick's face. Taylor wet his finger with a little saliva and rubbed the "blood" off: "This is ketchup. It is not a part of the photograph." Hurd did not know how ketchup could have gotten on it and called it an honest mistake. Hurd then made me out to be a dangerous and violent man. He told the jury, "Ladies and gentlemen, we have a good system here. The government is here to protect *you!* Would you believe, ladies and gentlemen, that the government, *your* government, would lie to you? What motive would the government have but the truth?" Finally, he let the jury in on a little secret: "Ladies and gentlemen, why was Pfersick beaten? Ladies and gentlemen, he was not beaten because he came uninvited, or because he brought drugs, or because he made a sexual pass at Mr. Crow

Dog's wife. No. He was beaten because they thought that Pfersick was an informer!"

After that Dan Taylor summed up for the defense. All through the trial the judge had tried to get things done in a hurry. And now, when Dan had his last chance to speak for me, he tried to rush him: "Mr. Taylor, you have exactly four minutes left. After that I'll cut you off." So ended the day. I was brought back to the jail. The Crow Dog party went back to their motel and had dinner. Dan assured everybody that the verdict would be not guilty.

The next morning the case went to the jury. The judge charged the panel fairly: "If Crow Dog acted in self-defense, you must find him innocent. The same holds true if he protected his home, his family, or even just his property. He cannot be found guilty if this was just a rambling, mutual fight which he did not start, if he has, in fact, not used a dangerous weapon. Then the jury can find him guilty only on a lesser charge—simple assault. Ladies and gentlemen, it is simply a credibility case. It is a matter of whom you believe."

The all-white jury believed Hurd and Pfersick. In less than an hour they came in with a guilty verdict, and I was right—five more years. So now I had been sentenced to ten years on the two aggravated assault and battery cases and the eleven-year sentence for the postal inspectors case was no longer suspended because of my later convictions. So now I was in for twenty-one years altogether. It took a lot of long, hard work and devotion to get me out of the hole the government had dug for me.

twenty-five

IRON DOOR HOUSE

They have taken everything from me.
They have taken Crow Dog's land.
They have taken my elements.
Most important of all, they have
taken my human body away
from my people. But they can never
take away my spirit: Let me be the earth,
let me be the wind for my people.
                              Leonard Crow Dog

I was dragged from one prison to another—Deadwood,
Pennington county jail in Rapid City, the holding tank in
Pierre, Minnehaha county jail in Sioux Falls, all in South
Dakota; Oxford and Cedar Rapids, Iowa; Terre Haute,
Indiana; Wichita and Leavenworth, Kansas; Chicago, federal correction institution; Lewisburg, Pennsylvania;
Richmond, Virginia; Sandstone, Minnesota; and, for one
night, a holding tank in New York City. The government
was trying to hide me so that my wife, my family, and
even my lawyer could not find me. In some joints I was
kept for only a few days, or even hours. Only in
Leavenworth, Lewisburg, and Terre Haute did I stay for
any length of time.

On November 30, 1975, when they took me away, I
was thirty-three years old. They put handcuffs on me,

along with waist chains and leg irons; I was like a walking hardware store. I was fingerprinted and given a number. Just before I was put into the holding cell inside the federal building at Pierre, I was allowed to make one short phone call to my wife, who was still at the Holiday Inn. She asked where I was going from there, but no one would tell me.

Twenty-five minutes after my sentencing I was taken by car to the Minnehaha county jail in Sioux Falls. I wished that I could go on a vision quest. Instead, I fasted for four days. During the eight days I was in Sioux Falls I met a number of inmates who had heard about me during Wounded Knee, in 1973. They said they never thought they'd meet a leader from the American Indian Movement. They said, "You are now one of our brothers." I answered, "Yes, I am your brother."

After Sioux Falls I spent a few days in a jail at Wichita, Kansas, and from there they transported me to Leavenworth, a maximum-security penitentiary. I was there for quite some time. They first took me through a maze of corridors and underground passages. Every few yards there was an electronically controlled grill. The guards had to push a button every time to open the grill to let us through. I felt like Jonah inside the whale. I wound up in a tiny room, really just a gray-green cement box. This was the hole, solitary. When I asked why I was being punished, the guards told me that this was a standard process before a prisoner was released into the general prison population.

The hole was like a grave. There was a narrow bunk, a washbasin, and the "toadstool." That was all. There were no windows, no clock. There was artificial, neon light that was never turned off. The whole two weeks I spent in the hole was like being buried alive. I didn't know whether it was day or night, or what day of the week it was, even what month. I didn't know whether the stuff they fed me was breakfast or supper. I became disoriented.

This was all done according to plan. In Leavenworth, the first thing they do with a new inmate is try to break his spirit through what they call sensory deprivation. I was so down that the first day or two I could not even pray. I was too angry, too numb. Then I roused myself and said, "Tunkashila, Grandfather, you are here with me. They cannot penetrate me or my mind. They cannot disable me." I started singing ancient ceremonial songs, peyote songs. Inside the hole I taught myself a new way of singing so that it sounded like two voices.

When they released me into the general prison population, the inmates already knew about me. They stuck their clenched fists through the bars and shouted, "Crow Dog, Crow Dog, Crow Dog!" In this way they welcomed me. They took one another by the hands through the bars, some whites, some Indians, some blacks. They chanted a prayer for me, a prayer for a Lakota medicine man.

The routine in the maximum-security prisons is always the same. You are in your cell, your "house." You just lie there and get bored to death. It's brain genocide. The whistle blows at five o'clock in the morning. That's the wake-up call. The noise is terrific. There's no sunlight, no fresh air.

There were close to five hundred seventy-five men in our "E" maximum-security unit. The inmates were considered dangerous because they were political, men who had been involved in movements. They made me a janitor. I cleaned up everything. I had an hour to do it. After that they locked me up again. They let me out for lunch, then they put me back in my house.

I made friends—a white friend, a black friend, a Chicano, an Asian. They often asked my advice on different things. They told me, "Our thinking is very weak. We've been here for too many years now. We don't know what's happening outside the fence. We get a glimpse of cars driving by in the distance, but we do not know what is happening to us. We don't know if our relatives still remember us. We do not know whether our friends outside are still struggling for the people." My black friend's name was Verge. He was a young man in his twenties. He was in the pen for forty-five years. He would be an old man when he would be released.

He made up a song about me. He sang it to my wife over the phone while strumming on his guitar.

In all the prisons I was in, the hacks were always the same. It takes a special kind of man to want to be a hack. They are uneducated and badly paid. Half of the time they are prisoners themselves, cooped up with us inside. Outside nobody respects them. If somebody asks them, "What do you do for a living?" they say, "I work for the state," or "I'm a peace officer." They are ashamed to admit that they are prison guards. The hacks have no culture. They don't have anything to tell their sons and daughters. They have nothing their kids could be proud of. Inside the joint they feel superior to the inmates because they have power over them. That's the only thing that makes them feel they're somebody. They get a kick out of humiliating the prisoners.

In every prison I had a case worker, a counselor, and a shrink. The shrinks have a "behavior modification" lab. They use "control medications." They love to have you on thorazine all the time. They tried to give me therapy—"logical therapy," "living in reality," "acculturation," reports, interviews, group sessions. "How are you? What are you? Why do you think you are here? Let's see, what did you say in your last interview? What's in your records? What did you say yesterday? What are you going to tell me today and tomorrow? If you cooperate, no problem. I could get you out of here in no time. Not cooperating you've got a problem, a brain problem."

One of them told me: "Let me research you. Let me analyze you. You've become a hobby of mine. You are my first Indian. I never met anyone like you. Let me crack your mystery."

"No," I said. "I am the native psychiatrist, I'll analyze *you*, brain-shrink you. Be my guinea pig. Let me figure out what makes you tick. Tell me about your sex life. Through spiritual thoughts of my mind I could teach you, make you understand the red man, who we are and what we represent. But, maybe, you're too retarded to be taught." He didn't like it. So we waged a kind of psychological warfare on each other.

I had a hard fight to practice my religion. When I was imprisoned they did not recognize the Indian religion or the Native American Church. A priest or a rabbi could visit the inmates, but not a medicine man. I asked to be given my sacred pipe under the Freedom of Religion Act, but at first, my request was refused. Later, my lawyers forced the warden to let me have my pipe. They brought me the bowl and the stem, but not the tobacco. I asked them, "Where is it?" They said, "You can't have it. It could be some kind of drug." I said, "How can I pray with the pipe, how can I smoke it without my sacred tobacco?" The warden told me: "We must first send it to a lab and have it analyzed." After many weeks the lab report came back. It said that the Indian tobacco was a "suspicious vegetable matter." Only at the very end of my incarceration was I allowed to use the pipe in the right way.

From Leavenworth I was taken to Lewisburg, Pennsylvania, a stone fortress on the banks of the Susquehanna River. It is one of six maximum-security prisons in the country, with cells for one thousand six hundred inmates. Again I was put on hold in an isolation cubby hole, so tiny that I could neither stretch out completely nor stand up without my head touching the ceiling. When they released me into the main prison population I found out that Lewisburg was the most dangerous of all the prisons I had been in. It was a killing place. The going price for murder was two cartons of cigarettes. I was told that if the place were thoroughly searched they'd find enough dope to feed the habits of all the junkies in New York for a month, and enough cash to found a bank. Every day, a young kid not strong enough to defend himself was gang-raped. Murders were done with a "shank," a two-foot-long piece of sheet metal sliced off by a machine in the prison shop. A shank was a fearful weapon. I walked in the yard and saw a group of inmates huddled together. Suddenly the group split up, everybody running in a different direction, leaving a man lying on the ground with his throat cut from ear to ear so that his head was dangling by a thin strip of skin. That was my welcome to Lewisburg.

So I kept to myself. I did not speak to anyone if I could help it, except two or three Indian inmates I could trust, one of them a Pueblo from Taos, New Mexico. I obeyed all the rules, both the prison rules and the unwritten ones made up by the cons. Luckily, most inmates looked upon me as a sort of oddball and gave me some respect. So I survived.

The next night, on the way to Richmond, I was kept in a New York City holding tank. It was the worst night of my life. I called up Richard Erdoes and Mary. I told them: "They are going to take away my mind. They are going to cut part of my brain out." Richard and Mary could have taken a cab and been with me in fifteen minutes, but the marshals would not allow them to see me. Richard said "They can't do that to you without special permission." I said "You don't know. At Lewisburg they can do with you whatever they want." We were on the phone from eight in the evening to six in the morning, until we were totally exhausted. I wept a lot during the night. The next day, Richard and Mary got in touch with my lawyer and we found out that, in fact, there was no plan to lobotomize me; strangely enough, the whole experience was a turning point for the better.

Richard Erdoes went to the "god box"—that's what they call the National Council of Churches boxlike building in New York— and persuaded them to take my case. They raised one hundred fifty thousand dollars for my defense. In addition to Dan Taylor they gave me two other lawyers: Bill Kunstler and Sandy Rosen. Later, they added Vine Deloria, Jr., so that a Native American attorney would be involved in my case. Vine is a Lakota from the Standing Rock reservation, a famous writer, and a professor at the University of Arizona. Kunstler was a great courtroom performer. Sandy Rosen was the lawyers' lawyer, very patient and painstaking, going over every detail. He took my case all the way to the Supreme Court. At times my defense team was joined by Ken Tilsen, of Minneapolis, who had been on several AIM-related cases and was a supporter of Indian rights. We also got an expert who could figure out which jurors might be sympathetic to our cause and which were not.

Even during my worst days in prison there were things to console me. I felt that wakan Tanka, the Creator, was with me. Grandfather talked to me. He came to me in dreams and let his power work inside me. He sent birds to console me. Birds are sacred. They are the Great Spirit's messengers. I saw them in my visions and in reality. I saw them outside my prison window. A crow spoke to me. I talked to a yellowhammer. I saw eagles in the sky. Several times during my imprisonment I thought I heard an eagle bone whistle. It came from the wind. It came from nowhere and it came from everywhere. The sound of the sun dance whistle gave me strength.

On March 10, 1976, I was released from Lewisburg, pending appeal. It came just in time. On the orders of the warden they would have taken me to the barbershop to cut my braids off the next day. Braids were not allowed in Lewisburg, not even on a Lakota medicine man.

Richard Erdoes, Mary, little Pedro, and some friends drove from New York to pick me up. They waited for me outside the fence. Laid out on a blanket were my sacred things—my pipe and pipe bag, my eagle wing and eagle bone whistle, my red and blue prayer shawl, my medicine bundle. We went to Richard's apartment and had a feast. Then I fell down on the couch and slept for almost twenty-four hours.

I was not free for long. My appeal was denied. On June 22, 1976, I surrendered myself at Deadwood, South Dakota. I picked Deadwood because the first Crow Dog had given himself up there in 1884, and I was following his legend. This time they took me to Terre Haute, Indiana, another maximum-security prison. The routine, the treatment, the boredom were the same as in Leavenworth and Lewisburg. Again I was a nameless number.

But I was not forgotten. My friends kept working for my freedom. In September 1976, my whole defense team went to Richmond to apply for a sentence reduction. When the defense team assembled in court they saw a long trestle table heaped with stacks of support letters and petitions. Judge Merhige said, "We have lots more, but we have no place to put them. There are letters here from Africa, from Austria, from Indonesia, and God knows from where else. I wonder how folks thousands of miles from here can know so much more about this case than I." He smiled and then rendered his decision: "I can't resist all this. I order Crow Dog to be immediately released and his sentence reduced to time served." Even though Merhige had ordered my immediate release, Hurd protested and it took months before I was finally let go.

When I finally got home the whole tribe honored me with a feast and giveaway. Two spiritual men, Wallace Black Elk and Bill Eagle Feathers, ran the ceremony. All my relations were there, all my friends. The tribal chairman and vice-chairman had come, and Father Witthoeft, who had supported me through all my trials. Richard Erdoes had flown in from New York. Many people wore their traditional outfits. Bill Eagle Feathers and Dallas Chief Eagle had their war bonnets on, besides wearing their beaded and quilled rawhide outfits. Many others wore their old fringed buckskins, breechcloths, and even ancient bone breast plates of their grandfathers. I wore my ribbon shirt and an old peace medal on my breast. In my hair I wore an eagle tailfeather together with the plumes of three other birds. My pipe bag hung from my belt. The women wore their beautiful white deerhide dresses or many-colored fringed dance shawls. It was a great sight. Black Elk and Eagle Feathers fanned me off with their eagle wings and smoked me up with sage and sweet grass. My father helped them. We smoked the pipe and partook of the sacred food. Black Elk blew the eagle bone whistle toward the four directions. The drummers pounded out the AIM song. They chanted the chief-honoring song for me. I led the dance around the circle with Wallace Black Elk on my left side and Bill Eagle Feathers on my right. Behind us came my parents and my wife. My old mother uttered the wichaglata, the pulsating brave-heart cry, and all the other women joined in.

Soon after came the sun dance, the most sacred of all our rituals. The sun dance has often been misrepresented as a ceremony to initiate boys into manhood or to show courage. But that is not why you suffer, why you pierce yur breast or hang from the tree; you do that because the sun dance is a sacrifice. You undergo pain to make a sick relative well, or to bring a son back alive from war. I danced so that my people should live. As old Chief Lame Deer put it: "The whites have made it easy for themselves. They let Jesus do the suffering for them, once, two thousand years ago. But we Indians take the pain upon ourselves, experience it in our own bodies. We make a vow: 'Grandfather, next year I will dance. I will pierce myself, to get somebody well, to make our people whole.'"

For many years, the government forbade the sun dance. They called it barbaric, savage, superstitious. Indians were jailed if they were caught sun dancing. Even to purify oneself in a sweat lodge was a crime. But it never stopped us from performing our sacred rituals. We danced in secret, where the wasichu could not find us. During all the long years when our religion was outlawed, somewhere, in hidden places, the Lakota were dancing. My father's chest is crisscrossed with the scars from many piercings. He danced in spite of the missionaries, government agents, and BIA police. He danced across the river, at Picket Pin's place. He danced up on the hills among the pines. He danced way out on the prairie, in hidden valleys, in clearings among ancient cottonwoods. If you look for them you can still find the traces of our old dance circles. My father always wanted his piercings to be prayers for all the people.

Ever since 1971, in early August there has been a sun dance at Crow Dog's Paradise. But the one in 1977, just after my release, had a special meaning for me. Bill Eagle Feathers ran it. The sacred tree was brought in, the tallest cottonwood they could find. They planted it in a hole filled with buffalo fat and the four kinds of sacred food. Chief Eagle Feathers prayed for an eagle to bless us, and at once a large bald eagle appeared, flying in from the east, circling over the sun dance ground, and then disappearing slowly toward the west. More than one hundred dancers had come, all in their red kilts, with wreaths of sage crowning their heads, blowing on their eagle bone whistles, making a sound of a thousand birds. The drum pounded, uniting us all in its heartbeat. The singers intoned the sun dance song:

Wakan Tanka unshimala ye,	Creator, have pity on me.
wanikta cha lecha mu welo.	I shall live, that is why I am doing this.

We danced so that our Lakota nation should live. We took upon us the sufferings of our brothers and sisters in the white man's jails. My wife and my sisters pierced on their arms and collar bones. Ten- and eleven-year-old boys pierced. Everywhere people made flesh offerings. My friend Jerry Roy hung from the tree. Seventeen-year-old Bobby Leader Charge dragged twelve buffalo skulls attached by rawhide thongs to skewers imbedded in the flesh of his back. He did this to bring back his half-brother, who was still imprisoned. I danced looking at the sun until my mind was filled by a bright light from another world. I danced with the tree. It talked to me. I was outside myself, way beyond myself, seeing the world with chante ishta, the eye of the heart, not the eyes in the face. All along the rawhide thongs reaching from the skewers in my chest to the top of the sacred tree, I communicated with the Grandfather Spirit and with the stars. Before I tore myself loose, I danced with the tree so that it swayed in rhythm with my movements. Nobody had ever done this. I called out to the eagles. When I finally finished, a great shout rose from the people. I had come home.

I end my story here, at the high point of my life. I will never dance again as I danced then. There will never be another Wounded Knee. I became what I had been before I gave myself to the movement—a medicine man performing the ancient ceremonies for my Lakota people. Pedro and my teenage son, Anwah, already run yuwipi and Native American church meetings. They know all the songs. They will follow on my trail when I am gone.

Clearwater and Buddy Lamont are looking down on me.
Raymond Yellow Thunder and Pedro Bissonette are looking down
on me. Much of what I am doing, I am doing for them.

Tunkashila wama yanka yo	Grandfather, behold me.
le miye cha nawajin yelo he	This is me, I am standing.
Tunkashila wama yanka yo	Grandfather, behold me.
le miye cha	This is me,
nawajin yelo he.	standing up.

Mitakuye oyasin.